A Therapeutic Journey

A Therapeutic

Journey

Lessons from
The School of Life

Alain de Botton

Published in 2023 by The School of Life
First published in the USA in 2023
This paperback edition published in 2024
930 High Road, London, N12 9RT

Printed and bound by CPI Group (UK) Ltd, Croydon, CR0 4YY

The School of Life publishes a range of books on essential topics in psychological and emotional life, including relationships, parenting, friendship, careers and fulfilment. The aim is always to help us to understand ourselves better – and thereby to grow calmer, less confused and more purposeful. Discover our full r ange of titles, including books for children, here:
www.theschooloflife.com/books

The School of Life also offers a comprehensive therapy service, which complements, and draws upon, our published works:
www.theschooloflife.com/therapy

www.theschooloflife.com

ISBN 978-1-916753-13-6

10 9 8 7 6 5 4 3 2 1

Contents

Introduction

This book describes the arc of a journey—from breakdown and collapse to convalescence and recovery. It is intended as both a practical guide and a source of consolation and friendship during what might be some of our loneliest, most anguished moments.

This is a book about getting unwell, imagining that we have let everyone down—and losing direction and hope. It's also a book about redemption: about regaining the thread, rediscovering meaning, and finding a way back to connection, warmth, and joy.

It's a book interested in sympathy, endurance, and how to build a life where, despite everything, we are once again sure we want to be here.

This is, ultimately, a book about resilience. It insists that we cannot allow terror, self-hatred, and sadness to have their victories over us and that we can always, so long as we think matters through with sufficient creativity and gentleness, identify reasons to live.

It can be easy to wonder for too long what books and ideas might be for. Their highest calling, which inspires what follows, may simply be to try to lend us—at our very worst moments—the strength and clarity to endure.

I : Challenge

For a long time, we may cope well enough. We make it to work every morning, we give pleasant summaries of our lives to friends, we smile over dinner. We aren't totally balanced, but there's no good way of knowing how difficult things might be for other people, and what we might have a right to expect in terms of contentment and peace of mind. We probably tell ourselves to stop being self-indulgent and redouble our efforts to feel worthy through achievement. We are probably world experts in not feeling sorry for ourselves.

Decades may pass. It's not uncommon for the most serious mental conditions to remain undiagnosed for half a lifetime. We simply don't notice that we are, beneath the surface, chronically anxious, filled with self-loathing, and close to overwhelming despair and rage. This too simply ends up feeling normal.

Until one day, finally, something triggers a collapse. It might be a crisis at work, a reversal in our career plans or a mistake we've made over a task. It might be a romantic failure, someone leaving us, or a realization that we are profoundly unhappy with a partner we had thought would be our long-term future. Alternatively, we feel mysteriously exhausted and sad, to the extent that we can't face anything any more, even a family meal or a conversation with a friend. Or we are struck by unmanageable anxiety around everyday challenges, like addressing our colleagues or going into a store. We're swamped by a sense of doom and imminent catastrophe. We sob uncontrollably.

We are in a mental crisis.

This is what might come next . . .

1 *Breakdown*

If we are lucky, when it feels impossible to carry on any longer we will know to put up the white flag at once. There is nothing shameful or rare in our condition; we have fallen ill, as so many before us have. We need not compound our sickness with a sense of embarrassment. This is what happens when you are a delicate human facing the hurtful, alarming and always uncertain conditions of existence. Recovery can start the moment we admit we no longer have a clue how to cope.

The roots of the crisis almost certainly go back a long way. Things will have not been right in certain areas for an age, possibly for ever. There will have been grave inadequacies in the early days, things that were said and done to us that should never have been, and bits of reassurance and care that were ominously missed out. In addition to this, adult life will have layered on difficulties which we were not well equipped to know how to endure. It will have applied pressure along our most tender, invisible fault lines.

Our illness is trying to draw attention to our problems, but it can only do so inarticulately, by throwing up coarse and vague symptoms. It knows how to signal that we are worried and sad, but it can't tell us what about and why. That will be the work of patient investigation, over months and years, probably in the company of experts. The illness contains the cure, but it has to be teased out and its original inarticulacy interpreted. Something from the past is crying out to be recognized and will not leave us alone until we have given it its due.

It may seem – at points – like a death sentence but we are, beneath the crisis, being given an opportunity to restart our lives on a more generous, kind, and realistic footing. There is an art to being ill—and to daring at last to listen to what our pain is trying to tell us.

Mental health is a miracle we are apt not to notice until the moment it slips from our grasp—at which point we may wonder how we ever managed to do anything as complicated and beautiful as order our thoughts sanely and calmly.

A mind in a healthy state is, in the background, continually performing a near-miraculous set of maneuvers that underpin our moods of clear-sightedness and purpose. To appreciate what mental health involves—and therefore what makes up its opposite—we should take a moment to consider some of what will be happening in the folds of an optimally functioning mind:

- First and foremost, a healthy mind is an *editing* mind, an organ that manages to sieve, from thousands of stray, dramatic, disconcerting, or horrifying thoughts, those particular ideas and sensations that actively need to be entertained in order for us to direct our lives effectively.

- Partly this means keeping at bay punitive and critical judgments that might want to tell us repeatedly how disgraceful and appalling we are—long after harshness has ceased to serve any useful purpose. When we are interviewing for a new job or taking someone on a date, a healthy mind doesn't force us to listen to inner voices that insist on our unworthiness. It allows us to talk to ourselves as we would to a friend.

- At the same time, a healthy mind resists the pull of unfair comparisons. It doesn't constantly allow the achievements and successes of others to throw us off course and reduce us to a state of bitter inadequacy. It doesn't torture us by continually comparing our condition to that of people who have, in reality, had very different upbringings and trajectories through life. A well-functioning mind recognizes the futility and cruelty of constantly finding fault with its own nature.

- Along the way, a healthy mind keeps a judicious grip on the drip, drip, drip of fear. It knows that, in theory, there is an endless number of things that we could worry about: A blood vessel might fail, a scandal might erupt, the plane's engines could sheer from its wings . . . But it has a good sense of the distinction between what could *conceivably* happen and what is in fact *likely* to happen, and so it is able to leave us in peace as regards the wilder eventualities of fate, confident that awful things will either not unfold or could be dealt with ably enough if ever they did so. A healthy mind avoids catastrophic imaginings: It knows that there are broad and stable stone steps, not a steep and slippery incline, between itself and disaster.

■ A healthy mind has compartments with heavy doors that shut securely. It can compartmentalize where it needs to. Not all thoughts belong at all moments. While talking to a grandmother, the mind prevents the emergence of images of last night's erotic fantasies; while looking after a child, it can repress its more cynical and misanthropic analyses. Aberrant thoughts about jumping on a train line or harming yourself with a sharp knife can remain brief peculiar flashes rather than repetitive fixations. A healthy mind has mastered the techniques of censorship.

■ A healthy mind can quieten its own buzzing preoccupations in order, at times, to focus on the world beyond itself. It can be present and engaged with what and who is immediately around. Not everything it could feel has to be felt at every moment.

■ A healthy mind combines an appropriate suspicion of certain people with a fundamental trust in humanity. It can take an intelligent risk with a stranger. It doesn't extrapolate from life's worst moments in order to destroy the possibility of connection.

■ A healthy mind knows how to hope; it identifies and then hangs on tenaciously to a few reasons to keep going. Grounds for despair, anger, and sadness are, of course, all around. But the healthy mind knows how to bracket negativity in the name of endurance. It clings to evidence of what is still good and kind. It remembers to appreciate; it can—despite everything—still look forward to a hot bath, some dried fruit or dark chocolate, a chat with a friend or a satisfying day of work. It refuses to let itself be silenced by all the many sensible arguments in favor of rage and despondency.

Outlining some of the features of a healthy mind helps us to identify what can go awry when we fall ill. At the heart of mental illness is a loss of control over our own better thoughts and feelings. An unwell mind can't apply a filter to the information that reaches our awareness; it can no longer order or sequence its content. And from this, any number of painful scenarios ensue:

■ Ideas keep coming to the fore that serve no purpose, unkind voices echo ceaselessly. Worrying possibilities press on us all at once, without any bearing on the probability of their occurrence. Fear runs riot.

■ Simultaneously, regrets drown out any capacity to make our peace with who we are. Every bad thing we have ever said or done reverberates and cripples our self-esteem. We are unable to assign correct proportions to anything: A drawer that doesn't open feels like a conclusive sign that we are doomed; a slightly unfriendly remark by an acquaintance becomes proof that we shouldn't exist. We can't grade our worries and focus in on the few that might truly deserve concern.

■ We can't temper our sadness. We can't overcome the idea that we have not been loved properly, that we have made a mess of the whole of our working lives, that we have disappointed everyone who ever had a shred of faith in us.

■ Every compartment of the mind is blown open. The strangest, most extreme thoughts run unchecked across consciousness. We begin to fear that we might shout obscenities in public or do harm with the kitchen knives.

- In the worst cases, we lose the power to distinguish outer reality from our inner world. We can't tell what is outside us and what inside, where we end and others begin; we speak to people as if they were actors in our own dreams.

- At night, such is the maelstrom and the ensuing exhaustion that we become defenseless before our worst apprehensions. By 3 a.m., after hours of rumination, doing away with ourselves no longer feels like such a remote or unwelcome notion.

However dreadful this sounds, it is a paradox that, for the most part, mental illness doesn't tend to look from the outside as dramatic as we think it should. The majority of us, when we are mentally unwell, will not be foaming at the mouth or insisting that we are Napoleon. We won't be making speeches about alien invasions or declaring that we control space and time. Our suffering will be quieter, more inward, more concealed, and more contiguous with societal norms; we'll sob mutely into the pillow or dig our nails silently into our palms. Others may not even realize for a very long time, if ever, that we are in difficulty. We ourselves may not quite accept the scale of our sickness.

The clichéd images of "madness"—with their obscenities, ravings, and bombast—may be frightening in themselves, but our collective focus on them suggests a concealed search for reassurance. We depict mental illness in colorful and extreme terms to convince ourselves of our own sanity; to put some clear blue water between our own fragile states and those of people we dismissively term "lunatics." We thereby fail to acknowledge the extent to which mental illness is ultimately as common, and as essentially unshameful, as its bodily counterpart—and also comprises a host of more minor ailments, the equivalents of cold sores and broken wrists, abdominal cramps or ingrowing toenails.

When we define mental illness as a loss of command over the mind, few of us can claim to be free of all instances of unwellness. True mental health involves a frank acceptance of how much ill health there will have to be in even the most ostensibly competent and meaningful lives. There will be days when we simply can't stop crying over someone we have lost. Or when we worry so much about the future that we wish we hadn't been born. Or when we feel so sad that it seems futile even to open our mouths. We should at such times be counted as no less ill than a person laid up in bed with flu—and as worthy of attention and sympathy.

It doesn't help that we are at least a hundred years away from properly fathoming how the brain operates—and how it might be healed. We are in the mental arena roughly equivalent to where we might have been in bodily medicine around the middle of the seventeenth century, as we slowly built up a picture of how blood circulated around our veins or our kidneys functioned. In our attempts to find fixes, we are akin to those surgeons depicted in early prints who cut up cadavers with rusty scissors and clumsily dug around the innards with a poker. We will—surprisingly—be well on the way to colonizing Mars before we definitively grasp the secrets to the workings of our own minds.

It is surely no coincidence that in many parts of Europe, asylums for the mentally ill were, from the Renaissance onward, opened up in converted monasteries, signaling an implicit connection between the solace sought from religion and from psychiatry. The best of these asylums, and there were very few, promised a dignified refuge from the pressures of society and the terrors of the mind. They may have had extensive gardens, most famously like the one at the Saint-Paul asylum in Saint-Rémy, where an ailing Vincent Van Gogh spent a year in 1889, sitting very still in his room for hours at a time and then painting dozens of sublime canvases of irises, cypresses, and pine trees, paintings that may to this day help persuade the inconsolable to keep living.

In its way, this book aims to be a sanctuary, a walled garden filled with nourishing psychological vegetation and with comfortable benches on which to sit and recover our strength, in an atmosphere of kindness and fellow feeling. It outlines a raft of therapeutic moves with which we might approach our most stubborn mental afflictions and instabilities. It sets out to be a friend through some of the most difficult moments of our lives.

Vincent Van Gogh, *The Garden of the Asylum at Saint-Rémy,*
May 1889, 1889.

A SELF-PORTRAIT

Our societies sometimes struggle with the question of what art might be for. Here the answer feels simple: Art is a weapon against despair. It is a tool with which to alleviate a sense of crushing isolation and uniqueness. It provides common ground where the sadness in me can, with dignity and intelligence, meet the sadness in you.

Perhaps for a long time, the man in the diner kept it together. As late as this morning, he might have believed that, despite everything, he would be OK. He'd taken his hat along with him, as always; he remained attached to appearances. Even as his anguish mounted, he kept going, one sip of coffee after another, an occasional pat of the mouth with a paper napkin, while looking out at the busy room: secretaries at lunch, people from the nearby construction site, a few exhausted mothers and their kids. Then, suddenly, there was no more arguing with the despair any longer. It swept him up without any chance of a rejoinder: the mess he had made, the fool he had become in everyone's eyes, the absurdity of everything. His head hit the table with a shocking clatter but almost at once it was absorbed by the dense murmur of the room and the city. One could die in public here and few would notice.

Except that there was a French photographer right opposite who was very much into noticing everything: an elegant, willowy man, with a name impossible for Americans to pronounce—he invited them to call him Harry—and a Leica 35 around his neck. Henri Cartier-Bresson had wandered the area all morning; he'd shot a group of women chatting outside on Ground Street and discovered a striking view of midtown Manhattan from the promenade. He had just begun his lunch when, without warning, there came that distinctive bang of a head hitting a table with force.

We need not feel ashamed, the photograph suggests, that we are in despair; it is an inevitable part of being alive. The distress that normally dwells painfully and privately inside our minds has been given social

Henri Cartier-Bresson, *A Café, 2nd Avenue,
Brooklyn, NYC, USA*, 1947.

expression—and no longer needs to be shouldered alone. Whatever a distressingly upbeat world sometimes implies, it is normal, very normal, to be in agony. We don't, on top of it all, ever need to feel unique for being unwell.

CURLING UP INTO A BALL

We cause ourselves a lot of pain by pretending to be competent, all-knowing, proficient adults long after we should, ideally, have called for help. We suffer a bitter rejection in love, but tell ourselves and our acquaintances that we never cared. We hear some wounding rumors about us but refuse to stoop to our opponents' level. We find we can't sleep at night and are exhausted and anxious in the day, but continue to insist that stepping aside for a break is only for weaklings.

We all originally came from a very tight ball-like space. For the first nine months of our existence, we were curled up, with our head on our knees, protected from a more dangerous and colder world beyond by the position of our limbs. In our young years, we knew well enough how to recover this ball position when things got tough. If we were mocked in the playground or misunderstood by a snappy parent, it was instinctive to go up to our room and adopt the ball position until matters started to feel more manageable again. Only later, around adolescence, did some of us lose sight of this valuable exercise in regression and thereby began missing out on a chance for nurture and recovery.

Dominant ideas of what can be expected of a wise, fully mature adult tend to lack realism. Though we may be twenty-eight or forty-seven on the outside, we are inevitably still carrying within us a child for whom a day at work will be untenably exhausting, a child who won't be able to calm down easily after an insult, who will need reassurance after every minor rejection, who will want to cry without quite knowing why and who will fairly regularly require a chance to be "held" until the sobs have subsided.

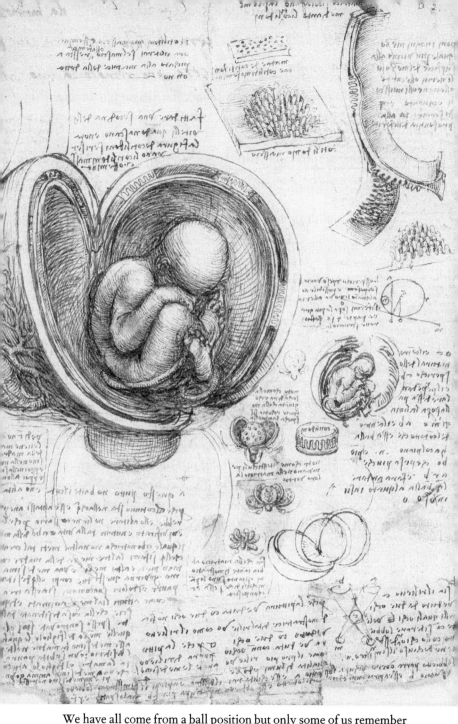

We have all come from a ball position but only some of us remember
to return there on a regular basis: Leonardo da Vinci,
Studies of the Foetus in the Womb, c. 1510–13.

It is a sign of the supreme wisdom of small children that they have no shame or compunction about bursting into tears. They have a more accurate and less pride-filled sense of their place in the world than a typical adult: They know that they are only extremely small beings in a hostile and unpredictable realm, that they can't control much of what is happening around them, that their powers of understanding are limited, and that there is a great deal to feel distressed, melancholy, and confused about.

As we age, we learn to avoid being, at all costs, that most apparently repugnant—and yet in fact deeply philosophical—of creatures: the crybaby. But moments of losing courage belong to a brave life. If we do not allow ourselves frequent occasions to bend, we will be at far greater risk of one day fatefully snapping.

When the impulse to cry strikes, we should be grown up enough to cede to it as we did in our fourth or fifth years. We should repair to a quiet room, put the duvet over our head, and allow despondency to have its way. There is in truth no maturity without an adequate negotiation with the infantile and no such thing as a proper grown-up who does not frequently yearn to be comforted like a toddler.

If we have properly sobbed, at some point in the misery an idea—however minor—will at last enter our mind and make a tentative case for the other side: We'll remember that it would be quite pleasant and possible to have a very hot bath, that someone once stroked our hair kindly, that we have one and a half good friends on the planet and an interesting book still to read—and we'll know that the worst of the storm may be ebbing.

THE SLEEP OF REASON PRODUCES MONSTERS

Goya's title is central. In case we were to miss it, it is even etched on the desk, and it sounds more eloquent still in the original: *El sueño de la razón produce monstruos*. As the artist knew intimately—he'd been manic

Francisco Goya, *The Sleep of Reason Produces Monsters*, plate 43 from "Los Caprichos", 1799.

depressive since late adolescence—night is when things can become properly unbearable if our mind is fragile.

Each of Goya's monstrous animals is really a thought of the kind that can assail us when we are exhausted. Such thoughts are an internalization of the most awful messages we've ever heard from other people—probably those we grew up around: *You are no good. You disgust me. Don't you dare to outsmart me.* The owl with outstretched wings might be shrieking: *You will never achieve anything.* The furry-beaked bat might be hissing: *Your desires are revolting.* The lynx-like thing at the bottom looks on judgmentally: *I'm so disappointed in what you've become.*

During the day, when we feel so-called monsters hovering as we talk to a colleague or have dinner with friends, we can fend the animals off with rational arguments: *Of course we've done nothing wrong. There's no reason to keep apologizing. We have the right to be.* But at night, we can forget all our weapons of self-defense: *Why are we still alive? Why haven't we given up yet?* We don't know what to answer any more.

To survive mentally, we might need to undertake a lengthy analysis of where each animal comes from, what it feeds off, what makes it go on the prowl and how it can be wrestled into submission. One beast might have been born from our father's mouth, another from our mother's neglect. Most of them get excited when we have too much work, when we're exhausted and when the cities we live in are at their most frenetic. And they hate early nights, nature, and the love of friends.

We need to manage our monsters—each of us has our own versions—with all the respect we owe to something that has the power to kill us. We need to build very strong cages out of solid, kind arguments against them. At the same time, we can take comfort from the idea that the night-time monsters will get less vicious the more we can lead reasonable, serene lives. With enough gentleness and compassion, we can hope to reach a point when, even in the dead of night, as these monsters chafe at their collars and strike at their bars, we will remember enough about ourselves to be unafraid and to know that we are safe and worthy of tenderness.

Goya's print isn't just an evocation of night terrors; it's also pointing us—more hopefully—to how we might in time tame our monsters through love and reason.

REASONS TO LIVE

When we say that someone has fallen mentally ill, what we are frequently indicating is the loss of long-established reasons to remain alive. And so the task ahead is to make a series of interventions, as imaginative as they are kind, that could—somehow—return the unfortunate sufferer to a feeling of the value of their own survival.

This cannot, of course, ever be a matter of simply telling someone in pain what the answers are or of presenting them with a ready-made checklist of options without any sincere or subtle connections with their own character. If we are to recover a true taste for life, it can only be on the basis that others have been creative and accommodating enough to learn the particularities of our upsets and reversals and are armed with a sufficiently complicated grasp of how resistant our minds can be to the so-called obvious and convenient solutions.

We can hang on to one essential and cheering thought: that no life, whatever the apparent obstacles, has to be extinguished. There are invariably ways for it to be rendered liveable again; there are always reasons to be found why a person, any person, might go on. What matters is the degree of perseverance, ingenuity, and love we can bring to the task of reinvention and remodelling.

Most probably, the reasons why we will feel we can live will look very different after the crisis compared with what they were before. Like water that has been blocked, our ambitions and enthusiasms will need to seek alternative channels down which to flow. We might not be able to put our confidence in our old social circle or occupation, our partner or our way of thinking. We will have to create new stories about who we are and what counts. We may need to forgive ourselves for errors, give up on a need to feel exceptional, surrender worldly ambitions and cease once and for all to imagine that our minds could be as logical or as reliable as we had hoped.

If there is any advantage to going through a mental crisis of the worst kind, it is that—on the other side of it—we will have ended up *choosing* life rather than merely assuming it to be the unremarkable norm. We, the ones who have crawled back from the darkness, may be disadvantaged in a hundred ways, but at least we will have had to find, rather than assumed or inherited, reasons why we are still here. Every day we continue will be a day earned back from death, and our satisfactions will be all the more intense and our gratitude more profound for having been consciously arrived at.

2 *Self-Knowledge*

A VISCERAL UNDERSTANDING

One of the great impediments to understanding our lives properly is our automatic assumption that we already do so. It's easy to carry around with us, and exchange with others, surface intellectual descriptions of key painful events that leave the marrow of our emotions behind. We may say that we remember, for example, that we "didn't get on too well" with our father, that our mother was "slightly neglectful" or that going to boarding school was "a bit sad."

It could, on this basis, sound as if we surely have a solid enough grip on events. But these compressed stories are precisely the sort of ready-made, affectless accounts that stand in the way of connecting properly and viscerally with what happened to us and therefore of knowing ourselves adequately. If we can put it in a paradoxical form, our memories are what allows us to forget. Our day-to-day accounts may bear as much resemblance to the vivid truth of our lives as a postcard from Naxos does to a month-long journey around the Aegean.

If this matters, it's because only on the basis of proper immersion in past fears, sadnesses, rages, and losses can we ever recover from certain disorders that develop when difficult events have become immobilized within us. To be liberated from the past, we need to mourn it, and for this to occur, we need to get in touch with what it actually felt like. We need to sense, in a way we may not have done for decades, the pain of our sister being preferred to us or of the devastation of being maltreated in the study on a Saturday morning.

The difference between felt and lifeless memories could be compared to the difference between a mediocre and a great painting of spring. Both will show us an identifiable place and time of year, but only a great painter will properly seize, from among millions of possible elements, the few that really render the moment charming, interesting, sad, or tender. In one case we know about spring, in the other we can finally feel it.

This may seem like a narrow aesthetic consideration, but it goes to the core of what we need to do to recover from many psychological complaints. We cannot continue to fly high over the past in our jet plane while refusing to re-experience the territory we are crossing. We need to land our craft, get out and walk, inch by painful inch, through the swampy realities of long ago. We need to lie down—perhaps on a couch, maybe with music—close our eyes and endure things, metaphorically, on foot. Only when we have returned afresh to our suffering and known it in our bones will it ever promise to leave us alone.

FIGURING OUT WHAT WE REALLY, REALLY THINK

What we really think about, for example, the character of a friend, or the next best move we should make in our career or our stance toward an incident in childhood . . . all of our conclusions on such critical topics can remain locked inside us, part of us but inaccessible to ordinary consciousness.

We operate instead with surface and misleading pictures of our dispositions and goals. We may settle, in haste or fear, on the most obvious answers: our new friend is very kind, we should aim for the most highly paid job, our childhood was "fun."

We ignore our truths first and foremost because we aren't trained to solicit them; no one ever quite tells us that we might need to exhibit the patience and wiliness of an angler while waiting at the riverbank of the deep mind. We've been brought up to act fast, to assume that we know everything immediately and to ignore the fact that consciousness is made up of layers, and it's the lower strata that might contain the richest, most faithful material.

We may also be hesitant because the answers that emerge from any descent into the depths and subsequent communion with our inner beings can sound at odds with the settled expectations we have of ourselves in daylight. It might turn out that in fact we don't love who we're meant to love, or are scared and suspicious of someone who is pressing us to trust them or are deeply moved by, and sympathetic to, a person we hardly know. It's the profoundly challenging nature of our conclusions that keeps us away from our inner sanctum. We prioritize a sense of feeling normal over the jolting realizations of the true self.

The steps we need to take in order to check in with ourselves are not especially complicated. We must make time, as often as once a day, to lie very still on our own somewhere, probably in bed or maybe in the bath, to close our eyes and direct our attention toward one of many tangled or murky topics that deserve reflection: a partner, a work challenge, an invitation, a forthcoming trip, a relationship with a child or a parent. We might need a moment to locate our actual concern. Then, disengaged from the ordinary static, we should circle the matter and ask ourselves with unusual guilelessness: *What is coming up for me here?* Holding the partner, work challenge, invitation, or disagreement patiently in mind, we should whisper to ourselves: *What do I really think? What is the real issue? What is truly going on? What is actually at stake?*

We should—to sound a little soft-headed—ask ourselves what our heart is whispering to us or what our gut is trying to articulate. We're striving to access a sincere part of the mind too often crushed by the barking, harried commands of the conformist executive self.

What we will almost certainly find is that, in a quasi-mystical way, the answers are already there waiting for us, like the stars that were present all along and only required the sun to fade in order to come to light in the dome of the sky. We already know—much more accurately than we ever assume—who we should be friends with, what is good and bad for us, and what our purpose on this earth is.

We need only a few moments in the dark at 11 p.m. or 5 a.m. to wander the corridors of the deep mind with the torch of consciousness and ask: *What have I looked at but never seen?*

FACING ANXIETY

One of the stranger aspects of feeling anxious is that we can be both suffering and markedly uninclined or unable to acknowledge that we are in fact so. We know of course that something isn't quite right, but a kind of bravery or pride keeps us running forward, unable to square up to the problem. It's as if, somewhere in our thoughts, we worry that looking at our anxiety directly will bring us harm: slow us down, cause us pain, or just be of no use.

It helps to note that our minds can easily carry more than one mood. They are like movie theaters with a variety of screens; there tends to be a foreground and a background to our emotional horizon in which very different things may be happening. In the foreground, we might— on a given day—be focused on achieving certain practical goals. Things might be fast-paced and relentless. We might keep opening tabs, scanning the diary, looking up emails—and diverting ourselves with glimpses at the news.

But then at another level, further back in the emotional sky, there might be something vast, eerie, and confused, a black sun we can't quite see or touch and yet also can't escape from. It tracks us everywhere; it is never not present but it doesn't ever clarify itself into anything with borders. If it had a soundtrack, it might be made up of distant bellowing occult horns. If it were a color, it might be a hazy dark burgundy and brown. If it were made of words, it would be about fear and doom.

It isn't, of course, very pleasant to be bearing this sort of diffuse anxiety within us. But we are not powerless before it and the way to defeat it is, paradoxically, to engage with it more directly than we probably have to date. Doing so is both easy and hard. Practically speaking, it requires nothing more than a few questions, questions which sound – at one level – utterly banal in their simplicity. But though such simplicity can be an insult to our pride, we should never do ourselves the injustice of assuming that our misery rests on something overly complex at a procedural level. We are sometimes like a high-powered aeroplane that can be grounded because a small screw is missing. We should be humble in the face of the ostensibly simple things that can ruin our lives.

With this caveat, we should step outside the ordinary flow of the anxious day for a moment, close our eyes, take a deep breath and ask ourselves this: *What am I really worried about right now?*

If we let the question resonate for a time, allowing its true profundity to emerge, we stand to find that, waiting until we have quietened the noise, there is a pain we knew all along, looking up at us with startled, wise eyes, like those of a tortoise we find hiding beneath a car or a fox burrowed in a corner of the garden.

We can continue the questioning: *Why is this thing so worrying?*

And then: *What could I tell myself to make this less bad?*

And finally, we can ask ourselves to complete a sentence: *I feel compassion for myself because . . .*

It sounds so simple and it takes only a few minutes, but it can decisively change the internal weather. Our minds are not obvious to themselves. We may be running for days, months, decades even, without pausing to wonder what is really the matter. We have so much misplaced composure, it can be dreadful to realize how fragile and scared we have been all along. We need to create a small safe place in which we can ask ourselves some basic questions—and whisper to ourselves what we are truly finding difficult.

3 Childhood

THIS FEELS LIKE AN INSULT

Modern psychotherapy is united on one point: Our problems require us to engage with our childhoods. This can feel profoundly offensive. How insulting to be told that childhood could matter inordinately to our adult lives, to our temperament, our chances of happiness, our sexuality, our levels of anxiety, and our self-esteem. Particularly if our childhood was difficult, we want more than anything to escape its dark centrifugal energy and to imagine ourselves as a free agent, able to determine the future without impediment. How dispiriting to be asked to believe that who we are was substantially determined by external factors before we reached the age of reason and, moreover, that if we are to have any hope of helping ourselves, we must undertake a painful and lengthy journey to understand the past in fine-grained detail.

It's clear why we might want to take out our annoyance on psychotherapy itself. Has this discipline not seen how broad and interesting the world is? How many grand and strange things there are in it? Hasn't it soared over the Western Australian desert or wandered the stately corridors of palaces and national libraries? Why does it so badly want us to return to, and circle, the messy claustrophobic start?

We understand. To take on the past, we don't need to be driven by a preternatural enthusiasm for self-exploration, we don't need to be self-pitying or dementedly furious with parents who were only trying to do their best. All that is required is a weary, dutiful realization that the principal way to overcome our history is to address it. We should try to remember not out of nostalgia, but in order to be able to forget, once and for all.

COULD IT MATTER SO MUCH?

Our unwillingness to look backward might have to do with more than just boredom or frustration; it might be a symptom of sheer incredulity that childhood could matter as much as it apparently does. Could this period be so critical? Could events in those short years have such an outsize influence on everything that comes after? Are children really so impressionable and so easily marked?

The short answer to all such enquiries is a weary, regretful but resounding *yes*. The human mind between the ages of one and ten is dauntingly receptive, infinitely attuned to its environment, which means that our whole identity can be decisively and near-permanently shaped by our young experiences. A somewhat cold, forbidding father or an erratic mother really may be all that is required to breed an elevated degree of anxiety or self-hatred that colors the next eight decades. This susceptibility has been present throughout history, but only now are we beginning to notice it and give it due attention. Every era had its share of childhood-damaged people, it's just that no one bothered to find out why the fishmonger was so sad, the merchant fell into rages, or the knight was impotent—just as no one bothered to investigate what might pollute water or how germs could spread. We are, finally, becoming a little more aware of causes and effects.

In insisting on the importance of the early years, it can help to think of the acquisition of language. Without having any memory of the phenomenon, all of us learned—between the ages of zero and five—many thousands of words and their seemingly limitless combinations. While we were innocently going about our business—doing cartwheels in the yard, drawing submarines at the kitchen table, eating cookies by the TV—a part of our minds was picking up and assembling, with extraordinary ingenuity, entire dictionaries of terminologies, declensions, verb endings, gerunds, and subordinate clauses. Without having any clue how it all happened, we became expert grammarians, far surpassing our mightiest computers in dexterity.

We should imagine that something similar was going on in the psychological sphere. We were acquiring an extensive command of emotional language: We were learning about trust, communication, esteem, kindness, cruelty, shame, anger, empathy, selfishness, and responsibility. And we didn't realize that this was happening any more than we realized that we were learning to speak. We were simply going about the ordinary business of childhood while being emotionally imprinted in a most permanent and comprehensive way by the people around us.

We now spare little time thinking of how relative our emotional language might be, just as we seldom reflect on the arbitrariness of speaking English or French rather than Sentinelese or Pirahã. We overlook that there are people for whom love is *mohabbat* (Hindi) or who bid each other goodnight with *hyvää yötä* (Finnish) or *wǎn'ān* (Cantonese). Or, to shift register, people who don't feel depressed every time they succeed or worry that any sexual encounter might end in shame.

And finally, as with standard language, with time we stand to realize how appallingly hard it can be to learn a new and different language, what a struggle we have ahead of us when we no longer want to speak in our allocated tongue—a tongue of anxiety, self-hatred, contempt, or cynicism—and seek to try to express ourselves instead in tones of trust, calm, and kindness.

THE DEFENSELESS IMPRESSIONABILITY OF A CHILD

To accept the importance of childhood, we need above all to take on board and inwardly feel the desperate impressionability and vulnerability of a one- or two-year-old child. Notice, first, their scale. The fingers are implausibly tiny, the wrists even more so. A modest bump to the head or three centimeters of water can finish them off. Notice, too, how out of control they are. Saliva dribbles from their mouth, their head bobs drunkenly when they are weary, they fall asleep in supermarkets or on the laps of near strangers. They're wholly, terrifyingly trusting. They lack all defenses. They take everything at face value. They'll follow you wherever you want to take them. You can tell them strange stories about who lives in the house next door, or why the trees look the way they do, or what sort of a human being you are. And they'll agree. They have no place from which to judge anything independently. They can't tell if Mommy is as nice as she claims, they simply know that she has supernatural powers and understands how to drive a car and make lumps of dough morph into cakes in the oven. They won't be able to determine whether what Daddy is doing is reasonable or kind until another decade has passed.

The vulnerability is both touching and—when you remember how damaged certain adults are—appalling. You can do anything with little people. Tell them you are their friend and then burn their hand, give them a lollipop and then separate them from their parents, whisper to them late at night that no one must ever know about this and ruin them for life. It sounds highly disturbing and it is.

We were those little people once. We aren't any longer. We know the ways of the world. We're tall and our voices carry. We can think freely. But this was once us—and the distortions of those years have a habit of remaining embedded within our minds for a long time, beneath a substratum of maturity. We owe it to ourselves to take a very patient look at what might have happened to us before we knew who we were.

WHAT IS A GOOD PARENT?

We can afford a few generalizations. First, and most importantly, a competent parent is someone who can feel inordinately pleased that their child has come into the world—and never ceases to remind themselves or their offspring of the fact, in direct and indirect ways, at small and large moments, pretty much every day. There is no risk of spoiling anyone by doing so: Spoilt people are those who were denied love, not those who had their fill of it.

Second, the good parent is attuned to their child; they listen—very closely indeed—to what the small person is trying to say. This means getting down on their knees and paying attention to messages that may sometimes sound extremely weird. Maybe the child is saying that they are very sad, even though it's their birthday and the parent has gone to enormous trouble with the presents. Maybe they are saying that they are angry with their teacher, even if education is in principle very important and the school was difficult to get into. Maybe they are explaining that they are fed up with Granny, though of course she means well and she's our mother too. Children are filled with complicated emotions that may have no place in the average adult's assessment of what is "normal," let alone convenient. Good parents suspend judgment and check their certainties. There is no danger of creating an entitled brat by doing so. People who cause a fuss don't generally do so because they have been listened to a lot; they start screaming—and later taking drugs and robbing stores—because their smaller, younger messages were never heard.

A good parent is, furthermore, not so fragile that they constantly need to be obeyed. They can take being sometimes called a fool because they lost their pride long ago. They're sufficiently on top of the unfairness of life not to mind being someone on whom a child, especially a teenage one, occasionally offloads their disappointments at the misery of everything. They don't need to instil terror; they have the self-confidence to be ignored or overlooked brusquely when a child's development requires it.

A good parent isn't envious of their children. They are strong enough to allow them to have a better life than they did. They aren't sadists: They never derive relief from making a child miserable. They don't feel any cleverer themselves by telling the child that they're an idiot, or more in control by monitoring the child's every move.

They don't want to pass on their sadness and regret. They don't think it's a good idea to make someone very unhappy because someone else made them miserable long ago.

They are sufficiently on top of their issues to be able to warn their children about them. They make it easy for the child to work out what the family madness is—and to move on from it. They don't insist on their normality and then challenge the child to determine where they've been lied to.

They don't inject their poison into anyone: Their jealousy, terror, ambition, or disappointment remains a matter for them alone.

They don't need attention from their own children because they have enough of an audience elsewhere.

They don't demand admiration—and certainly not gratitude. They know how to be calm and even boring. They absorb the child's excitements and terrors without adding to them. They show up day after day and act with reliable dullness. Of course they have drama going on beneath the surface, it's just that no child wants to think of their parent as overly complicated or three-dimensional. The good parent doesn't mind being, in a benign sense, a caricature.

The good parent knows how to play because their imagination is free: the doll can be a princess, the couch can be a ship and dinner might be pushed back by half an hour without peril. They're solid enough inside not to need to impose rigidity on the world. Sometimes, they can allow themselves to be very silly.

They know about boundaries. The game was hilarious for a long time, but now it's the moment to wind down, to put the paints away, to get back to work or to go up to bed. The good parent doesn't mind being hated for a time in the name of honoring reality.

Around the good parent, the child is, at the same time, allowed to utter "no" about certain matters, being a center of sufficient autonomy to disagree. It should not have the final say but should invariably have a voice.

The good parent is tender: Of course teddy's lost eye doesn't matter in the broad run of things, but the child's world is small and minor things loom large in it. Good parents therefore have the patience to respond to the child's minor crises and delights from a sure sense that maturity will emerge through precisely targeted indulgence.

We might think back to our past and give our carers a score to measure how things went. It isn't unfair or mean sometimes—in the privacy of our own minds—to hold people to account.

WHAT A BAD PARENT CAN DO
TO A CHILD

The power of a bad parent is almost without limit. Within only a few years, a bad parent might be able to create an offspring who:

is convinced that they are unworthy

hates themselves without limit

is perpetually certain that they have done something very wrong

constantly anticipates catastrophe

loathes their own appearance

fears everyone's rage and envy

cannot enjoy sex

is unable to explore their mind

always feels they need to agree, comply, and people-please

can't show their true self for fear of revolting everyone

will never put a stop to their own abuse, in whatever form this comes

has to puff themselves up with money and acclaim to feel acceptable

is compelled to torture others as they were tortured

cannot tolerate ambiguity and criticism

cannot play

must always be right

has to sabotage anything promising, kind, and good that enters their life

And that's just to start the list.

THE PARENTS WHO LIVE
INSIDE OUR MINDS

It's a measure of how invisible the process of parental imprinting can be that most of us would be highly surprised to think that a parent or two might be living inside our heads. The way we think seems to us to be the result of our own will. We seldom come across any voices or attitudes that feel actively foreign or externally sourced.

Nevertheless, given how long we were exposed to them and at what formative stages, our parents may have left more of a mark on us than we normally recognize and may be constantly commenting on our lives from inside like a chorus of unhelpful marionettes.

When we fail, a voice inside us may say: *You should never get above your station.* When a relationship breaks down, an inner voice might whisper: *Never expect anything from others.* When a nasty rumor spreads about us, we hear: *You were always too impulsive.*

It can help to ask ourselves a number of questions about our parents' views—as experience has taught us to conceive of them. We might, without thinking too hard and thereby allowing our defenses to choke our spontaneous insights, finish the following sentences:

My father gave me a feeling that I am . . .

My mother left me with a sense that I am . . .

My father would now think that I am . . .

My mother would now think that I am . . .

What our inner parents have to say is often not especially enlightened or in line with what we want for ourselves. And yet even so we can observe how deeply such ideas sink into us.

We can continue the exercise:

If I really needed him, my father . . .

If I really needed her, my mother . . .

To disagree with my father would mean . . .

To disagree with my mother would mean . . .

If I made a mistake, my father would . . .

If I made a mistake, my mother would . . .

Our parents' views rarely stick out in our minds. Instead, they merge with our own; they lose their identifying labels and become sides of everyday consciousness, indistinguishable from what we more broadly want and believe.

Yet we should try to reverse the process of absorption and recover some distance between ourselves and impulses and attitudes that may bear no relation to our healthier aspirations. It's bad enough to suffer; it's even worse to do so at the hands of what we might as well term, with no supernatural associations, a coven of unfriendly ghosts.

THE EXTREME LOYALTY OF CHILDREN TO THEIR PARENTS

We hear a lot about ungrateful children: offspring who lack respect and deference, who don't appreciate how much was done for them, who complain without reason and lament with unfair bitterness.

But what is often missed is how deeply children are, for the most part, loyal to their parents. They will go to enormous lengths to try to think well of those who brought them into the world, isolating things that are good in them and focusing on these wholeheartedly at the expense of memorizing what was mean-spirited or painful.

As psychotherapists have long observed, the worse the childhood, the greater and more manic the filial loyalty tends to be. There are no more tenacious defenders of their parents' legacies and reputations than those who were maligned, ignored, or physically harmed. In a choice between thinking that we might be bad ourselves or accepting that a parent was the disappointing and cruel one, self-hatred tends to win most of the time. It is, in the end, less devastating to deem ourselves ungrateful and awful than to imagine that we were brought up by small-minded mediocrities who were too ill or troubled to care.

ARE WE MODERNS UNIQUELY SELF-OBSESSED?

To compound our sense of irritation at needing to look at our child-hoods, we may have a nagging sense that doing so is a uniquely modern luxury. It can seem like evidence of a particularly regrettable kind of decadence and weakness that we should be spending so much time thinking of "Mommy" or "Daddy" while outside bigger and more important issues await us. We may enviously suspect that earlier, less cosseted and more martial ages had no time for any such non-sense. They were too busy surviving to indulge themselves in idle, circuitous thoughts about their ancestors and progenitors.

But we should be wary on this score. People in other ages may not have had the language of Freud; they didn't know about projection, the superego, or repression. And yet they thought a lot about mommies and daddies nonetheless—and worried intensely about the impact they had on their lives. Even while they were spearing enemies, tracking deer, or setting off in longboats, they were never far from extraordinary absorption in their own families' stories. They simply framed their interests in different terms.

In any premodern culture we might study, we can identify an obses-sion with the well-being and management of "ancestors." Every illness, perturbation of the mind, obsession, incapacity, or sorrow will imme-diately be ascribed to the work of the spirit of a dead family member; it is always about the past. And every society therefore learns to manage these figures from yesteryear with extreme care, with an understanding that an ancestor who has not been properly processed and put to rest will end up taking bitter revenge on us: we might become impotent or grow depressed, marry the wrong person, or fail in our careers.

A group of devotees and Buddhist monks pray inside Wat Lang Ka pagoda during Pchum Ben festival, September 23 2014, Phnom Penh, Cambodia.

In Cambodia, during the annual fifteen-day festival of Pchum Ben, the whole society turns its attention to its ancestors, stretching back as many as seven generations, and makes extensive and costly food offerings in their names, as well going to temples to carry out rituals and to chant songs for them. It's understood that the gates of hell have been opened at this time and any ancestor with a difficult character may be on the loose, looking to cause trouble, unless they are appeased by the strenuous efforts of the living.

We may not go about matters in exactly this way—we may head for the couch rather than the temple. But the underlying dynamics are strikingly similar. We are in essence always striving to ensure that figures from our pasts are not allowed to ruin what remains of our lives.

4 *Love*

The main ingredient on which any recovery from serious mental illness depends is also one which, curiously and grievously, never makes an appearance in any medical handbook or psychiatric diagnostic, namely love. The word is so fatefully associated with romance and sentimentality that we overlook its critical role in helping us to keep faith with life at times of overwhelming psychological confusion and sorrow. Love—whether from a friend, a partner, an offspring, or a parent—has an indomitable power to rescue us from mental illness.

We might go so far as to say that anyone who has ever suffered from mental illness and who recovers will do so—whether they consciously realize it or not—because of an experience of love. And, by extension, no one has ever fallen gravely mentally ill without, somewhere along the line, having suffered from a severe deficit of love. Love turns out to be the guiding strand running through the onset of, and recovery from, our worst episodes of unwellness.

What, then, do we mean by love, in its life-giving, mind-healing sense?

UNCONDITIONAL APPROVAL

What frequently assails and derails us when we are sick in our minds is a continuous punishing sense of how terrible we are. We are lacerated by self-hatred. Without any external prompting, we think of ourselves as some of the worst people around, even the worst person on earth. Our own charge sheet against us is definitive: we are "awful," "terrible," "nasty," "bad." We can't really say much more—and efforts to get us to expand in rational terms may run aground. We often can't even point to a specific crime, or if we do it doesn't seem to onlookers to merit quite the pitiless opprobrium we devote to it. In our illness, a primal self-suspicion bursts through our defenses and overtakes our faculties, leaving no room for the slightest gentleness. We are implacably appalled by, and unforgiving of, who we are.

In such agony, a loving companion can make the difference between suicide and keeping going. Such companions do not try to persuade us of our worth with cold reason; nor do they need to go in for any showy displays of affection. They can just demonstrate that we matter to them in a thousand surreptitious yet fundamental ways. They keep showing up by our bed day after day, they make pleasant conversation about something that won't in any way make us anxious, they've remembered a favorite blanket or a drink, they know how to make a few jokes when these help, and they suggest a nap when they feel us drifting away. They have a good sense of the sources of our pain, but they aren't pushing us for a big conversation or confession. They can tolerate how ill we are and will stick by us however long it takes. We don't have to impress them and they won't worry too much about how scary we are looking or the weird things we might say. They're not going to give up on us. The disease might take a month or six years or sixty, but they're going nowhere. We can call them at strange hours. We can sob or we can sound very adult and reasonable. They seem, remarkably, to love us in and of ourselves, for who we are rather than anything we do. They hold a loving mirror to us and help us to tolerate the reflection. It's pretty much the most beautiful and useful thing in the universe.

NON-JUDGMENT

Part of what can make the attentions of others oppressive is the note of patronizing pity we may detect beneath their apparent kindness. They— the well ones—have come to see us in order to help, but we sense how much they cling to a fundamental difference between the mess we are in and who they think they are. We are the insane ones and they will always fly the flags of health, rationality, and balance. They feel sorry for us from afar: We are the proverbial drowning man and they the observer on dry land.

Loving companions bear no such hints of superiority. They do not judge us as beneath them when we lie crumpled in our pyjamas at midday because they do not fundamentally see themselves as "above" someone who has fallen through the floor of sanity. We may happen to be very ill at the moment, but it could just as easily have been them if not for the accidents of psychology and of neurochemistry. They don't oppress us by covertly clinging to a belief in their own inviolable solidity and competence. They throw in little sentences that indicate that they too find life very taxing, that they too are very strange and that they too might one day be in our place.

LOYALTY

At the heart of many mental traumas is an early experience of abandonment. Someone, when we badly needed them, was not present and their neglect has thrown us off balance ever since. We may find it hard to depend on others in adult life and lack faith that someone won't run away, or take advantage of us, in turn.

A loving companion intuits this about us and is ready to fight to earn our trust. They know that they cannot blithely assert their loyalty, they will have to prove it, which means not deserting us at moments when others would be tempted to give up. We may try to incite despair and frustration in them as a way of testing the relationship; we may say some awful things and pretend to be indifferent. But if the companion is wise, they will listen and remain unruffled—not because they are weak, but because they understand that a basic piece of repair work around trust is under way.

We have to be given the chance, which we may have missed out on in childhood, to be a bit more demanding than usual in order to witness conclusively that this isn't enough to destroy love. We can be ill and still acceptable to another person. How much more real love will feel once it has been shaken by our disease and survived.

REASSURANCE

The future for a mentally ill person is a source of ongoing and limitless torment. A thousand questions hover: *What if someone gets very angry with them? What if someone wants to take them away? What if someone tries to kill them? What if the voices in their head never go away?*

The loving companion does their best to quieten the panic by presenting the future as unknowable in its precise details but fundamentally safe and bearable. They hold open options: it will always be possible to leave town, to live very quietly in a small cottage, to be at home and lead a domestic existence. No one expects them to perform great feats any more, just being is enough. There doesn't have to be pressure to earn money, to impress strangers, or to be heroic. Surviving is all that matters.

More importantly, the loving companion insists that they will be there to personally ensure that the future is manageable. When things get terrible, they can be in each other's presence and hold each other's spirits.

The loving companion doesn't get bored of instilling the same fundamental message: I am here for you and it will be OK. Even if this OK isn't what one would ideally want, still it will be all right, it will be better than death—which probably remains the alternative in the sufferer's mind. Quite how the years ahead are going to pan out can't be determined yet, details will have to be examined later, but what is known already now is that the future won't need to be unendurable, for a huge basic reason: because there is love.

PATIENCE

We are, when mentally ill, often extremely tedious in relation to the number of anxieties we desperately need to go through with others. We may want to return again and again to the subject of whether or not we said something terrible to someone at a party hosted by our workplace seven years ago. Or whether we might have unwittingly upset a sexual companion five years before. Or if we might go bankrupt because we didn't warn our accountant of a small move in our tax affairs.

Loving parents know that the minds of little children are similarly filled with anxiety-inducing and sometimes peculiar questions: *Is there a tiger under the bed? What happens if one of the trees comes into the room and takes me away? What if someone laughs at me at school?*

The temptation can be to rush in and give an answer full of blustering, impatient confidence. Of course it will be fine! Nonsense, there's no tiger! And so on. But the properly loving response is to take the worry as seriously as its progenitor does and address it head on, without scoffing or denying the scale of the concern. We might get out a pad of paper and a pen and run through all the many anxieties. It doesn't matter if this is the first or the fifteenth time we have done so. Love gives us the patience to enter imaginatively into the other's worried mind and to try to settle it by sensible examination of what there might be to fear.

We may be called upon to inspect for imaginary tigers night after night and, on the floor with a torch, should always be ready to go through the many reasons why these big cats have—after all—decided to leave us in peace.

JUST THE WAY YOU ARE

Many mentally ill patients have suffered all their lives from a feeling that they are not, in and of themselves, good enough. They are likely to have worked hard for decades and become extremely high achievers in order to prove to someone who was skeptical about them at the outset that they are respectable and worthy after all. They may have craved money and status and power to shore up a ghastly feeling of not being able to matter to people unless they had first attracted society's baubles and prizes.

When they break down, what remains unbelievable to these exhausted warriors is that they could ever be loved outside of their performance in the worldly race. Surely it is only their earning potential that counts? Surely it has to be their popularity that matters?

But now that they are ill and without any of the usual tools to impress, the mentally unwell stand to discover a more complex and salutary lesson. According to the values they have been subsisting on, they are a disgrace and should kill themselves. But with any luck, in the presence of a loving companion, they can start to believe in something far more nuanced and miraculous: that they could be loved without prizes, that true love isn't about impressing or intimidating someone, that an adult can love another adult a little like a good parent loves their child: not because of anything they have done, but simply and poignantly just because they exist.

INDEPENDENCE OF MIND

A good loving companion looking after a mentally sick friend heals through their power not to care very much about "what other people think." Of course, out there, some people are sniggering. Of course, out there, some people judge and say that the illness isn't legitimate or that it's deserved and that the sufferer was awful to begin with. The good companion knows enough about the perversities of the human mind not to worry in the least when they encounter everyday prejudice and meanness; daftness is to be expected. The hasty judgments of thousands of people will, of course, be askew and lacking proper understanding. But that is no reason to panic or give up our original analysis. Let them laugh, let them feel superior, let the idiots be idiots: These are the consoling messages of love that we need to hear when we are defenseless before the judgments of an unkind world. Our loving companion knows where their loyalties lie and isn't going to give up on us because a mob is jeering. They aren't democrats when it comes to love. They don't care if they are in a minority of one in cherishing us.

PARENTAL REPAIR

Both we and our carer may be deep into adulthood, but if their tenderness heals us, it is likely to be because, in covert ways, what they are doing through their ministrations is repairing a deficit of early love. They will be reparenting our broken child selves.

One of the eternally paradoxical things about babies and small children is that they need love as much as they need milk and warmth in order to develop properly. They need to be cuddled, spoken and sung to, played with, held close and looked at with enthusiasm – and will as good as die inside without such care. Every child needs to experience what one could term "primary parental delight," a basic feeling that they are limitlessly wanted by those who put them on the earth and are capable of generating intense pleasure through their very being. Without this, a child might survive, but they can never thrive. Their ability to walk the earth freely will always be somewhat in doubt. They will grow up with a sense of being superfluous, disruptive and, at heart, unappealing and shameful.

Such emotions feed directly into a broad range of mental illnesses: chronic anxiety, self-harm, suicidal ideation, depression. All of these have roots in a sense of not having mattered enough to anyone over long childhood years.

This defines the challenge for the carer in adulthood. Some of the work will involve making good failures of early provision. The wounded inner child will need to be convinced that what they didn't receive decades ago could still be available today; that there might still be joy, reassurance, play, and kindness.

It might seem highly patronizing to tell an adult that they need to be reparented. In fact it's the height of maturity to recognize that the small version of us must, if we're ever to get better, allow ourselves another chance to experience what it could feel like to matter limitlessly to a kindly companion.

COMPANIONSHIP THROUGH THE NIGHT

Way back, the night was when we were especially afraid, and especially needed love and reassurance. The same will be true in our periods of acute mental illness. The night will terrify us, stretching out as a vast and threatening space in which our worst fears and most critical voices will have unlimited dominion.

We need someone who can help us during these torturous hours, perhaps by remaining awake next to us, or by sleeping in an adjoining bed or room, or by giving us permission to call them whenever panic descends.

We will know we are properly loved when we can wake up at 3.30 a.m. and have the right to no longer be completely alone with our racing hearts and fearsome anxieties.

We shouldn't be so surprised at the enormous levels of mental illness at large in society. We just need to understand how bad we are collectively at love, how poor we are at being sympathetic, at listening, at offering reassurance, at feeling compassion and at forgiving—and conversely how good we are at hating and shaming and neglecting. We consider ourselves civilized but display levels of love that would shock a primitive tribe or a den of thieves.

Furthermore, we've opted to wash our hands of the issue of love and handed responsibility for healing wholesale to the scientists, as though they could culture a complete solution to mental unwellness through their pills. We ignore the fact that the cure largely lies in the emotional realm: in getting better at appeasing each other's fears, at being generous about our transgressions, at no longer tormenting and maltreating one another for our failures and at sitting together through the darkness in a spirit of care and kindly forbearance.

We should of course be under no illusion that the love described above will be easy to find. But at least by defining what it could consist of we can grow more clear-eyed about, and less ashamed of, the loneliness that has surreptitiously contributed so much to our suffering.

5 Community

One of the cruellest aspects of mental illness is that it strips us of our ability to believe that other people might be suffering in the way we are. We aren't being wilfully egocentric or arrogant; we are condemned by our illness to a feeling that we are uniquely pitiful, uniquely unacceptable, uniquely awful. The central legacy of mental illness, and a major contributor to our suicidal impulses, is a feeling of exceptionalism.

Once ill, we start to run away from other people. Gatherings become impossible, for we grow pre-emptively terrified of the presumed invulnerability and judgmentalness of those we might meet. We can't possibly make small talk or concentrate on what someone else is saying when our heads are filled with catastrophic scenarios and an intrusive voice is telling us that we should die. There seems no easy or acceptable way to share with old friends what we have been going through. They knew us as chatty and optimistic, so what will they make of the tortured characters we have become? We start to assume that no one on earth could possibly know—let alone accept—what it is like to be us.

This is especially tragic because the best cure for mental illness is company. Our disease denies us access to precisely what we most need in order to get better.

In 1892, the Swiss artist Ferdinand Hodler exhibited *The Disappointed Souls*. Five figures are pictured in varying states of dejection. We don't know quite what has gone wrong in their lives, but Hodler's talent invites us to imagine possibilities: a marriage here, a social disgrace there, a depression, a feeling of overwhelming anxiety . . . However awful the individual stories might be, the true horror of the painting emerges from the way each crisis is unfolding in complete isolation. The disconsolate figures are only millimeters away from one another, but they might as well be in other countries. It should be so

Ferdinand Hodler, *The Disappointed Souls*, 1892.

easy to reach out, to share the burden, to lend a comforting hand, to swap stories—and it would be so life-giving. But no fellowship seems possible in this insular hell. Sadness has wrapped each sufferer up in a pitiless sense of their own singularity.

Hodler wasn't painting any one scene. He intended his work as an allegory of modern society as a whole, with its absence of community, its lonely cities and its alienating technologies. But in this very depiction lies the possibility of redemption. We will start to heal when we realize that we are in fact always extremely close to someone who is as wretched as we are. We should therefore be able to reach out to a similarly broken neighbor and lament in unison. We should learn to come together for a very particular kind of social occasion the whole focus of which would be an exchange of notes on the misery and lacerations of existence.

In an ideal gathering of the unwell, in a comfortable safe room, we would take it in turns to reveal to one another the torments in our minds. Each of us would detail the latest challenges. We'd hear of how others were going through sleepless nights, were unable to eat, were too terrified to go outside, were hearing voices and had to fight against constant impulses to kill themselves. The material would be dark no doubt, but to hear it would be a balm for our stricken lonely souls.

Ideally, we would keep meeting the same people, week after week, so that our lives would grow entwined with theirs and we could exchange mutual support as we traveled through the valleys of sickness. We would know who was in particular difficulty, who needed tenderness and who might benefit from an ordinary-sounding chat about the garden or the weather.

It isn't possible that we are as alone as we currently feel. Biology doesn't produce complete one-offs. There are fellow creatures among the seven billion of our species. They are there, but we have lost all confidence in our right to find them. We feel isolated not because we are so but because we are unwell. We should dare to believe that a fellow disappointed soul is right now sitting next to us on the bench, waiting for us to make a sign.

6 *Psychotherapy*

The discipline of psychotherapy has a deserved place at the center of most accounts of a return to mental health. But what might it involve; what should we expect?

TRUE NORMALITY

Part of the reason why we may have fallen ill is because of the scale of the lies we have had to tell the world about ourselves—not in order to deceive, more in order not to shock or offend. Our illness masks a truth that is struggling to break through a compliant exterior. There is so much that we are meant to be but are not and are meant to feel but don't. And in the gap between our notion of respectability and our own reality, there grow silence, shame, anxiety, and guilt.

We may—in private—be terrified of being exposed as incompetent at work, while having to maintain an aura of poise in front of colleagues. Or we may be hugely frustrated with a partner or a parent while under pressure to show only consideration and calm. Or there may be a secret in our sex lives that seems wholly incompatible with what we hear discussed in the media or among our friends.

Therapy should at last allow us to be honest. We can finally tell someone else the secrets that have pained us for too long. We can tell a non-judgmental, judicious, wise observer about the appalling terrors that we have been assailed by and the incongruous thoughts that run through our minds. We don't need to be afraid of upsetting or surprising the therapist; they have seen all this before and much more. We can tell them about the crying in the night, the longing to be dead, the anxiety that strikes every morning, the fear of failure, the nature of our sexual tastes. We don't have to be cheerful, competent, restrained, or admirable. We can be ourselves, in all our complexity and strangeness. We can regress, complain, and lament, without fear of censorship and condemnation. We can start to heal ourselves through honesty.

TRUE AND FALSE SELVES

The psychoanalyst Donald Winnicott made a distinction between what he termed a "true" and a "false" self. In order to be healthy, a baby and developing child needs to be allowed to express and experience its true self: that is, it has to be honest about its actual wishes and desires, without fear of censorship or any pressure to compromise. If it is feeling furious, it should have a tantrum. If it's sad, it should weep. If it's envious, it should gnarl. It should be allowed the luxury to express its genuine emotions in all their raw intensity. Later on, of course, the child will have to be taught about manners and the feelings of others. Gradually, but only gradually, it will be shown the way to adopt—at points— a false self that knows how to smile, say thank you and not let on about its disagreements. But only if the true self has had its say for a good long while can development be healthy—and Winnicott knew that too many of us are wandering the world without having had the chance to be appropriately awkward and tricky with others before the demand to be polite set in. Going "mad" for a while may be our attempt to return to some of the feelings that we had to surrender too soon in the name of not angering or upsetting parental figures. Therapy can offer us a second chance to recover contact with the true self and rage and cry as much as we need to.

QUESTIONING OUR STORIES

We tend to be imprisoned by a set of stories and judgments that we repeat to ourselves without even noticing how partial, and usually unfair, they are to us, and how open they might be to being questioned and nuanced. For example, we may tell ourselves: *Respectable people don't have those sorts of sexual urges*, or *Good jobs are always unenjoyable*, or *No really good person would ever want to leave this kind of relationship*, or, more bluntly and definitively, *You are an ugly failure*.

We may not even know we're carrying such narrow and punitive notions within us, but a good therapist will identify them and gently probe at their logic, opening a sanity-restoring degree of space in our imaginations. They will raise new possibilities with us: *Might it not be OK to want something different sexually? Why not contemplate leaving a job that is evidently making us miserable? Must this relationship be for ever? And why? Is it really true that we have never done anything with our lives? Might we not be deserving and attractive?*

We may never have revealed to anyone the peculiar arguments that reverberate inside us and make us feel so hemmed in. But speaking these arguments aloud to an outsider can help us to see their absurdity and cruelty—and ultimately break their unwarranted spell over us.

THE STRANGLEHOLD OF THE PAST

Small children are incomparable learning machines, picking up language, motor skills, and social skills at an exponential rate in their early months and years. They are wholly porous to their environment so that they can learn French and European table manners in Paris and Inuit and fishing techniques in Iqaluit. But it's this very porousness that also makes them perilously vulnerable to the emotional peculiarities of their host families. We generalize outward from dubious premises. One particularly difficult father or mother can shape our expectations of men or women over a lifetime. Being emotionally neglected by a distracted parent can instil a lasting sense of worthlessness which no amount of later attention or fame can easily contradict. Fear of a volatile parent's temper can mold a whole personality in the direction of meekness and compliance.

The therapist's role is to incite the patient to get curious about the strangeness and partiality of their introduction into the world. What they might have believed was "normal" was in fact the result of a very particular, and problematic, set of circumstances. We are granted the right to question the sanity of our early caregivers and, in the process, to recover some of our own.

We may have inherited a script from childhood that dictates that we should only ever fall in love with people who leave us emotionally unfulfilled, or that we should start to panic that we will be attacked and humiliated the moment we do well professionally. Our script may tell us that no one will understand if we level a complaint against them or if we betray anyone on whom we have come to depend.

A therapist can open our eyes to how we may be following a script simply because it feels familiar, not because it is rational or in any sense connected to our satisfaction, and thereby offer us a chance to invent newer and more satisfying ways to lead our lives.

SORROW FOR OURSELVES

We may learn that we are ill because we have been brave for far too long. We have not been allowed to fully appreciate the difficulties we navigated—a depressed parent, a jealous sibling, a bullying classmate—and so have not shown ourselves the compassion and sorrow we have always been owed. We may need to cry long and hard about the past until the present ceases to seem so universally dark.

ANGER AT OTHERS

We may likewise need to feel a past fury that has grown cold and congealed inside us. Small children tend never to blame those who have harmed them. They depend on them far too much to dare to question their authority. They turn the hurt in on themselves: they wonder, for example, why they aren't good enough, rather than wondering what business an adult has in humiliating and crushing the spirit of a four-year-old. The intervention of a therapist can bring an earlier cruelty and illogicality to light and therefore permits some of the anger to be redirected from the self—where it might have been the source of depression and suicidal longings—back toward its true target. No longer needing to worry about retribution from an overbearing or fragile parent and assured of the justice of our feelings, we can take the risk of being, for a time, as angry as our mental health requires.

A SECOND MIND

It may sound odd or impolite to suggest that most of us, when we are in the grip of mental illness, are no longer capable of thinking. That's not how it feels of course. From the inside, our minds have probably never seemed so busy and so focused. From the moment we wake up in panic and self-disgust, we are ruminating, pondering, exploring catastrophic scenarios, scanning our past, attacking ourselves for things we have done and not done, questioning our legitimacy, talking to ourselves about how repulsive we are, paying attention to strange voices telling us that we are evil and sick and headed for the worst—and wondering whether and how we should kill ourselves. Our minds don't give us a moment of respite. We may rub our temples to cool them down but when we eventually fall asleep we are exhausted by the marathons our thoughts have run inside us.

Nevertheless, we may still want to insist—for the kindest and most redemptive of reasons—that we have not been thinking at all, that none of this hive of activity deserves the title of thinking; it is just illness.

To be mentally ill is to be swamped by secretions of fear, self-hatred, and despair that, like surging seawater through a pumping station control desk, knock out all our higher faculties, all our normal ability to sensibly distinguish one thing from another, to find perspective, to weigh arguments judiciously, to see the wood for the trees, to correctly assess danger, to plan realistically for the future, to determine risks and opportunities, and, most importantly, to be kind and generous to ourselves.

None of these faculties function any longer, but—and this is the true nastiness of the illness—we are never and nowhere alerted to our loss. We are both very ill and very unaware. It looks as though we are continuing to think as we have always done, with all our usual intelligence and reliability, but that we just have a lot more to worry about. Nowhere along the way does our mind do us the honor of telling us that it has begun to look at reality through a distorted lens, that it has, at some point in the day, to all intents and purposes stopped working. No bell goes off, no hazard lights flash.

Yet the truth is that we have lost command of about a third of our minds and are pulling together our ideas from the most degenerate, traumatized, unreliable, and vicious aspects of ourselves. It's as if a group of terrorists had donned white coats and were impersonating prestigious scientists in order to lay out a set of vicious theories and prognoses.

Once we have been through a few cycles of distorted thinking and finally recovered contact with reality, we should do ourselves the kindness of accepting that, on an intermittent basis, we will lose command of our higher faculties. There is nothing embarrassing in recognizing the possibility and accommodating ourselves to it very carefully.

We should get better at detecting when illness might be drawing in, what the triggers for it might be. Then, when it is upon us, we should do and decide nothing. We shouldn't send emails or deliver judgment on our lives or plan for the future. We should, as much as possible, stop all mental activity and rest. We might listen to music, have a long bath, watch something untaxing on television, and perhaps take a calming pill.

We should also try to plug our brain into the brain of someone else, to benefit from their greater powers of reason. If we have a trusted friend or therapist on whom we can call at such moments, we should ask them if they might help recalibrate and regulate our thoughts with an injection of their wisdom and insight. We should willingly put them in charge of determining how things are for us. They should be allowed to tell us what we are worth, what we have done, what there is to worry about—and that we should do our best to discount the doom-laden signals that emerge from inside us. They may be able to come up with innovative ideas that we're no longer capable of recognizing—and that could save us. They might tell us that it's OK to have secrets or that compromise is not always a disaster—concepts that our panicked minds would have had no way of conceptualizing.

We should strive to become thinkers who can acknowledge when they are no longer able to think.

FOREBODING VS REMEMBERING

Mental illness—which doesn't present itself as an illness to us of course, it's far too clever for that—frequently leads us to worry incessantly about the future: about bankruptcy, disgrace, physical collapse, abandonment. What is pernicious about this kind of worrying is that it attaches itself to genuine features of the here and now, presenting itself as reasonable. But on closer examination it clearly isn't. There is always something to be alarmed by: turbulence in the economy, things that go wrong with our bodies, reputations rising and falling . . . But what should eventually alert us to the peculiarity of our position is the duration, scale, and repetitiveness of our worries. We should learn to see that we are essentially worried all the time about something. The focus may shift, but what is constant is our insecurity about existence. It is in such situations that a therapist may make a hugely useful intervention, pointing out that the way we worry about the future is in fact telling us a huge amount about our past. More specifically, we are worried right now in a way that mirrors the panic we once felt as children; we are greeting the challenges of the adult world with the defenseless panic of the child we once were. What we are doing in the process is exchanging the pain of remembering the difficult past for a sense of foreboding around the future. The catastrophe we fear is going to happen has already happened.

So sealed off are our memories, we project them forward, where they greet us as apprehensions of what is to come. Instead, we should identify them as legacies of unmasterable past anxiety. The good therapist becomes aware of the correct source of the anxiety—and doesn't let go of their insight. They will listen politely and generously to our description of our current panic: *What will happen in our job, have we studied enough, what if our enemies gang up on us?* But then they will gently try to shift the conversation to the past, to show us that the future looks so fearful because we are being counterproductively loyal to the terrors of an earlier age, which we now need to remember, to feel sad about, and then eventually to mourn and move on from. We should be disloyal to those who brought us up in an atmosphere of fear in order to save what remains of life from always appearing doom-laden. We may be trying to stay close to them by continuing to panic alongside them, but we owe it to ourselves to break the circle of worry and to make our future different from the past by remembering, localizing, and mourning what belonged to yesterday even as it pretends to be about tomorrow.

REVISITING OUR YOUNGER SELVES

For many of us, childhood was a traumatically confusing and lonely time as we were placed in circumstances that far outstripped our ability to understand, contextualize, and properly apportion blame. As a result, we have grown up fundamentally mistaken about who we are and what we might deserve.

Returning to health can involve learning to go back to the child we once were, seeing ourselves in all our early helplessness and confusion, and bringing ourselves the benefit of adult compassion and insight. A visual metaphor for what this might involve comes in the work of the Japanese photographer Chino Otsuka, who, in a project called

"Imagine Finding Me," located old pictures of herself in a variety of childhood settings and then inserted her current self next to the child she once was. Thirty-three-year-old Otsuka slipped in beside ten-year-old Otsuka outside a boulangerie in Paris, popped up next to her on a beach in Japan, and, one winter, gave her a hand with a snowman she was building after a heavy snowfall.

This deceptively simple idea latches on to a powerful fantasy: that the older us could go back to help the younger us. How extraordinary it would be if we could give our comparatively frail and bereft tiny self the benefit of our adult strength, experience, poise, and confidence. If only we could return to provide ourselves with answers, to explain the adults around us and sometimes just to offer ourselves a consoling hug. We would be much more able now to navigate what we endured with such pain then. We would tell ourselves not to worry, we would guarantee that we were lovable and precious, we would hold ourselves through the long nights.

This might sound merely fantastical, but in fact it has practical applications in therapy. The reality is that our childhood selves still exist: their ghosts still wander around the old vacation destinations, they're still having bath time in the old house, they're still at school on winter mornings, and they are still crying at night in bed. No part of us ever really dies; our younger selves continue at some concurrent level in the unconscious and will cause us pain for as long as they remain fearful and abandoned.

The priority is therefore to go back and, just like Otsuka in her project, stand beside our younger selves in all their difficulties. We should slip into our bed the night we were sobbing after having been shouted at. We should take ourselves to school and sit at the desk next to ours and tell ourselves what we so needed to hear but never did. We should stand up to particular adults and make the speeches we were too inarticulate to utter. Our lost sad child is still inside us and won't let us rest until we have been able to witness and appease them.

Through therapy, we will get better once we have located the scenes

Chino Otsuka, *1982 and 2005, Paris, France*, from the series
"Imagine Finding Me," 2005.

Chino Otsuka, *1976 and 2005, Kamakura, Japan*, from the series "Imagine Finding Me," 2005.

Chino Otsuka, *1980 and 2009*, *Nagayama, Japan*, from the series "Imagine Finding Me," 2009.

that truly matter and then comforted and reparented ourselves back to health.

For all these life-saving functions of therapy, we should add that most therapists will not match the exalted hopes we have of them. This merely reflects the realities of the distribution of talent—which we should be ready for and accommodate ourselves to. Just as we can have the highest estimation of art but still find most practicing artists mediocre, so most therapists we come across are likely to be less than what they should be. We shouldn't despair or blame the profession as a whole; we should trust our instincts, politely leave, and keep searching until we find someone with the kindness, intellectual grit, humor, insight, and warmth we need. We will be very lucky if we find this therapeutic figure at once, but the eventual prize should make even the longest search worthwhile.

7 *Modernity*

People have fallen prey to mental illness for as long as our species has been in existence, so it could sound naive or punitive to single out any one era as especially responsible for generating mental troubles. Nevertheless, certain periods of history seem capable of bringing together such a confluence of aggravating factors and of so perfectly testing our emotional limits that they deserve to be considered as causes of mental unwellness in and of themselves.

Such may be the case with our own era, a time known as modernity which, notwithstanding its extraordinary technological creativity, overall peaceability, and increasing wealth, has imperiled our mental health as few ages before it ever have. The illnesses bequeathed to us by modern times may manifest themselves very personally within us, but a great many of their causes lie in the broader dynamics of society, economics, and politics.

We would do well to identify the myriad ways in which our age renders our mental lives more challenging than they should be—and then find techniques to sidestep the worst of our contemporary ills.

LIMITLESS AMBITION

The hallmark of modernity has been its impatience with anything that might set limits on human achievement. Whereas past ages resigned themselves to offering modest destinies to most of their citizens, modernity has insisted that everyone—whatever their background or families of origin—should be capable of realizing the most stellar feats. No longer should anything—education, background, race, creed—stand in the way of ambition.

This has been in its way an incomparably generous philosophy. But it has also, in the background, set up the ideal preconditions for mental instability. It is one thing to promise us all a chance of success, it is another to hint—as our era constantly does—that a modest destiny is essentially unacceptable. While praising lives of outsized accomplishment, our era has thrown a shadow over the ordinary lives that most of us will by necessity continue to lead. The norm has ceased to be enough. We cannot be average without at the same time having to think of ourselves as being what our age resents above all else: losers.

MERITOCRACY

For most of history, it was accepted that what happened to people in their lives was, to a critical degree, beyond their control or responsibility. The matter lay in the hands of the gods or of fortune, of luck or, more likely, of rigged odds. No one expected the world to be "fair," so it was natural to offer sympathy to oneself and others at the inevitable moments of failure.

Modernity has refused to accept this state of affairs. It has fought with unparalleled energy, whether in education, business, politics, or family life, to create a world that can be deemed just, one in which those who deserve to get to the top are able to rise and where rewards are rightfully apportioned to the most deserving candidates.

Though this too may sound like an advance, it carries a nasty sting in its tail, for if one is committed to believing in an order of things whereby those who achieve success invariably deserve to do so, then one is simultaneously signing on to a vision of existence in which those who fail must, with equal fairness, be deserving of their fate. In a meritocracy, an element of justice enters into the distribution of punishment as well as rewards.

The burden of personal responsibility grows exponentially and explains why this age has seen a corresponding increase in rates of suicide, since the blame for a life that has gone awry can only reside narrowly within each of us. We can no longer look elsewhere to explain why we have floundered; we can no longer blame the gods or bad luck. Winners make their own luck, goes the modern mantra, so we must logically also pay the full, unmitigated price for our failures.

ENVY

For most of history, we were protected from the ravages of envy by a class structure that denied most of life's advantages to all but a narrow and preselected few. Most of us had very little, but we also knew that there was no alternative to penury and that it was therefore not for us to gape with longing and desire at those with finer homes and carriages, horses and titles.

Modernity has freed us from such class-bound strictures. We are repeatedly informed that everyone is born equal and therefore we can and should aspire to the most gilded of lives, comparing ourselves to everyone else in our societies. We no longer believe in innate aristocrats or born peasants; we are runners on a notionally level playing field, able to reach whatever we aim for depending on our investments of imagination and energy. This means that the eventual gaps in social status and material wealth are no longer, as they used to be, an unremarkable feature of the natural order; instead they are a devastating reminder that the good life has eluded our grasp.

It becomes painful and at points intolerable to hear about old school acquaintances who are now scaling the heights while we remain, for causes we cannot overcome, tethered to more lowly stations. We are condemned to perpetual inadequacy in a radically unequal world of self-declared equals.

CHEERFULNESS

Past ages understood the need to leave a wide space for sadness and melancholy in the experience of every human being. Life was understood to be, for the most part, a matter of regret, longing, failure, incompleteness, and sadness. Buddhism declared that life itself was suffering; the Judaeo-Christian tradition emphasized that we were all the heirs of Adam and Eve, broken and tarred by sin, condemned to grief outside the gates of paradise. The situation was dark but, crucially, communally so. There was no danger of feeling isolated with one's woes; to exist was automatically to sign up to suffering.

Modernity has heroically thrown off such inbuilt pessimism. It is an age of resolute good cheer, of faith in the future and in our ability to overcome whatever challenges we face through willpower and technology. Pessimism has been recategorized as a disease.

But though the trajectory of humankind may, arguably, be on an upward curve, the arc of every life never manages to escape fearsome degrees of pain and loss. The human race may be getting happier, but each one of us remains exposed to a devastating range of sorrows. Except that there is now an added burden in weeping when we are meant to smile and in wanting to hide when others are insisting that we step out and celebrate. Our sadness starts to seem like a personal curse rather than what it more fairly always is: an inevitable feature of being alive.

SECULARISM

To further aggravate our emotional woes, modernity has cast aside what had been, since the dawn of time, a central resource for coping with life's vicissitudes. God has died and there is now little we can turn to, intone in front of, or beg for deliverance from when times grow hard. We dwell in a world ruled by the pitiless laws of science in which relief is on offer only from psychotherapists or psychiatric doctors, who equate our problems narrowly with our own personal histories and biology. It feels, for most of us, impossible to weep in temples and churches. We scour the universe for clues as to why we are here and what we are meant to do with our troubles, and hear back only static and silence.

At the same time, the disappearance of religion means that

humankind looms ever larger in our own imaginations. There is nothing left to relativize us. We used to be put in our place by contact with the spiritual realm. Every weekend, we would be shepherded into gloriously rendered halls and reminded of what a puny thing mankind was, how ridiculous were all our achievements, and how flawed and frail we were next to the majesty of God. The differences between human beings were as nothing next to the differences between us and the Almighty. We were usefully relativized by the shadow of the divine.

Now mankind is the measure of all things. Our heroes are drawn only from our own kind, our myths reference only ourselves and our strengths. We receive few lessons in perspective and modesty, losing our sanity in the gap between what we are meant to be and what almost all of us end up remaining.

LONELINESS

We could not in the past survive without the clan or group. Our natural frailty meant that we would need to lean on the family and community in order to survive. It made for oppression at points, but it also spared us modernity's recurrent risks of alienation.

We have grown ever more capable of subsisting without others. We can endure for days in cities of 10 million people without uttering a word. Yet we have lost the art of admitting our sorrows to others and of building connections based on vulnerability. We are lucky if we can lay claim to even one or two people we can call on when disaster strikes.

Our age attempts to cure loneliness through romantic love with the promise that we may, each of us, find one very special person to whom we can tie ourselves for life and who will spare us the need for anyone else. But this emphasis serves only to aggravate our isolation and renders our relationships more fractious than they should be, for no single person, however extraordinary, can ever replace our need for a more broadly based circle of support. We fail to bring the most important parts of ourselves to our friendships; we starve ourselves of the solace and salvation of the many in a misguided search for the one.

THE CHATTER

So seriously does our age take itself that it doesn't cease talking of its own melodramas and triumphs with a mesmerizing and maddening intensity. We have surrounded ourselves by gadgets that give us minute-by-minute insights into the perturbed and excited minds of billions of others—and that along the way deny us all necessary access to stillness, distance, and perspective, let alone time for self-knowledge and reflection. We grow convinced of the unerring importance of everything in the near term and can set nothing in its broader context. We pass our own mental perturbations on to one another under the guise of keeping ourselves "informed." The media spreads our madness virally and without respite. We come under pressure to know at all times "what is going on," without realizing how much we have abandoned ourselves to an enervating collective frenzy at the cost of our serenity and self-possession.

So pernicious are the trends of modernity, so greatly do they affect our chances of mental well-being, that sanity demands we exercise immense caution around our era and, as quietly as we need to, enter a state of what could be termed internal exile from some of its pressures. We may continue to benefit from the advantages of the modern age while simultaneously creating a wide berth between ourselves and its more destructive and cruel psychological ideals.

To do so, we might draw on a range of counter-cyclical ideas.

MODESTY

We know the attractions of extraordinary lives well enough: the glamour, the acclaim, the material abundance . . . What can be less familiar to us is their costs: the destruction of emotional stability, the frenetic activity, the lack of time in which to absorb experiences, the envy and hostility that success arouses, the fear of retribution, and the dread of downfall.

Once we have properly surveyed the merits and demerits on offer, we may willingly choose to side with what the modern age typically considers to be a disaster: a quiet life. This is not from any lack of ambition, but from a more focused aspiration for what we now recognize to be the primordial ingredient of happiness: peace of mind.

We might choose to live outside a large metropolis, not to push ourselves forward for promotion, to avoid the limelight, and to do a satisfactory but undramatic kind of work. We can discover the subtle greatness of a life in which we exercise our virtues on a domestic canvas, in which we do not seek to be known by people we don't ourselves know and in which the intricate love of a few carefully chosen souls replaces the hurried attentions of a host of unfaithful strangers. In such quiet lives, we can go to bed early, avoid functions with people we despise, work only for the money we need to secure a materially adequate standard of living, drop out of the status race, and refuse to assess ourselves according to the alien standards of a corrupt media.

We will have liberated ourselves from the madness of the age when we can look on loud and heroic lives—perhaps led by people we once knew—and with good faith say that this is not for us, that we are happier where we are, because we at last understand what we really require to survive mentally: cosiness, connection, and an ongoing lack of drama.

SELF-ACCEPTANCE

We know well enough the modern mantra that we are what we earn and that we count only in relation to the scale of our achievements. But it is open to us also to question this so-called meritocratic logic and to adopt a more generous point of view, one in which we count simply because we exist, and that our achievements, be they stellar or doomed, should not be the measure of the whole of us. We can throw off the idea that we always get what we deserve and that any reversal has to be judged as earned and therefore labeled just. We can accept the truth of an extraordinary redemptive idea that the modern age cannot tolerate: that it might be possible to fail in the eyes of the world and yet to remain valuable and deserving of love.

COMMUNITY

Every time we share a piece of our pained inner self with a like-minded friend, we defend ourselves against despair and self-hatred. This should matter to us far more than whether we have found one special romantic partner. What we need is a network of non-judgmental souls who have known enough of their own suffering to be ready to show us compassion and tenderness when we stumble.

PERSPECTIVE

We need to puncture the self-importance of the age with regular contact with older, deeper, wider sources of feeling: through contact with a natural world that pursues its own priorities with little reference to our own sagas, through the reading of history books that shrink our modern-day adventures and convulsions to a more manageable and rightful size, and through travel to countries that take no interest in our own peculiar national preoccupations, scandals, and triumphs.

AN INTERNAL HUT

We might, in order to escape modernity totally, seek to move to a hut somewhere far away. We would dwell amid nature with our own thoughts and, ideally, a circle of supportive friends. We would not need to be harried and pressured to conform to foreign ideals of success. But moving ourselves physically may not be necessary. What we may need is not so much an actual hut as a hut inside our own minds, one to which we can retreat when we know that we are being assailed by values that are inimical to our sense of balance and self-love. We may continue to wander through the modern world, to all intents and purposes just another obedient citizen of its value system, while internally highly suspicious of the messages we are receiving and committed to re-placing them with ones imbued with far greater kindness and justice.

We can blame ourselves too much for our mental suffering. It is not that we are personally fragile but merely that we are living in a high-tech age that routinely smashes its more sensitive members to pieces through adherence to what will one day be recognized as a grossly primitive and unimaginative ethos.

8 *Self-Compassion*

If there is one generalization we can hazard about those who end up mentally unwell, we could say that they are masters at being very nasty to themselves.

The worst kind of nastiness doesn't have to involve shouting at oneself or calling oneself an idiot, though this might happen too. It means that one part of us continually drives the other toward self-doubt, fear, paranoia, shame, and despair, without revealing that it is doing this or that there might be other options available. Panic and self-flagellation become identified with safety and virtue. No attention is drawn toward the partiality of the choices that are being made internally—otherwise the game would be up. Self-loathing may be the order of the day but it is never presented as such. We just think that we are "normal," hard-headed and interpreting reality as it truly is.

Release from the grip of self-loathing therefore has to start with an awareness of what we are doing to ourselves—and what the alternatives might be. For example, we might start to notice that no sooner has something nice happened to us than we set about wondering when something awful will strike in revenge; that every success has to be ruined by a feeling of foreboding and guilt; that every potentially pleasant day ends up marred by panic or a sense of loss; that we spontaneously imagine that everyone must hate us and that the worst things are being said about us the moment we leave any room.

None of this looks on the surface like "nastiness." We could just say that we have a "worried mind" or a "regretful temperament." But it is useful to group these ideas under a single title in order to fully identify the direction in which they point: toward the systematic destruction of any pleasure in being ourselves. This is, when we think about it, a very nasty thing indeed to do to someone. Without realizing it, we are committed to throttling our chances of contentment. We dwell inside a mind in which every good element has to be spoilt and every vicious, destructive, alarming, and cruel thought has to be honored.

As an experiment, we might imagine trying to be as kind as possible to our own minds, in order to see how differently things might unfold. Rather than dragging every last deformed and mean idea into the theater of consciousness, we could dare to be vigilant about only presenting our minds with the very kindest and most reassuring ideas. The moment we leave a room, we could ruthlessly prevent thoughts about our unacceptability from manifesting themselves in the usual way; they might beg to be let in, claiming all sorts of reasons why they should be, but for once we could give them a firm "no." If they keep trying to force their way into our minds, we might put on a piece of music or do some gardening—anything other than allow destructive thoughts to have their normal hold over us.

Likewise, when the old familiar thought about the future being terrible knocks at the door, we might refuse to let it in. When we wake up with the traditional burden of guilt about our past mistakes, we might decide to pay no attention. We then realize that we have agency over the things that fill our minds and that we don't have to surrender control to our masochistic stage manager at every turn.

We might along the way start to appreciate that other people do not give their worst thoughts unlimited sway. They don't give endless time to ideas of their own dreadfulness or their likely destruction. They don't allow whole days to be lost in catastrophic forebodings. And one way to make sense of the reason for this is that they are fundamentally, without being aware of it in this way, *kind to themselves*; they are not in the business of torturing their own spirits.

Where does this unconscious impulse to be unkind to ourselves come from? How is the choice to torture ourselves made? We can hazard another generalization. The way we treat ourselves is an internalization of the way others once treated us, either directly in the sense of how they spoke to us or indirectly in the sense of how they behaved around us, which could have included ignoring us or openly displaying a preference for someone else.

Our early caregivers did not literally instruct us to worry about our right to exist or tell us to panic constantly about what might happen next. But the way that our minds now work bears the imprint of their relationship to us; it is an extrapolation from their messages of fear and ridicule, humiliation and shame, which we have absorbed as careful students.

To get a measure of where we stand on the spectrum of self-love, we need only ask ourselves a very simple question—one that we have nevertheless ignored for far too long: *How much do I like myself?* If the answer immediately and intuitively comes back that we feel we are loathsome, there is a history that we urgently need to consider and are, conveniently for our self-torturing minds, choosing to ignore. The contempt we habitually show ourselves is neither fair nor right. We should spot the oddity and partiality of treating ourselves with a viciousness that we wouldn't accord to our worst enemies.

This self-hatred breeds low self-confidence and a continual fear of disaster. Terrible things must, after all, happen to terrible people. We are denied any confidence in ourselves as workers, parents, friends, and humans more broadly, and are terrified both when things go well, because our comeuppance is sure to be just around the corner, and when we contemplate the future, which must be filled with dreadful and threatening prospects. It's one of the more unexpected features of mental life that what manifests itself as "anxiety" is really, at heart, a form of intense self-suspicion.

For a long time, self-hatred can be disguised within an outwardly normal life. The destruction blends in. But just how dangerous and unfair we are being to ourselves is likely to come to the fore when we hit a crisis, making some sort of a mistake or encountering a reversal. At moments when anyone might experience a dip in their degrees of self-love and confidence, we enter a completely different and more perilous zone. The bad news confirms every one of our savage impulses and self-suspicions. It kick-starts efforts to conclusively tear ourselves apart. Not only are we somewhat in trouble and responsible; we are, as we tell ourselves, a catastrophe and despicable, foul and damned. Self-torture can quickly end up with compulsive thoughts of self-extinction.

People who commit suicide aren't those for whom a few things have gone very wrong; they are people who have encountered some otherwise survivable reversals against a background of fierce self-hatred. It is the self-hatred that will end up killing them, not the apparent subjects of their panic and sorrow.

As ever, salvation comes through self-awareness. There is nothing inevitable about self-hatred. We are treating ourselves unkindly because people were in the past not especially kind to us—and we are being touchingly yet dangerously loyal to their philosophies of derision. Harshness can have a glamour all of its own; it can seem the more serious and powerful approach to take toward our characters, as though we were doing ourselves a favor, and even securing our safety, by whipping our consciences as hard as possible.

But if we're to stay alive, we need radically to redraw our moral code and return to kindness the prestige that it should always have had. Kindness to ourselves is the single most necessary quality for success and endurance. That we spent so long on the side of cruelty is a sign not of its utility, but of the scale of the distortions we have inherited from the past. We have learned far too much about a lack of mercy, about panic, about self-suspicion and finding oneself pitiful. Now, when we have felt the temptations of suicide, we need to rediscover the virtues of forgiveness, mercy, calm, and gentleness. And when we panic and feel intensely anxious about the future, we need to remember that we are in essence worrying about our fundamental legitimacy and lovability. Our survival depends on a swift mastery of the varied arts of self-compassion.

9 *Gratitude*

A particularly unfortunate consequence of mental illness is its power to close us off from the world, from its beauty, its interest, and its power to distract us from ourselves. We are liable to be so engulfed in what feels like a life-or-death struggle, we forget that there is anything outside the walls of our own minds. Every morning is likely to begin with fear and trepidation; it feels like a close-run thing whether we will make it to evening. In the circumstances, there is little chance to observe the dawn, we don't hear the birdsong, and we miss the way the rising sun briefly dressed the horizon in a mantle of purple gold.

Once upon a time, when we were children, we were champions at observation. A simple walk to the park offered a treasury of discoveries. There was the brick wall along which we liked to run our hands; there was an ant that we saw on the sidewalk and followed until it disappeared into a mysterious hole just wide enough to take its body; there was a small yellow flower growing in some rubble whose stem we caressed and whose petals we rubbed against our cheek. There were the clouds we observed, stretching and distending themselves like swirls of milk in coffee; there were the three gigantic trees whose weathered bark we ran our nails across and wanted, if we'd been able, to knead and wrap ourselves in.

It can feel as if there is no time for such frivolities now. Adult life has grown drained of delight. We spend hours poring over our emotions with therapists, we visit psychiatric doctors, we sit in ugly rooms discussing our pains with strangers.

It isn't that we have resolutely turned our minds against appreciation. We simply lack encouragement—and, we might say, permission. We need to have it confirmed to us by some external source that it is not trivial to look up from ourselves for a while, that the capacity to find delight in so-called "small things" is at the core of recovery and strength. Appreciation may once have been automatic but that isn't an argument against a little artificiality in restarting its engines. We may need to be nudged, occasionally, to pause with our travails and take a moment to look around. The huge things won't be solved quickly. We're going to be with anxiety and despair for a little while longer yet. But that is no reason to shun moments of relief.

It is artists who may best stimulate our appetite for observing the world through the evidence of their own heightened sensitivities. We might consider, for example, the work of Gustave Caillebotte (1848–94), an exceptionally generous observer of our place on the earth. He looked closely at summer fruit, skies, the view from the window in mid-afternoon, the atmosphere in the park. In 1875, while staying in his family's home in Yerres, south of Paris, he went down to the river on a gray day and grew fascinated by the patterns made by large drops of summer rain on the surface of the water. We have seen such a sight hundreds of times before, but are unlikely—for a long while at least—to have given it its due, to have grown appropriately mesmerized by the complex geometries of interlocking circles, by the refractions of light, by the variegated sounds of water falling into water.

Caillebotte's painting isn't about our distress. It doesn't know anything about the broken relationship with our spouse, our troubles with lawyers, our financial anxieties, our fear of the future . . . But it seems to grasp that such things might exist and yet insist that they do not, right now, need to swallow the whole of our lives. For a moment or two, we can slip out of ourselves, pause on our walk by the riverbank and take in something that will remind us that it is worth keeping on with existence.

We might, following the example of Caillebotte, sometimes interrupt our internal dialogue in order to study daisies in jars, someone's hands, an old map, a photo from childhood, a pencil on a new sheet of paper. We have suffered so much, we are so aware of all that is difficult and arduous, but we have not been barred from adopting the wide-eyedness of children and artists. Indeed, it is against the backdrop of

Gustave Caillebotte, *Yerres, Effect of Rain*, 1875.

The Yongzheng Emperor Admiring Flowers, c. 1725.

our difficulties that beauty becomes not just pleasing but moving—a reminder of our true home, to which we so long to return.

In our efforts to appreciate what is still good, we might also take a lead from the exceptionally busy Yinzhen (1678–1735), fifth emperor of China's Qing dynasty, who was much preoccupied with reforming his country's taxation system and rooting out corruption in local officials, but nevertheless found the time to take his son and a few of his favorite courtiers out for a picnic in the fields near Beijing, in order to look at the flowers, at some point around 1725.

It is touching to note the solemn expression of the Emperor, who has interrupted the affairs of state for something as easy to overlook as some spring flowers. Yinzhen was known to have been a deeply pious and serious man, but he evidently retained a secure hold on life's real priorities, nudging us to recalibrate our own hierarchy of importance in the direction of the overlooked beauty of the everyday. If an emperor can do this, then we—for all our afflictions—can too.

Much remains imperfect; most of us have lives that are not as we would want them to be. But this should not become a reason to refuse modest pleasures. We should be sure to carve out moments when, despite everything, we can still savor incidental arguments for hope, sweetness, and an end to suffering.

10 *Routines*

We understand that in order to create a world-class athlete, it isn't enough to work on someone's muscle strength. We need to watch how they sleep, what they eat, the company they keep, the clothes they wear. Similar care is taken when trying to train elite soldiers or musicians; a whole way of life has to be examined and adjusted in order to deliver the right results. The foremost example of this totalizing approach can be found in the history of religions. Behind the invention of the monastery is the notion that, in order to fashion a mind that can focus appropriately on the divine, a great many details will need to be considered and rethought: what sort of hairstyle someone has, the kind of material their tunic is made out of, what time they have breakfast, how they sit when they read or contemplate and what the view should look like out of the window.

Underpinning such interest is a conception of the human being as immensely susceptible to the influence of what we in the secular realm tend to call, with fateful neglect, "small things." It seldom occurs to us to trace the connection between apparently incidental sensory and physical routines and what passes through our minds. We treat the mind as a more or less wholly isolated organ that can continue to function as we would want it to whatever food we serve it, however much rest we give it and whatever the architectural or natural vistas that lie before its eyes. We implicitly deem it impossible that our thoughts could be heavily colored by the sort of light we are exposed to, the articles we read, or the kind of exercise we take. No such indifference was ever permitted in Zen Buddhism or Catholicism. These careful belief systems developed elaborate traditions around posture, tea drinking, breathing, and gardening because they did not subscribe to our walled-off vision of the mind. They saw continuity between beliefs and, among other elements, how we bathe, the words we say on waking up, the kind of crockery we use, and the speed at which we eat our dinner.

We should take inspiration from this spiritual vigilance in the quest for our own mental health. We should borrow from the manic sensitivity of religions to imagine spaces and routines that can give our minds the best possible chances of finding and then holding on to robust reasons to keep living.

Here are some of the elements we might consider.

SLEEP

Part of the reason why many of us have a tangled and unhelpful relationship with sleep can be traced back to the way we first learned about the subject many years ago. Parents of small children tend to be very careful about bedtimes. They favor early nights, give their babies plenty of naps throughout the day, think a lot about black-out curtains, are quick to diagnose many instances of bad temper as stemming from a background deficit of rest and, while they may be indulgent in some areas, are likely to be entirely implacable in any negotiation over routines.

None of this is remotely altruistic: tired small children are a nightmare to look after. Every reversal becomes a drama, every disappointment turns into a catastrophe, and every excitement shifts into mania. A halfway decent adult existence is impossible alongside a tired child. Self-interest necessitates totalitarianism.

But while a draconian philosophy is useful in the early years, it can set up an awkward dynamic in an offspring's mind as adolescence sets in. Growing up and asserting their independence and individuality can then become associated with a newly defiant and cavalier approach to bedtimes. Not for a newly empowered young adult the strictures and denying rules of the past. Why bother to put the light out by ten or even midnight, given that they are so obviously no longer a toddler? And as they have no more use for nappies, why worry that they are still finishing something on the computer as the first signs of dawn appear in the eastern sky?

What is thereby missed is how much every adult shares in a young child's sensitivity to a shortfall of sleep. Just like our younger selves, we do not automatically have a reasonable view of our own prospects or condition. There are many different ways of telling the stories of our lives, ranging from optimistic accounts of progress mixed with noble defeats to tragic narratives of thoroughgoing stupidity and unforgivable errors. What determines the difference between madness and sanity may be nothing grander, but then again nothing more critical, than how long our heads have been allowed to lie on a pillow in the preceding hours.

It's especially unfortunate that this connection is so easy to miss. No bells go off in our minds warning us that we are running low on nocturnal nectar; there are no parents around any longer to nag us up to our rooms; plenty of well-meaning friends invite us out for meals that begin at 9 p.m.; our screens never fail to have something new and interesting to tell us at every hour. What's more, no stylish or authoritative figures in the public realm ever seem to urge us to turn in early or proudly show off their cautious bedtime routines. Being meticulous about sleep is something that only a very dull or defeated person would care about.

As a result, we start to believe many dark things with doomful ease: that our relationship is over, that everyone hates us, that our lives are meaningless, and that human existence is a cosmic joke. As Friedrich Nietzsche knew, "When we are tired, we are attacked by ideas we conquered long ago." We go mad from tiredness long before we notice the role that exhaustion is playing in stealing our sanity.

We need to recover some of the wisdom of our early years. We may be a sizeable height, holding down an important job, and capable of performing impressive feats, but in terms of our vulnerability to emotional chaos, we are no more robust than a very young infant. Whenever we sense our spirits sinking and folly and anxiety pressing in on us, we should abandon all endeavors and head to the bedroom. We should be as proud of our regimented sleep patterns as we are of a neat house or a flourishing career.

Underpinning our care should be modesty. While thinking through our problems is crucial to our health, to attempt to think without enough sleep is worse than not thinking at all. The thinking we do when tired is vindictive and sloppy. It misses important details, gives the advantage to our enemies, and hands victory to the evangelists of sadness. It isn't disrespectful to the power of the mind to insist that we shouldn't attempt to fire up this machine unless and until it has been adequately restored to health—like a powerful rocket or exquisite motorboat that we wouldn't dare to activate unless we could be sure of a clear sky or a calm sea.

Understanding our vulnerability, we should never take seriously any worry that suddenly appears extremely pressing after ten in the evening. What we panic about in the early hours should automatically be discounted. No large conversation or argument should ever be undertaken past nine o'clock.

Being careful doesn't just apply to the night. At varied points in the day, when we are overwhelmed, we should know to stop and hoist a white flag. It may look as if we should keep trying to fight our demons. In fact, we need to sidestep them with a nap. We may feel guilty, but it is lazier and more irresponsible to try to keep going than it is to know the game is up for now. There is never anything shameful in admitting we can't cope. It's this very knowledge that guarantees us a chance to fight another round soon.

When we lie in bed, it makes sense to think of ourselves as akin to a smaller, furry mammal, a rabbit or perhaps a squirrel. We should lift our knees up very close to our chests and pull our duvets over our heads. We might soak a whole patch of the pillow with our tears. We should metaphorically stroke our own weary foreheads as a loving adult might once have done. Grown-up life is intolerably hard and we should be allowed to know and lament this.

We shouldn't feel weird in our weepy-squirrel position. Other people go to immense lengths to hide that they do, or would like to do, the very same sort of thing. We need to know someone extremely well—better than we know 99 percent of humanity—before they will let us in on the scale of their despair and anxiety and their longings for a cozy, safe nook. It looks childlike but it is in fact the essence of adulthood to recognize and make space for our regressive tendencies.

What the curled-squirrel position indicates is that not all mental problems can be solved by active reasoning. Not thinking consciously should also be deemed a part of the mind's work. Being curled up in bed allows our minds to do a different sort of thinking, the sort that can take place when we are no longer impatiently looking for results, when the usual hectoring conscious self takes a break and lets the mind do what it will for a time. It is then, paradoxically, that certain richer, more creative ideas can have the peace and freedom to coalesce, as they may do when we are out for a walk or idling in a cafe. Thinking isn't what we do best when it's all we're meant to do.

There remain plenty of reasons to live. We simply may not be able to see them until we have allowed ourselves the privilege of a weepy nap or a long night's sleep.

FOOD

Mental illness is often bound up with a sense of shame, self-disgust, and self-flagellation. We scour our past for reasons to hate who we are. We appear in our own eyes as unworthy and despicable candidates who should never have been allowed to be.

It's a measure of the close connection between diet and mental health that such thoughts are particularly likely to come to the fore following certain sorts of meals. After a lunch or dinner soaked in trans fat and sodium nitrate, processed sugar and corn syrup, saccharin and palm oil, potassium benzoate and butylated hydroxyanisole, reasons for our non-existence can appear especially persuasive.

In a quest for mental health, we would be advised to take in only those ingredients that help dampen our anxiety, weaken our self-hatred, and strengthen our sense of hope. Some of the following are especially to be recommended in a diet for a vulnerable mind.

Camomile tea

We, the ones forever on the edge of madness, hardly require anything to stimulate us further. We have visions aplenty without the fluorescent colors added by caffeine or alcohol. What we require above all else is something that can slow our racing thoughts and hold us to our most sensible and quiet mental pathways. With a cup full of hot camomile tea, we will be forced to sip slowly, the steam will gently caress our eyelids and we will treat ourselves as who—without any pejorative connotations—we really are: convalescents.

Figs

We should incline toward foods that have been tampered with as little as possible by the artifice and wiliness of chemists, foods that would have been around in much the same form when the world still had some of its original innocence and quiet. The fig seems to understand sadness and vulnerability. It keeps its appeal muted and it may not be until after we have eaten one that we properly appreciate how nourishing and flavorful it was beneath its serene, unshowy exterior. It urges us to follow it in its attitude of humility and reticence.

Nuts

Especially sympathetic to mental health are handfuls of walnuts and hazelnuts, cashew nuts, and (unsalted) pistachios. They seem to rein in the ambitions that ordinarily torture us. They satisfy us with little and thereby urge us to quieten our restlessness and ignore the chatter and excitement of the public square. They reach a special pitch of sanity-inducing goodness when accompanied by three or four dried apricots.

Dates

A good life can't be free of moments of delight and ecstasy and the date knows this. There has to be room for a degree of excitement. The date delivers ravishment when required, but it is also limited in its power to derail us. It will never render us manic. We could not—even though it can seem as though we might—become addicts of this fruit. It won't allow us to escape ourselves for too long but it will, for a few moments at least, reorient us toward the light.

Feta cheese, Kalamata olives, and bread

This should count as a meal for us in moods of mental torment, taking us back to a basic existence and reassuring us that this can be tolerable and wholesome. We don't need very much to survive. The walls may have closed in and yet pleasure can be drawn from the most apparently insignificant elements. We may lose everything but there will still be this, and alongside it the love and care of a few imaginative and loyal people.

Dark chocolate

It can be as black as the night we fear, but it is—without melodramatic sweetness and with a grown-up understanding sternness—on our side. It leaves behind an almost metallic taste that endows us with courage and resolve without adding guilt or judgment.

In our ill moods we're unlikely to have the energy to cook or even think about food, so we can end up highly vulnerable to the blandishments of processed dishes. Yet we should take care that food never becomes yet another reason why we might hate ourselves or regret decisions. We should lean on a few simple menus to carry us across the most difficult, frightened phases of our inner lives.

BATHING

It is a sign of our lack of civilization that we insist on thinking of baths primarily as tools to clean ourselves with rather than honoring them as what they truly are: instruments of mental health.

The Romans would have been astonished by our modern plumbing, our ability to summon up a flawless cauldron of piping-hot water at the turn of a tap inside almost every home at negligible cost. Our boilers would have awed them, our pipework would have been the envy of their engineers. These were people who did not consider a country or province properly colonized until public baths had been constructed, who moved mountains and cut through forests to ensure a regular supply of water, who left behind elegant bathing establishments from northern England to the edges of the Sahara desert, from Mérida in the Iberian West to Palmyra in the Levantine East.

And yet it would have puzzled the Romans how silent we are on the deeper resonances of bathing, how few poems and odes there are to our moments in the tub, how unimaginative we tend to be about the powers of hot water to heal our souls.

All of us have come from warm, watery encasements and, when mental troubles strike, we should immediately head back into the bath to be held, as the womb once did, in a tight aquatic embrace.

Hot water is a symbol of love and care. It allows us to let down our guard and, as at so few other moments, to be at once defenseless and safe, naked yet cozy. We can bolt the door, turn down the lights, and allow ourselves to do nothing for a time other than watch the water lap at our knees and occasionally up the temperature with a small scalding infusion.

We don't need to force ourselves to arrive at any great conclusions. This is a time to idle and free-associate. We can let the mind wander, perhaps backward to more innocent days or to the moment when the troubles began. We can float over our lives without our usual critical inclinations. We can drown our pain in the heat, cauterize our mental wounds, and let our tears lose themselves in the steam.

We may want to keep a small towel and a pad of paper and a pencil by the bath, in case something strikes us that could put a better spin on our travails. Or we can simply float and wait for some of the panic to subside, as it surely will.

Those of us who suffer in our minds should not be embarrassed to have as many as three baths a day, each one lasting up to an hour. They will be the enamel ships that carry us over the worst of our griefs.

EXERCISE

One of the great impediments to taking exercise is the idea that being unwilling to do so must be caused first and foremost by something called "laziness." The reason why we are sitting on the couch a lot, or are spending a considerable time in bed, or are seriously reluctant to run is that we are, in essence, bone idle.

But we must get to the root of what is really going on with the mentally unwell. They don't sit around because they are lazy but because they are ill, and it's a specific feature of mental illness that you may be especially hampered when it comes to the matter of moving your body with any degree of vigor.

One might say that mental illness makes one retreat – from the world in general, its trees, its people, its sagas and concerns and joys. But it also makes us retreat from our own body, from its limbs, its skin, and its right to be. One might say that illness squats at the front of consciousness in pain and is reluctant to let anything carefree or mobile or fluid get through.

Many varieties of mental illness freeze us, not with fear necessarily, though that too, but with self-hatred, shame, anxiety, and regret. With such moods coursing through us, we are in no position to stretch, to run, or to gambol. We are rooted to our spot, a place of sadness, misery, and dread.

We know all the arguments in favor of exercise—they are incontestable. Our limbs need to move, our lungs need rapid oxygenation, our skin needs to sweat vigorously. But when we are ill these arguments end up feeling punitive and accusatory. They remind us of all that we are incapable of, of how badly we have failed and of how awful we are.

To have any chance of exercising, we need a different, more forgiving approach, one built first on a lot of modesty. Because we are ill we can't be an athlete, certainly not for now. So by "exercise" we mean something far gentler than might ideally be recommended. The only exercise we are capable of will be mild in the extreme—realistically, we are talking about going for a walk and not much more. This doesn't sound like any sort of feat, but nor do many of the achievements of those who are in recovery. They become heroic only once we know what the individual had to go through to pull them off.

The walk might be only once or twice around the block, but it will still be extremely valuable, especially if it's repeated every day. In many forms of mental illness, such is our degree of shame we don't feel we have permission to leave the house. We feel it is illegitimate to be outside "enjoying" ourselves, worried that we will be seen and negatively judged. We want to hide because we feel like a monster in the eyes of others. So it's an enormous feat to put on a coat and, against all our instincts, wander out as though the world could be a habitable, welcoming, and safe place.

Yet how salutary it can be to take the risk, because there is healing to be found in the sight of the trees on the horizon, the starlings in a hedge, a duck by the meadow, a dog next to the supermarket. What we are seeing is soothing evidence that the world exists beyond our own cruel, mean-spirited ill minds. There is so much that knows nothing of us, that is gloriously indifferent—those stars appearing in the dusk sky—and that isn't there to shame us. We slowly reinhabit our bodies. Outside seems so much more normal than what is inside our heads and we can take inspiration: Someone is moving house, a child is playing with a stick, there is a cat on a wall resting in the sun.

Things may not be as awful as we had assumed when it was just us in the bedroom, going through the narrow, dark corridors of memory. We can feel our feet taking slightly longer steps, our lungs working a little harder. We have walked once around the block already and no one has attacked us, no one has mocked us, no one is laughing. We are doing extremely well.

We shouldn't push it. Exercise can be very minor and still wholly beneficial. We aren't going to be marathon runners, but we have managed something extraordinary nonetheless. We're athletes of a different sort, tackling a different enemy, and our battle is already well under way.

SILENCE

The news media serves two essential constituencies: people who are running nations and businesses; and people whose lives are a little too quiet, a little too undramatic, and a little too serene for their own tastes.

These two broad categories are unlikely to comprise anyone who self-identifies as mentally unwell. The last thing that we need when things are going awry in our minds is yet more evidence of folly, melodrama, chaos, aggression, partisanship, and an absence of forgiveness. We owe it to ourselves to become willingly more ignorant of what is going on in our highly disturbed and disturbing media.

The minds of the mentally ill are already engaged in titanic struggles and battles. While there may be no outward movement, inside heroic efforts will be taking place to answer back against the monsters of self-hatred and to hold the door against the hounds of self-contempt. They will be facing floodwaters of anxiety that try to sweep away every last hope in their path, crushing like toys elements placed in their way, like plans and affiliations and a sense of identity. If we could hear this struggle it would have some of the melodrama of a Wagner opera; and if we could see it it would have the turbulent quality of a Turner painting. Someone could be sitting down on the couch, looking sad, occasionally

J. M. W. Turner, *Valley of Aosta: Snowstorm, Avalanche, and Thunderstorm*, 1836–7.

putting a finger to their lips, while inside their benighted mind scenes might be unfolding akin to *Valley of Aosta: Snowstorm, Avalanche, and Thunderstorm* set to the sound of "Ride of the Valkyries."

In the circumstances, we don't need to have our nerve endings further shocked or titillated. What we urgently need, and may die without, is quiet. Despite the pressure to "stay informed" and know "what is going on," our real responsibilities lie elsewhere: in not knowing a great many things in order to keep faith with life itself. We will have our hands full reviewing our past, battling despair, and hanging on to reasons why it might be worth surviving until next summer. This leaves no time to be curious about the parliamentary elections or the latest dilemmas facing an actor and her partner. The apparently innocent activity of reading the headlines now counts as a hugely reckless act.

We should tell those who love us and are living in our vicinity to help us direct our minds toward hope and kindness. We should beg them to switch off all media and not bring any papers into the house. Let them not refer to anything that hasn't been around for 200 years at least. We should focus on eternal verities and on small sympathetic, generous ideas nearer to home.

We need serenity in which to challenge our beliefs that we are awful, that the worst will happen to us and that we won't be able to survive. We need calm in which to rebuild faith in ourselves and in existence more broadly. To assist us, we need interiors like those depicted in the works of the great Danish master of stillness Vilhelm Hammershøi, rooms in which the sun washes on to clean, empty surfaces and all that can be heard in the distance might be the sounds of a child playing in the yard or some pigeons on the roof opposite. We don't need any further arguments in favor of chaos and nastiness. We have enough of this in our heads for twelve lifetimes. We don't need to titillate ourselves with the thought that the world might boil or be rocked by a nuclear accident or that a new disease might ravage us. Let someone else keep an eye on the bigger picture, calling us only when the crisis is at the door; for now, leave us to fight our inner world-shaking struggles in a corner of a quiet, sunlit room.

Vilhelm Hammershøi, *Interior in Strandgade, Sunlight on the Floor*, 1901.

HOUSEHOLD TASKS

A traditional approach to mental healing stresses the need to face up to our demons—at all times and with full courage. The underlying idea is that we fall ill when we attempt to back away from certain painful but necessary truths about our inner lives: that we are in a very unhappy relationship, that we were traumatized in childhood, that we are addicted to a substance, or have not dared to do justice to our sexuality. We will only get well, so the theory goes, once we cease to crowd out our own reality; the glare of honesty will save us.

But while we can amply recognize the toll of certain forms of denial, we can still make a nuanced case for the other side, for the occasional need—especially when we are very unwell—to take some time off from self-analysis. We should do so not in a spirit of escape but rather from a feeling of consciously giving ourselves a few hours away from our problems so that we can return to them with renewed creativity and strength. Distraction intelligently handled can be a part of mental healing.

We might therefore want to recommend that the mentally fragile make soup or freeze batches of pasta sauces; weed the garden and seed flowers for the spring; scour the internet for new kinds of peripherals for the computer; ensure that the stairs are spotless and the windows free of all finger marks; or invest in a strange kind of sanding machine with which to finally sort out the door that doesn't close properly.

Of course it's important to talk about key figures of childhood and try to trace the origins of our fears of disgrace. But it could be equally important at other moments to run away from the incessant pain inside us by making fishcakes or raking the garden.

Small household tasks offer us a metaphor for the sort of fixing we're interested in but can't yet quite manage inside ourselves. They give us the courage to imagine a day when we might be as tidy inside our minds as the linen cupboard outside currently is—thanks to what we did all afternoon.

There is kindness in making sure a mentally unwell person has a few untaxing duties to take care of every day. Monasteries understood the unruliness of the mind and the kindly role of chores in assuaging it. They allowed the monks to think head on of God and their responsibilities within a spiritual life for many hours at a time. But they also gave them moments to think of something that was simpler and more exhausting. Hence the emphasis on working in the vegetable garden and the kitchen, the laundry room, and the pantry.

It can be the height of generosity to ask someone who isn't well to help us change the sheets and prune the artichokes. It won't be work; it is in reality a minor vacation from the exhausting labors that must soon resume within.

MENTAL CONVALESCENCE

It's one of the benefits of most physical illnesses that they are immediately observable and hence command a ready degree of respect and kindness from those around us. We know to prop a pillow beneath the person with a broken arm, we immediately open the door to someone on crutches.

But without anyone meaning to be thoughtless, it is harder to keep this caring attitude in mind when dealing with a mentally unwell person. As sufferers, we may ourselves forget our condition, launching into tasks and situations for which we are not ready and which will undermine our efforts at recovery.

To get well, we need to recognize fully that we are ill and therefore that we must endure a period, which could be very lengthy indeed, of convalescence. This will mean rigidly patrolled and regulated routines, an absence of stimulation, a huge emphasis on rest, and a close monitoring of visitors. We should be as careful with ourselves as we might be if we were recovering from a cancer or lung operation. We may have no physical scars but we should do ourselves the kindness of accepting— simply based on our symptoms—that we are as sick as those in intensive care wards or those for whom sirens wail across the city at night.

We need to be selfish about the state of our spirits and ruthless in removing ourselves from situations that sap us. We should go to bed early, eat lightly, bathe often, go for a walk every day, have something pleasant to distract us, and, most of all, be kind to ourselves because of the mess we are in.

We should learn from physical rehabilitation how long it will probably take to feel well again. Recovery from a broken wrist might take six months; it can be a year before a new hip is fully functioning once more. A mind that's broken can take longer still; it could be one or two years, even four or five. We shouldn't be surprised. The mind is a far more complex organ than any bone or muscle and so warrants a correspondingly lengthy period of recuperation. Nor, as with other injuries, should we expect progress to be linear. There will be many days when we go sharply backward, when we're catapulted back into the sort of despair we had hoped to leave behind for ever. We should not be discouraged, though. What matters is the overall trend as measured across months, not a bad day here or there. There will be periods of darkness just when we had started to hope once more and we should greet them without panic.

We have become experts over many years in a distinct language, a language of illness and self-torture. It will take a great deal of time to unlearn it and become fluent in the language of generosity and self-compassion.

We may not be living in an institution, but we should proceed with as much care and seriousness as if we were. We should construct hospitals for the mind within our own homes and educate those around us about our needs. We will gradually grow well again as we learn to lead the peaceful, warm-hearted, kindly, and well-regulated lives that our minds have craved for so long.

11 *Work*

Even without knowing the specifics, we can hazard that work—somewhere along the line—will have heavily contributed to our falling mentally ill. But at the same time, we can suggest that work, if correctly rethought and reconfigured, may play a central role in our recovery. We should learn to handle this double-edged sword with particular care.

WORKING TO IMPRESS

Our emotional difficulties with work tend to begin with the way that it apparently offers us an unparalleled chance to impress those who do not, or did not, originally believe in us. It is the favored tool of all those who start in life with a feeling of being under-loved, under-appreciated, and overlooked. It is the instrument of vengeance of the once-ignored. Under the guise of a merely practical pursuit, it carries a heavy emotional mission: it is the means by which we try to earn our right to be.

It may for a while seem to fulfill this purpose very well. Success can earn us preferment, a higher income, honor and fame, which can assuage our underlying sense that we are undeserving and shameful.

But the healing is only ever cosmetic, temporary, and subject to constant reversals. All success necessarily brings with it envy and criticism. The moment we have achieved a prominent position, dissenting voices will emerge to claim that we are illegitimate and unworthy, and thereby remind us of precisely the negative self-image we are pedaling so hard to outrun. We'll be torn between listening to praise and focusing on the thread of denunciation—and the latter will be the only one that mesmerizes us.

No amount of success will be able to expunge our inner sense of baseness and unlovability. We may work monstrously hard, not because our material needs are so elevated but because we are only ever a few steps ahead of a chorus of inner voices telling us that we are futile and ludicrous.

Over time, we will fall prey to exhaustion. The source of our tiredness won't be the work itself, it'll be the constant effort to keep at bay a confrontation with our original lack of self-love. It'll simply be too tiring to spend a whole life insisting through our labors that we are not bad people.

IMPOSTOR SYNDROME

Related to such symptoms will be a continuous feeling, while at work, that we are about to be unmasked as not up to the job that we are claiming to know how to carry out. Whatever our technical competence or years of experience, our emotional state will imbue us with a conviction that we do not deserve the respect and trust of those who depend on us. The gap between what we are claiming to be and what we suspect we deep down are will lead to an increasing sense of anxiety and dread. We may fear being suddenly and publicly unmasked, denounced anonymously or humiliated at a time of our colleagues' and enemies' choosing. Paranoid thoughts will haunt us; we may have moments of blind panic and be unable to speak in public. In the end, it can feel easier to fail and so prove our inner voices right rather than continue to defy our latent self-suspicion.

THE BREAKDOWN

If we are extremely lucky, a breakdown does not need to be merely the end. We will be failing in certain eyes of course, we will be letting down a lot of people and dashing the hopes of those who need us to perform in a certain way.

But if accompanied by the right sort of care, a breakdown can allow us to review the role that work was playing in our lives and to cease using it as compensation for an emotional wound. We can see that the real tragedy isn't that we messed up our impressive careers but that we so badly needed to have them in the first place in order to make up for early and unexplored deprivation.

Our failure may have stripped us of chances to impress in the worldly sense. At a stroke, though, we'll be liberated from those false friends and colleagues who pegged their attention to our money and status. And all we will have to fall back on are those who understand love and are willing to be concerned with us not because of anything we can do for them, but simply because we are alive. This may be the first time we have ever witnessed such unconditionality—and it will correct a lingering misapprehension that we can only earn care through performance.

The breakdown will offer us a path toward a more authentic way of living, where who we really are, shorn of our trappings, can feel acceptable. The failure we always dreaded would happen has unfolded and we are liberated, no longer having to worry about it as a feared spectre.

In the ruins, we may be able to ask ourselves new questions: *What do I actually want to do? Whose opinion do I really care about?* We'll have slain the dragon of prestige and may now be ready to live on our own terms for the first time.

AUTHENTIC WORK

We may have to go back as far as childhood to ask: *What did I really enjoy doing? When did I feel most alive?* There may be clues to what our future should be in the way we used to play as small children, when impressing and earning money were far from our minds.

We should allow ourselves to think in original ways, casting aside any prejudices about what a respectable or reasonable job might be. We should be unbothered by fears of failing, for this is a seam we have now fully explored. We should go back to what work should always have been for us, which is a source of intrinsic satisfaction, before it got saddled with the task of assuring us of our value as a human being in the eyes of an imagined hostile and skeptical audience.

HELPING

Our mental troubles will have opened up fresh territories of pain for us. We'll be aware from first-hand experience that a whole subsection of the population is laboring under mental torment and we may be newly motivated to help them as others have helped us.

We may be able to use our own history of pain to help strangers in their agony, lending our time, empathy, love, and curiosity. We may have doubted that we could ever be of true use to anyone—we fell ill partly because of a basic sense of superfluity. But by targeting work where helping others in grave distress is the priority, we can derive a visceral sense of the difference we can make to someone else's world. We may not be earning as much and people at large may not care a jot, but we'll have all the affirmation we need for ourselves in the knowledge that we are—on a good day—able to lend someone else a reason to live.

SMALL IMPROVEMENTS

Much work seeks to have an impact on a large scale over an extended time period, involving hundreds and perhaps millions of players.

Given our fragility, we might be counseled away from vast and complex efforts. We need tasks that can leave us feeling, at the end of every day, as if we have made a small but notable difference in someone else's life. Perhaps we have in a modest way improved their command of a language, or cleaned up their garden, or given them something nourishing to eat. We may not have pushed the boundaries of know-ledge or be remembered in a thousand years, but we'll have done something more substantial still: kept ourselves steady against enor-mous odds and made an honest contribution to the welfare of a few ailing fellow humans.

12 *Pessimism*

It may be hard to imagine that the word "pessimism" could have any role to play in mitigating the effects of mental illness. But that would be to underestimate the covert persecutory aspects of its opposite, optimism. The expectation that our life *should* be well, that we *should* be forever free of anxiety and despair, paranoia and loneliness, is both understandable in its ambition and confidence and yet quietly tormenting.

Those of us who have been visited by severe mental illness need to cling to darker counsel. We, members of a not insubstantial minority, have been stricken by a fragility that will not lightly ever leave us alone again and so we need to be ready henceforth always to greet life with particular care: grateful for whichever days go well, serene in the face of those that don't, appreciative of the small gains we are capable of, and permanently vigilant as to the possibility of relapse. We have been denied the easy-going lives we would have loved to lead and should not add insult to injury by continuing to regret them. They should be mourned rather than lamented.

We should accept with grace that things are, naturally, not as we would wish them to be. We will have to hobble when we would have loved to gambol freely. We'll need to be creative about exploring how life could be bearable in circumstances far less rosy than anyone would have wished. We will have to give up our pride: that is, our assurance in our own competence and automatic right to dignity. We have been humbled and ridiculed by our own minds.

At the same time, we should take steps to make ourselves at home in the darkness. We should willingly expose our reason to our worst, nastiest, and most invalid thoughts rather than let them steal up on us at a time of their choosing. We should practice thought exercises that strip our fears of their unexamined hold on us.

The anxious should defiantly accept that they can never eradicate certain risks but that these can be shouldered—and a habitable life made among the ruins. Our relationships may never go right, certain family members will always resent us, particular enemies will never come over to our side, we cannot correct mistakes in our career, there will invariably be doubters and outright sadists. But none of this should surprise us and we should not let undue innocence aggravate our mood. We should explore the unbudgeable sadness on sunny mornings, when our reasoning faculties are lively and calming, instead of letting matters unnerve us in 3 a.m. confrontations when we are too groggy and worn down to know what to answer our demons.

We should heed the fact that it has already been very bad and, if it were to be so again, we would cope as we have already done. We should take comfort from the thought that we have suffered what some would consider to be the worst scenario—we have actually gone "mad"—and yet we are still here, more or less coherent, still able to enjoy one or two things, still capable of gratitude and occasional appreciation. We should, simply on the basis of what we have survived, not be very scared of anything much at all again.

We must accept with grim cheer that it wasn't to be our fate to belong to the mentally robust cohort. When the angels were distributing brains in the upper atmosphere, we were accorded one of the more sensitive, erratic, brilliant, tumultuous ones, which we will have to continue to watch like anxious nurses for the first signs of fracture till the day we die.

But the troubles we feel so personally are not in reality ours alone. We are a community of the ailing and the more we can discover and connect with its other fascinating, consoling members, the less our troubles will weigh on us as singular punishments. The mood of society as a whole may tend remorselessly toward cheeriness. We have access to a dark cheerfulness of our own, shared among fellow sufferers, who are equally resolute in meeting a fate they never asked for, do not deserve, but refuse to be cowed by.

13 *Skepticism*

Few things come more naturally to us than trust in our own minds: their first impressions, the feelings they summon up for us, their judgments about people and situations, their assessments of who we are, what we are worth and what the future may be like for us. It feels right and normal that we should accept, without hesitation or compunction, whatever response our minds put forward to our consciousness. Why would we go to the trouble and tedium of starting to doubt what we innately and automatically think and feel? We must surely be able to trust our very own thinking machines.

Yet at the core of recovery from mental illness is the continually bewildering realization that our minds are, at key moments, objectively extremely unreliable and illogical. And, to compound the problem, they give us no sign at all that they might be any such things. They insist on their reasonableness even while they are behaving in what we can only much later deduce, with great patience and effort, is a foolish, harmful, or demented way. We have a grave enemy and deceiver right between our ears.

For example, these minds will tell us with total sincerity that the future holds something entirely awful for us and will thereby ruin decades of our lives in paranoid obsessions and compulsive rituals. They will tell us with supreme confidence that we face grave danger by doing something that actually doesn't imperil us at all, and might even bring us a chance to flourish. They will encourage us to sabotage relationships filled with love and possibility, driving willing partners from our arms. They will tell us to give up on hugely promising work projects for fear we'll annoy someone and will inform us that there is grave danger in building up faith in ourselves.

Our brains cannot think straight because they are reasoning via experiences in the past that were anomalous, unfair, unrepresentative, and unreliable. These brains claim to know that we are useless because that is how we happened to be viewed by one or two caregivers when we were very small and our neural networks were being laid down. They have complete assurance that achieving success will be dangerous for us because it once was, for a little while, around a jealous and inadequate relative who died many years ago. These brains keep sabotaging our relationships because of one relationship that hurt us immensely when we were too young to know how to defend ourselves. Or they keep us in a subservient position vis-à-vis someone in the present because this was once the safest way to be, when we were under five.

Our flawed brains are fateful generalizers from their earliest moments. They take the raw material of our young lives and extrapolate universal theories from it which can destroy our chances of responding adequately to the diverse and novel conditions of adult reality.

Recovering mental health depends on doing something utterly counter-intuitive: doubting our first thoughts on pretty much all topics through an appreciation of our innate biases, how they are structured and where they come from. We should put a large distance between ourselves and any impulse that washes over us. Strong feelings—that we have found our ideal life partner after ten minutes, that we must leave a person immediately, that we are about to be destroyed, that everyone hates us, that disaster is upon us—should invariably be resisted, placed in a safe zone and inspected with the utmost rigor, calm, and skepticism. We should develop an ingrained suspicion of our greatest, most spontaneous certainties, asking a whole series of questions of them: *Is it really true that they told me they hate me? Did they actually say they wanted to end the relationship? Is there real evidence that everything is over?*

It's a curious way to live, and a humbling one too, to have to pass our certainties through a constantly skeptical sieve and to demand that we sleep on conclusions and discuss them with a reliable friend before acting on them.

At given moments, especially when we are tired, we should realize that we are not capable of thinking correctly and should therefore stop thinking altogether rather than mangle our conclusions any further. We should hold on to the idea that when we are especially distressed and upset, we will have lost our hold on the fragile thread of reason.

There will be certain ideas that enter consciousness with which, politely, we should just refuse to engage—because we have done so too many times before and know they are futile and disconnected from anything real. There really is no point in thinking, for the millionth time, about how ugly we are, how bad we are, how guilty we are. These aren't thoughts that have anything sensible to tell us about our lives today. With due respect to our minds, we'd be better off putting on some music, counting to a hundred or calling up a friend.

We'll be on the road to recovery and sanity when we see that one way to be properly reasonable is to appreciate how much of the time we aren't able to be so. We aren't disrespecting ourselves; we're properly honoring our complex histories and the congenitally flawed thinking patterns they have unwittingly led us to.

II : Love

Central to the process of overcoming mental turmoil is learning more about what love really is, so that we can detect its absence in the way we treat ourselves and start to nurture and honor its presence in those we decide to be close to.

We are often sold a fundamentally and unhelpfully romantic view of love, which proposes that love is the reward given to a person for their strengths: it is what someone can expect to receive when they are supremely beautiful, rich, impressive, or popular. The most lovable person on earth is—according to this philosophy—simultaneously the most gifted and consummate one.

But there is another, broader, nobler conception that understands love not as a reward for strength but as a sympathy for, and commitment to attending to, weakness. Love is what we feel when we see a small baby, helpless before the world, reaching out for our finger, clasping it tight and pulling a frail and grateful smile. Love is what we register when our partner, usually composed and competent, comes to us with apology and confusion, begging for our help.

However impressed we may be by beauty and flawless achievement, what we should truly love is vulnerability. We begin to love, rather than merely admire, when others no longer have to exhibit perfection to seem worthy. Simultaneously, the people we should put our faith in are those who do not recoil from us in our frightened or hesitant moments, those who don't just want to clap at us and be awed by our triumphs. They are those who can be moved by our crises, who are on hand in the dark hours, who will still be around when the rest of the world is jeering.

Similarly, the properly self-loving person isn't the one who congratulates themselves when they have pulled off an astonishing feat; it's the one who knows how to speak to themselves in a kind voice when everything has gone wrong, who can remain kind in the face of ill fortune, who doesn't have to berate or criticize themselves without mercy. We should feel proud of having attained a capacity for such love. It isn't weakness or charity; it is an achievement founded on the most dignified understanding of what we must do to accede to our full humanity.

We will have finally learned to love—ourselves and others—when fragility and imperfection touch us and incite our desire to assist, to understand, and to console.

1 *Learning to Love*

To begin with the love of others . . . A melancholy paradox lies at the heart of modern relationships: We know that to thrive emotionally must involve love, but on the ground contented unions are dauntingly rare. It is tempting to believe that those for whom love works out have been granted a form of divine favor. But we cannot build a decent life on the hope of randomly distributed heavenly munificence.

There is no need for superstition or despair. Good relationships are neither mysterious nor random. There are solid, rationally structured explanations for why some people do well together while others, despite powerful initial hopes and touchingly idealistic intentions, do not. Success seems random simply because we have to date operated with an insufficiently firm grip on the actual mechanics of true love.

There are, in reality, only a small number of fundamental factors that account for the well-being of every robust, loving couple. Though relationships might seem infinitely varied, whether they succeed or fail comes down, in essence, to the presence—or absence—of five anchors.

(I) NON-DEFENSIVENESS

However sweet and fascinating two people might initially be, it is inescapable that they will also with time, and the birth of true intimacy, stumble upon aspects of one another's characters that cannot help but generate difficulties and a degree of dismay. Each partner could be determined to be only kind, but the way that they shell an egg, leave the bathroom, deal with their suitcase on returning from a trip, handle the household keys, or tell an anecdote will gradually unleash powerful degrees of frustration or puzzlement in those they must share their lives with.

One of the most basic features of our natures is that we are defensive. That is, we seek to ward off psychic pain and defend ourselves against perceived attacks. Our minds are squeamish. We try to uphold a bearable picture of ourselves in the face of any possible insights or criticisms that others may direct toward us—or that could emanate from the more perceptive recesses of our own minds. We are not keen on feedback. Our defensiveness is a profoundly understandable tendency, yet it is also behind a predominant share of the failure of all relationships.

The problem starts when we, as partners, venture to air what we have noticed. We might start out politely and tentatively, gently mentioning the strands of hair in the basin or the muddled telling of anecdotes in front of strangers. But thoughtful receptivity can be hard to come by. Our partner is in danger of treating our remarks as if they were a direct attack, as something no sound adult could ever really be bothered by; they might go strangely quiet or immediately accuse us of being hugely unkind or malevolently judgmental. Or they might slyly turn the tables and start listing—with less and less good humour—certain things that they find awful about us and that they have been holding on to privately for a long time. Whatever strategy they adopt, the underlying meaning tends to be the same: that being found in some way imperfect is entirely unacceptable and deeply contrary to the spirit of true love.

"Love me for who I am" is the fateful rallying cry of all lovers headed for disaster. It is in reality a monstrously unfair—though entirely understandable—demand to be loved just as we are, with our panoply of faults, compulsions, neuroses, and immaturities. But with a modicum of self-awareness and honesty, we should only ever expect to be loved for who we hope to be, for who we are at our best moments, for the good that lies in us in a latent and not-yet-realized state.

The spirit of true love should require that whenever there is feedback, we turn gratefully to our partner and ask for more, that we continuously search to access a better version of ourselves, that we see love as a classroom in which our lover can teach us one or two things about who we should become—rather than as a burrow in which our existing errors can be sentimentally endorsed and encouraged.

In order to overcome defensiveness, we need to understand its sources; we have to think about defensiveness not in its obdurate, dismaying present manifestations but in its greatly more benevolent and engaging origins. Defensiveness is almost invariably founded on an intimate history that no defensive person consciously chose and that, compassionately recounted, might move us to tears. Defensiveness is a legacy of early pain. There might have been a shy six-year-old with a robust, confident parent who was ashamed of their timid, lonely child. No one much seemed to care for this soft-cheeked, large-eyed creature at home. There were criticisms and hints that another sibling was favored. Love, as this poor soul encountered it, was a scarce, easily lost commodity. For anything to be pointed out to them was, as they came to think, a harbinger of fresh contempt and renewed exclusion from everything sustaining and kind. Or else a parent was intermittently admiring and then terrifyingly angry at their offspring if there was the slightest drop in performance at school. Defensive people did not magically acquire their ferocity in relation to our comments, but rather suffered from some form of early neglect or encounter with unsteady, fluctuating warmth. No wonder that such a person might respond with alarm, even viciousness, when the slightest negative thought about them rears its head in a lover they felt ready to entrust with their whole being. There could, in the mind of the unfortunate sufferer, plainly be no such thing as *affectionate* criticism, no such thing as *helpful* feedback, no possibility of being at once adored *and* upbraided. Love cannot be conceived of as coexisting alongside occasional moments of evaluation. It is on the basis of such awkward, emotionally scarred internal associations that defensiveness is built.

A less-defended attitude isn't a random gift; it is something we can aim for every bit as much as we can aim for a flatter stomach or a tidier house. Even if we didn't have an ideal introduction to life, we can access ideas that dismantle the equation between love-worthiness and untouchable perfection. We can begin to become less defensive when we take some of the following on board.

Our early experience isn't a guide to the present

Our defenses were the best we could do in the face of early harshness. We were confronted with problems and demands far beyond our strength. But a decent partner, if we let them know our background troubles, will be moved by our tender desperation and hasty fear. And they can, so long as we master our panic, help us to see that the thing we should be afraid of now is not criticism but an inability to accept its occasional kindly manifestations.

By the background standard of the defensive person, no one could ever be loved

If love really required an absence of even the most minor flaws, no one could possibly qualify for a relationship. Yet in reality, we are love-worthy not because we are perfect, but because none of us ever can be.

Irritation isn't objective

We need not feel overly targeted by criticism. Every partner has their own particular fixations and preoccupations that make them latch on to certain features of another's character. That a partner is annoyed with us over something is no sign that we are doing anything appalling per se, so we can afford to feel unpersecuted by their judgment. Some people wouldn't mind a messy cupboard; not everyone cares about a lengthy anecdote. An issue can be worth discussing amicably not because it is a fundamental failing but simply because it happens to bother someone we love.

In the defensive person's mind, the least comment is like the small rock-fall that announces an avalanche. There seems no way to trust that it really is just about how long pasta should be cooked or the right way to make a bed. The underlying intention seems always to be to inflict a devastating wound and speed the entire relationship to a close. The defensive person has not had a chance to experience the robustness of love—how it is possible to call someone the worst names in the lexicon and then, ten minutes later, want to lie softly in their arms, tenderness having been renewed and reinvigorated by an opportunity to purge frustration. There can be ruptures—and repair. True love is resilient. It is not destroyed by a detail but only ever by the way that a detail can't be acknowledged or processed.

Defensiveness can be outgrown. We can learn to measure in our hearts the difference between a complaint and an existential rejection. We can come to hear a criticism without connecting it to damnation. That love once seemed fragile doesn't mean it must be today. We can trust that we may on occasion irritate a partner without concluding that they will for that matter hate everything about us unto eternity.

When searching for a partner, we need to look out for someone who can join us in the noble quest to recognize and overcome defensiveness. We might even raise this ambition on an early date—"I'd like one day to move to the country, learn Spanish and, with a lover's help, get over my defensiveness," we might declare by way of introducing our goals. We could frame the attempt to listen to criticism without fury or hurt as belonging to one of life's mightiest challenges—alongside sporting excellence or business success. Eventually, with a lot of effort, we would hope to reach the stage when a partner could point out with tact and humanity that we had bad breath or that our shoes didn't match our sweater and, rather than reacting as we have grown up to do, we could simply turn to them, smile benignly and say what flawed humans should always respond with when another member of the species deigns to help them to grow into a better version of themselves: *Thank you*.

(II) VULNERABILITY

There's a second criterion crucial for relationship success: The person who is good at love is good at being vulnerable.

We make ourselves psychologically vulnerable whenever we let a partner know some of the ways in which we are weak, needy, scared, immature, incompetent, or just plain odd—that is, some of the ways in which we are human. To be vulnerable is to dare to take off the usual cloak of normality and sensibleness with which we navigate the world and, for once, to show someone who we really are, with all the fragility and unusualness implied. We might, as vulnerable people, admit to having unsteady minds; to being prone to terror, despair, paranoia, and self-hatred.

It's a hugely complicated step to confess—especially in front of someone we fundamentally want to impress and secure the affection of—that there are basic ways in which we fall short of what a sane adult is meant to be like. A certain kind of no-nonsense partner might well tell us sternly to grow up, complain about us to their friends and make hasty moves to end the relationship.

As a result, we often lie, not for advantage or thievery, but in order to keep hold of a love we desperately want to rely on. We pretend to be strong and unafraid. We disown our needs and longings. We put on a show of being someone else. Such acting works in many contexts. An uncomplaining, breezy competence and unemotive intelligence probably make for an ideal employee, an admirable committee member, and a thoroughly respectable citizen of the modern world. But in an intimate relationship, this form of barricaded caution is fatal. Our fears and inadequacies don't vanish because we have hidden them; we don't get any less childlike or odd because we have learned to appear sensible. We simply end up making it impossible for a partner to know us—and, because they are likely to take their lead from our own reserve, they will be unable to show themselves to us in turn. We enclose ourselves in the high walls of our deceptions.

To dare to be vulnerable involves a faith that whatever we are inwardly most afraid and ashamed of in our own natures must have counterparts in other people. We cannot be alone in our oddities and our symptoms. The only people we can assume are "normal" or "sane" are those we don't yet know very well. But once we are past the flawless exterior, every person we meet—and especially the person we are now dating—will have their share of follies and tender spots: they will be unable to temper their panic, they will fear disgrace, they won't remember how to soothe themselves. We are guaranteed not to be alone in our terrors and neediness. And what is more, it's only on the basis of mutual disclosure of susceptibility that a true bond can be built. We may admire paragons of strength and stoicism; we can never properly love them.

To be vulnerable is in essence to let a partner catch sight of a side of us that dates back to childhood: the distant time when we feared Mommy would never come back, when we cried and no one comforted us, when Daddy shouted at us and we were frozen with dismay, when a rough friend told us we were a baby for still loving our stuffed elephant, when no one wanted to play with us in the playground, when we tried and tried to explain but Granny was still angry. To be properly, fully vulnerable is to take the other into the frightened, small places of our past and let them see that we're still in significant ways the little, distressed people we once were. Honest, vibrant love is an encounter between two vulnerable children who otherwise do a very good job of masquerading as adults.

What makes people reject the offer of vulnerability? The strength they insist on displaying to the world is an indicator of how punishing they have had to be toward their fragile inner selves; it's a measure of how fast they have had to grow up. If Mommy dismissed their night-time fears they will have had to try to tell themselves—desperately—that Mommy was right and that crybabies really are disgusting. They perhaps deflected the rough boys' taunting of Minko, who had been knitted by Granny while they were still in the womb and whose trunk had half disintegrated under the intensity of their hugs, by throwing the little soft toy in the bin. They managed their traumas by siding with those who had hurt them. They focused on keeping their room tidy, passing exams, and learning how to do business. And so they came to fear the very thing that they now most need: an enfolding, restorative, and profoundly understanding tenderness toward their traumatized early selves. In a grim paradox, to have words of empathy whispered to them lovingly in the dark only reinforces their deepest fears; their protective shell snaps ever more tightly shut at the approach of sympathetic love; they respond to their own needs with panic and self-disgust.

We learn to be vulnerable by understanding that those who conveyed the imperative of a tougher—non-crying, non-fragile, loving—self were profoundly incorrect and, in their own way, deeply traumatized. Mommy was dismissive of our fears not because she was impressively astute in her theories of human development but because she was struggling with her own history of unattended need. The anti-Minko "friend" wasn't showing us the real path to being a grown-up but inflicting on us some of the unkindness that had in other contexts been directed at them. We need to go back and convince ourselves—perhaps with a touch of anger—of how misguided the agents of our "growing up" really were.

Finding a partner with whom we can be vulnerable constitutes a supreme act of restoration. After a lifetime of denial and false strength, we stand to find in another the sympathy that was sorely needed but unavailable to us in the past. The old wounds can be gently tended; we become stronger by learning to speak the language of weakness. By letting our hurt, mentally fragile selves into the relationship, we open the way to a more nuanced, fruitful, creative, and accurate way of being an adult.

(III) TENDERNESS

Love has a third important but not always easily recognized ingredient: tenderness. Tenderness often gets overlooked because what it really involves is compassion at the very moment when compassion isn't obviously deserved. Relationships succeed when it is precisely a partner's less edifying and unworthy behaviors that remain capable of arousing, alongside a deep sigh, doses of unearned redemptive empathy.

In theory, we all have plenty of time for compassion, but we tend to have some specific notions of where and when this quality should really be deployed. We typically reserve it for the most obviously blameless candidates: those who are sad but entirely good, those who have lost their livelihoods through no fault of their own, those who were born into unfortunate circumstances, struck by lightning or rendered homeless by earthquakes.

What we find much harder to do is to forgive someone who appears to be behaving suboptimally on purpose, who seems to have made an active choice to mess things up, who looks as if they have taken a negative path out of wilfulness, idiocy, or nastiness; someone who had options to be successful or respectable, calm or grown up, but instead—for reasons we have no energy to investigate—decided to shout, to be mean, to respond ungratefully or to display immaturity. We know we are kind people, but we surely cannot be expected to love where love is undeserved.

And yet that is exactly where love should and must be deployed if relationships are to survive. True love cannot be directed solely toward those who are admirable and virtuous. It has to soften our judgments in relation to people who are at points undeniably maddening and plainly wrong.

A way to conceive of love is as a willingness to look beyond the obvious damning grounds for bad behavior in search of deeper, more forgivable reasons why someone messed up. We see this most clearly in the way that a good-enough parent loves a child. When a three-year-old throws a tantrum and pushes their dinner plate on the floor, scattering pasta everywhere, a parent knows not to slap their offspring and declare them "evil." The parent will search for reasons why their child acted as they did. Perhaps they have sore gums. Maybe they are extremely tired. Perhaps their rivalrous feelings toward a sibling have reached a pitch. The parent searches for something other than sheer "badness" to explain a departure from good sense and decorum.

A little of this curiosity and empathy should, with caveats and boundaries, enter our adult relationships as well. Here, too, there will be plenty of occasions when we cannot easily imagine why our partner acted as they did: their moodiness seems to have no rationale; there can be no blameless explanation for the way they spoke to our friend; nothing seems capable of excusing their persistent lateness . . .

But though outrage may feel liberating, it is no friend of love. In order to stand any chance of working, a relationship has to involve—on both sides—a continuous attempt to drill beneath difficult words and actions in search of their more complicated, and occasionally touching, origins. Perhaps our partner is feeling sexually insecure; maybe they are unduly threatened by a friend's financial success because they were never allowed to believe that they could matter in themselves. It's possible that persistent lateness is a protest against a bullying, coercive, time-obsessed parent . . . Someone may often be a pain—and yet still be worthy of a lot of thought and kindness.

At the core of the tender person's outlook is a simple-sounding but love-sustaining fact: they treat the other as no less fragile, flawed, and sensitive than they remember themselves to be—only around slightly different things. Tenderness taps modestly and perceptively into self-knowledge.

When love is tender, two partners can together develop an impetus for change: the most easily bruised parts of who they are can dare to be exposed because they know that the other's touch will be gentle. The things we despaired of anyone understanding about us become, at last, possible to admit to. The strange, sweet aspects of our complicated, troubled minds open up to being explored and accepted in all their lonely oddity and shame.

(IV) A THERAPEUTIC ATTITUDE

To state it boldly, and to risk sounding a bit strange, all good lovers are in a way good psychotherapists: that is, the success of modern romantic relationships critically depends on the degree to which both partners can, at crucial moments, adopt a therapeutic attitude toward the other's compulsions, blind spots, rages, and eccentricities.

This sounds odd to say because we usually see therapy as something only a professional could do in a consulting room after years of training, not as anything that we and a partner might be able to offer one another in the kitchen, the bedroom, or over a cocktail in a small but rather elegant bar.

Yet if we drill down into the true nature of psychotherapy our perspective changes. At base, the discipline relies on a theory about how emotional life works. Powerful emotions, therapy says, are triggered in the present by traumas and difficulties that began in a distant and usually largely forgotten past.

The essence of psychotherapy lies in a willingness to get systematically interested in why we constantly respond in the bizarre and uncalled-for ways we exhibit. It asks by what sequence of formative experiences an otherwise perfectly decent and intelligent person could be led to sob on the floor or threaten to jump out of the window after an argument. It's less disturbed by a tantrum, a sulk, or a cold withdrawal than curious about *where* such over- or under-reactions might be coming from.

In therapy, there is always a good—and often moving—story about why someone ends up shouting "Fuck off" to the person they most love or gets icily dismissive when another is pleading for warmth. Perhaps far back, in the old house decades ago, there were genuine, urgent emotional terrors that had to be countered by aggression or evaded by massive psychological withdrawal. While the body has grown, the deep patterns of the mind have stayed the same, so that one now reacts not to what is presently happening but to an old threat that has been unknowingly re-evoked. The brutish words or cold facade are, when the logic of the mind is properly disentangled, directed not at a partner but at a carer, parent, or rival in a now hazy, convoluted back story.

In the consulting room, disturbed feelings can gradually be repatriated so that we no longer unleash them, haphazardly, on whomever happens to be most prominent in our lives. We grow appropriately therapeutic when we can be genuinely interested in the long history that might be standing behind the least alluring and at times appalling emotional conduct of which we and our partners are capable. As therapeutically minded lovers, we no longer always ask why *they* are being so horrible to *us*, we try to work out what *other people* might long ago have done to and around *them*.

We realize that we've come along late in the history of others' souls. They are fighting emotional battles that commenced many years before they could have suspected our existence. They had dug themselves into defensive positions or honed their offensive tactics—to which we are now exposed—by the time they were mastering the eight times table. It isn't their fault. They didn't ask to have the childhood they did, they coped as best they could, and now we are simply the haphazard targets for their largely unconscious, albeit often genuinely off-putting, strategies of defense.

Along the way, psychotherapy teaches us that direct confrontation is seldom a good idea. A therapist might know, pretty much from day one, what a client is suffering from. They might have a solid thesis that the client is mentally scrambled because their mother's abundant love carried with it a secret command that they must never acknowledge any sexual feelings. Or that they are paranoid because of their father's displays of violence and cruelty. What counts, though, isn't that the therapist has developed an accurate diagnosis but that the patient is allowed to recognize it for themselves, by a process of carefully designed prompts, in a way that they can absorb without fear, in their own time. That is why therapists tend to proceed via gentle questions—"I wonder how it felt when Mom went away"—instead of blanket assertions: "Let me tell you why you are so messed up."

In relationships, too, therapeutic kindness should mean avoiding direct lectures on the issues we sense in our partners. We try—on a good day—not to say: "I've seen through you, I know what's wrong with you—and why you are running away from me as you are." And we strive instead to nudge the other toward greater self-knowledge at a pace they can benefit from. There are no prizes for trying to initiate others into varieties of self-awareness they have no strength for.

Furthermore, in relationships that work well, the burden of analytic interpretation never falls on only one person; we're both prepared to see each other through an even-tempered therapeutic lens. We can mutually promise: "I'll be less frightened of what's disturbed yet disguised in you, if you can begin to imagine doing the same for me and my foibles."

Everyone, during the close-up, prolonged inspection all relationships entail, is sure to reveal themselves as being substantially disturbed. Which is why we so much want and need to be with someone who grasps, with reference to the complexities of our early emotional lives, the essential normality of our oddities. They might win our hearts by saying, on an early date: "I'll tell you about how mad I am, and where it all began, if you'll tell me how crazy you are, and how Mom and Dad messed you up." We'll thereby be deploying the possibilities of a therapeutically minded perspective to help secure the long-term sympathetic love we are looking for.

(V) ENTHUSIASM

When relationships start, enthusiasm for our partners tends to be at a pitch. We think of them constantly, we want only to spend more time in their company, we delight in their many skills and accomplishments. We can't quite get over the way they know how to glide on a dance floor, prepare such tasty soups, read interesting novels, sweet-talk our hard-to-please mother, or calmly perform a life-saving operation on an ailing horse or poodle.

But this early phase of powerful admiration and longing rarely lasts. A few years in, our partner may still be an administrative whizz, a stylish dancer, a good cook, a knowledgeable thinker, a fixed favorite of our mother, or a superlative vet—and yet we now find it hard to feel or express too much wonderment. A sullenness has taken hold of us that does not lift. There is, somewhere deep inside us, a gigantic, stubborn "but . . ."

The corrosion of romantic enthusiasm is one of the grand, intimate, tragic, and rarely told stories of love. It seems to happen almost without our noticing; we gradually slip into a position of no longer being able to admire very much. With time, we may feel loyal to the union we've built; we may harbor a deep friendship toward our partner—we'd give them a kidney; but we can't relish and celebrate their merits as we once did.

The world often explains this cooling as a sheer and inevitable result of exposure. It is, they say, typical to neglect what is always around. But the true reasons seem more complicated, more psychologically rich and, in their own way, a lot more hopeful.

If we stop admiring, it is not because we are ever really bored or because it is "normal" to take someone for granted; it is chiefly only because we are, at some level, *furious*. Anger creeps into love and destroys admiration. We cease to delight because we unknowingly grow entangled in various forms of unprocessed annoyance. We can't cheer them on because, somewhere deep inside, we are inhibited by trace memories of certain let-downs, large and small, of which they have been guilty without their knowing. Perhaps they caused us immense difficulties around a work crisis—and never apologized. Maybe they flirted with a friend of ours—and left us feeling tricked and unsure. They may have booked a vacation without asking us—and then insisted that they'd done nothing wrong.

None of these infractions was, on its own, necessarily particularly serious, but taken cumulatively a succession of minor disappointments can acquire a terrible capacity to dampen and ultimately destroy ardor. Yet it is not the simple fact of being let down that counts very much; the true problem is created when there hasn't been an opportunity to process our disappointment. Irritation is only toxic when it hasn't been extensively and thoughtfully aired.

Perhaps we tried to explain what was wrong but we got nowhere. Our partner lost their temper and we gave up. Or, more subtly, we might have felt unentitled to make a fuss over so-called "small things" and therefore stayed silent even though, in our depths, the small things mattered immensely to us. With great unfairness to our partner, we may have forgotten to admit to our own sensitivities even as we developed a steady burden of resentment against their unknowing offenses.

What follows from such buried anger is something that can be mistaken for lack of interest but is in substance very different. We no longer want to celebrate their birthday, we withhold sexual attention, we don't look up when they walk into a room. This could seem like the normal impact of time and proximity. But it is no such thing. It is evidence of cold fury. We do our anger an honor, and can start to dismantle its deleterious impacts, when we recognize the full impact of unexamined frustration on our emotions. We never simply go off people; we only ever get very angry with them. And then forget we are so.

To refind our instinctive enthusiasm for our partner, we need to accurately locate our suppressed distress. We have to allow ourselves to be legitimately upset about certain things that have saddened us and then raise them—for as long as we need to—in a way that lets us feel acknowledged and valued. Because anger inflicts an ever-increasing toll the longer it is left unaddressed, a good couple should allow for regular occasions when each person can—without encountering opposition—ask the other to listen to incidents, large or small, in which they felt let down of late. There might be an evening a week left free for this form of "processing." The mission should be bluntly known to both parties: *an opportunity to pick up on areas in which we feel let down*—not, we should add, in the name of killing love but rather to ensure its ongoing buoyancy. It goes without saying that we might not immediately see why a given thing should matter so much to our partner; but that isn't the point. The object of the exercise is not to listen to complaints that seem utterly relatable to us; it is to let our partner know that we care because these are problems to them.

To ensure that our desire never suffers, this kind of hygienic ritual might be placed at the center of every relationship. If couples too often ignore the requirement, it is because they operate under an unfair burden of bravery: they are far more susceptible than they let themselves think. They assume that it cannot be sane to get "upset" so often, to experience so much hurt, to be so easily ruffled. They can't summon the courage to make a complaint about things that they don't even admit to themselves have caused a sting—and so stay silent until it is no longer possible for them to feel. Wiser couples know that nothing should ever be too small to cover at length, for what is ultimately at stake in a marathon conversation about a single word or a minuscule event in the hallway can be the fate of the entire relationship. These lovers are in this sense like wise parents who, when a child is sorrowful, are patient enough to enter into the imaginative realm of the child and take the time to find out just how upsetting it was that there was a loud bang in the street or that one of Nounou's eyes came off. They will devote three and a quarter hours to understanding why a partner got silently immensely upset by the way we said the word "ready" to them at breakfast the day before or how it felt to them when we were a touch slow at laughing along with a mildly unfunny story they shared about a train and a suitcase at dinner with our aunt. The gratitude that will flow from such an effort to understand them will be amply repaid the next time we feel abandoned because they forgot to put the lid back on the olives or omitted to add a second x at the end of an email.

To complain in love is a noble and honorable skill very far removed from the category of whininess with which it is sometimes confused. The irony of well-targeted and quickly raised complaints is that their function is entirely positive. Honesty is a love-preserving mechanism that keeps alive all that is impressive and delightful about our partner in our eyes. By regularly voicing our small sorrows and minor irritations, we are scraping the barnacles off the keel of our relationship and thereby ensuring that we will sail on with continued joy and admiration into an authentic and unresentful future.

2 *Love and Psychotherapy*

Lovers and psychotherapists might, at first glance, seem to have very little to teach one another, but an unexpected way of helping our relationships to flourish can be to study how therapists speak to, and approach the troubles of, their patients. The truths of psychotherapy don't belong only to clinical practice; they have widespread application in the bedroom and especially outside the bathroom door at midnight during heated arguments about ostensibly very little. When relationships get difficult, as they invariably will, therapeutic ideas can give us ways to understand and cope sympathetically with many of the stranger parts of ourselves and our partners.

The following therapeutic ideas can prove of particular relevance.

REFLECTIVE LISTENING

Life constantly brings us into contact with people we care about who— for a range of reasons, perhaps some of them having to do with us—have grown immensely angry or profoundly distressed. We would very much like to calm them down and relieve them of their symptoms, but our techniques for doing so tend to badly miss their targets. When we try to tell them "not to worry," they slide into even greater panic. When we say that, all told, "it doesn't really matter," their irritation heightens. When we explain to them in a warm voice that they could afford to calm down, they pick up a pencil and snap it in two in frustration.

We would at such points be advised to lean on a technique pioneered and much favored by psychotherapy known as "reflective listening." The theory behind it is that an important share of our most serious problems have no solutions in any practical sense. There are simply no "answers" to losing lots of money, being excluded from a social circle, or failing in a job. Of course, there might be a few steps that could be taken—applying for a loan, throwing a party, or going on a training course—but these are unlikely to be things that we have not thought about before or that could, if implemented, shave off more than a fraction of our pain.

What psychotherapy realizes is that, in our agony, what we desire more than anything, more than we usually even understand, is companionship: for someone else to know that we are suffering and to feel a measure of our pain more or less as we experience it. We yearn to feel that another person appreciates the scale of our despair and the magnitude of our sense of injustice, while at the same time being deeply suspicious of, and alert to, anyone who might too hastily be trying to make our distress go away. "Answers" and "solutions"—because they seek to remove a problem at speed—may in our panicky moments seem indistinguishable from being asked to shut up and talk about something else.

Having fathomed our longing, psychotherapy introduces a key innovation: it proposes a way of behaving around a person who is incensed or sad that can give them a strong feeling that they are being understood. Saying "I know" or "oh yes" won't—as psychotherapy knows—be quite enough. What we need to do instead is to *paraphrase* what our ailing companion has said, to build sentences that repeat back to them the essence of the difficulty they have expressed but in different words. This form of precis deftly signals two things: first, that we have precisely grasped what they have gone through, and second, that we have been doing more than listening passively. We haven't dumbly and distractedly echoed their exact language, as a recording device would; we've taken the trouble to find a fresh set of words for the same story. Their woes have passed, and been sympathetically filtered, through the distinctive channels of our own minds.

An episode of reflective listening might go like this. We hear them say: *I hate the bloody lecturers at university so much. They ramble and make no sense. I'm taking on huge debts to be there and I might as well be asleep for all the good it will ever do me.* To which we might respond: *I'm hearing that your course is proving deeply disappointing. You're finding it hard to understand what's really going on. And the faculty don't seem in any way interested in explaining things properly. You're worrying about how much all this is costing and what contribution, if any, this is going to make to your career goals.*

Or someone might tell us: *I don't see why you jump to such unfair conclusions about me. Why can't you believe that something just slipped my mind? You're always accusing me . . .* To which a reflective listener might answer: *I'm sensing that you don't feel trusted. You think I don't have enough faith in your good nature and intentions.*

The genius of reflective listening is that, on the basis of paraphrasing alone, we can leave our speaker appeased and becalmed. Without anything ostensibly changing, the incensed or sad person's levels of fear and irritation ebb. The squall passes; hope returns. This teaches us just how much "solutions" may ultimately be overrated. All that we are chiefly in search of when we are at our lowest point is evidence that we are in company.

ROOM FOR DARKNESS

Whenever people tell us their problems, one of our most common, quasi-automatic—and subtly dispiriting—responses is to try to deny the severity of what they have just said to us. Someone tells us that they haven't been sleeping very well and we respond, with the best of intentions, that not getting a certain number of hours "doesn't really matter." Another person tells us that they didn't get a promotion and we try to be nice by reminding them that they are "already doing very well" as they are. Were someone to reveal that they were dying, we might—*in extremis*—be tempted to say, "But you can't be . . ."

Parents are often to be heard performing this maneuver with their upset or angry children:

CHILD: I'm feeling sad.
PARENT: Don't be silly, no you're not. It's the holidays.

CHILD: I'm really worried.

PARENT: Darling, that's ridiculous. There's nothing to be scared of in your bedroom.

The reason for our cheerful rejoinders lies in our unresolved relationship with our own despair, fear, and sadness. We seem so unable to square up to awful things in our lives, we have no option but to try to deny that they might have a place in the lives of others. We become sentimental—that is, addicted to airbrushing away the uncomfortable aspects of reality, out of fear, not deafness.

A more evolved relationship to ourselves—of the kind psychotherapists seek to promote—can assuage the itch to deliver upbeat messages by prompting us to make our peace with sorrow. Someone might say that they are sad and we could in time learn simply, and more helpfully, to answer, "I hear you." Another might insist, "Everything is awful," and we might look them warmly in the eye and respond, "Yes, it really can feel like that at times."

The more we listen to the "sad" messages our companions send us, the less hard they will have to push them. The more we hear, the quieter they can be. Someone who says they want to burn the country down doesn't really want to burn the country down; they want to be heard for the deep frustration that their job or their family is causing them. They will become an arsonist only if we continue not to listen; but not if we do so amply with empathetic good humor. Feelings get less strong, not stronger, once they've been acknowledged. It is a move of exemplary generosity and maturity to let someone be sad and desperate around us without falling for the cruel temptation of saying something cheerful.

SOFTENING LANGUAGE

Much of our trouble in relationships comes down to the force with which we try to assert certain of our ideas to other people: ideas about who they are, what they've been up to and what they are likely to need in order to be happy. An idea of ours may be entirely correct, but the directness with which we attempt to insert it into another's mind can lead them to recoil and reject it almost as a matter of course, with violence and outrage. The truth, if ever it is to reach another's consciousness, has to travel in the softest, most hesitant layers of doubt.

This explains why we'll so often notice psychotherapists talking to their clients in a way that deftly avoids all powerful assertions or declarations. We won't—or should never—catch them saying: *You're immature* or *There's no point complaining*. They are unlikely to utter: *It's your mother's fault* or *Leave that no-nothing wastrel!*

They will, instead, typically go in for elaborate circumlocutions to ensure that their ideas feel like being stroked by weightless feathers. They will pepper what they say with markers of graceful and mild intent, repeatedly using terms like *perhaps* and *maybe*, *somewhat* and *slightly*, *a bit* and *a touch*. There will be *a bit of regret* and *a touch of sadness*; things will be *somewhat difficult* and there's *maybe a reason to fight back*.

These therapists will at the same time be powerfully alive to the benefits of saying "*I feel*" ahead of any analysis of their client's behavior or attitudes. They know how easily we can be panicked by universal judgments and how much we prefer it when ideas are framed as though they were only ever the thought of one person as opposed to a verdict of the whole community or the fruit of the mind of God himself. They hence opt for digestible suggestions over thunderous generalizations: "*I feel* you're withdrawing somewhat . . ." over "You're in denial"; "*I feel* you might be a touch angry . . ." over "You're in a rage." They know that there is a vast difference between "You're wasting your time" and "*I feel* you might no longer be getting the results you need . . ."; between "Don't always blame other people" and "*I feel* you might be tempted to hold your friend responsible . . ."

It is common to have vibrant insights into other people's characters that we would deeply like to share with them. It may suddenly strike us that the whole nature of their problem comes down to their mother. Or that all they need to do is break free from the baleful influence of their younger sister. The issue is not that such insights are necessarily flawed but that they are too potent and threaten to engage, in a ruinous way, the other's defense mechanisms. Most of what we don't listen to is far from worthless, it just asks too much of us and therefore has to be expelled from the mind to preserve the emotional status quo. There are truths too true to be heard.

A central way to disarm the danger of suffocating others with reality is therefore to resist the urge to tell them what we suspect is wrong with them. Whatever the provocation and however late the hour, we must never sink to giving out overly direct diagnoses or grand summaries of their condition. There is strictly no point in saying, "It all comes down to your father . . ." or "You're afraid of intimacy . . ." The novice student of psychology may well be tempted to throw around such fascinating and theoretically highly valid ideas, but if their goal is to be listened to, they would be well advised to reconsider the way they are opting to share their learning.

Rather than delivering verdicts, we must—in the name of winning over our audience—signal clearly that we are merely advancing musings, tentative, wholly speculative ruminations that have nothing firm, decisive, or tenacious about them. We really have no clue; we're just throwing something out and we are, almost certainly, quite wrong.

It is here that we should have recourse to one of the most emotionally compelling formulations in the psychotherapist's vocabulary: "*I wonder* . . ." We must take a brute statement such as, "You're trying to seduce someone who doesn't want you . . ." and carefully recast it with an introductory, "*I wonder* if you're attempting to seduce someone who . . ." We might start with, "Stop being so rigid about deadlines" but end up, far more usefully, with, "*I wonder* if you're not putting a bit too much emphasis on routines . . ."

Such moves may be apparently small, but their impact can be enormous. That it should be so tells us something very poignant about us. We don't want anyone to be too certain about our situation, especially those things that might be decisively true but are very hard to take on board. We need the gentlest words to help us come to terms with the most arduous insights.

It is a bathetic but unavoidable reality of human nature that what can separate our absorption of a truth from its angry and incensed rejection may be nothing more or less than a very small, soft, gossamer-light yet entirely crucial "maybe."

THERAPY KNOWS THAT THE TRUTH TAKES TIME TO ACCEPT

To an onlooker, one of the strangest aspects of therapy is the sheer length of time it requires. This is especially puzzling because an experienced therapist can typically diagnose the essentials of a person's troubles in one session. And yet a course of therapy can last two or three years, sometimes five or six, at a rate of one appointment a week, if not more.

As therapy sees it, the chief difficulty is not to identify someone's problem but to help them see, feel, and accept it. Were the truth to be baldly laid out before most clients, they would leave at once in a mood of incensed fury: we have only limited strength to hear that, for example, our levels of confidence might be connected up with our father's behavior toward our sister during our early teenage years or that our anxiety relates to a trauma that occurred before we were three. The trick is to divide a diagnosis into such small portions that it can start to sound like common sense and be benevolently absorbed over a lengthy timescale.

Therapy knows that trust is essential, too, if the truth is to be rendered bearable. We have to like our therapist very much, and have experienced them across a range of topics and developed a comprehensive faith in their personality, so that, when it comes to truly confronting ideas, we can—on a good day—maintain the belief that they are on our side and not simply putting certain thoughts before us in order to cause us pain and bewilderment.

Likewise, we need a partner to have shown us repeated kindness and forbearance before we'll listen when they tell us important but confronting things that our best friends never dared to raise with us—not because they were any kinder, but because they didn't care enough.

Therapy is a school of patience. It changes our notions of plausible time frames. In a therapeutically minded relationship, we're not going to be outraged that after a few weeks with us and two long conversations, our partner still shirks certain responsibilities, still has a wayward notion of punctuality, and still can't shed certain sexual inhibitions. These challenges are conceived of as deeply embedded in emotional dynamics that might, quite reasonably, take years to dislodge themselves. With the example of therapy in mind, we will in our own relationships look for tiny signs of progress rather than rapid, radical change around all those behaviors and thoughts that we so wish would vanish at a stroke.

WHAT IS NOT BEING SAID

Therapists famously listen to their clients carefully, but as much as they are listening to what's being said, they are equally attuned to what is not being said, to emotions that should be expressed given what is being recounted—for instance, a terrible story about loss or neglect—and yet have somehow drifted out of the story, relegated to the unconscious under the weight of untenable psychic pain. Someone might tell a therapist about their father's sudden arrest and six-month stay in prison, then end with a small laugh and the remark, "It was all quite funny really." But the therapist won't be laughing back.

Their aim will be to reunite their client with their exiled feelings. So they might pause, at the end of an ostensibly cheery tale about something dreadful, and say, "That must have been very frightening . . ." or "It seems so unfair really"—and hope thereby to help the client recover contact with their authenticity and truth.

Likewise, a skilled lover will know that pride and misplaced bravery might frequently lead their partner into diversionary behaviors and stories that mask their actual feelings. After returning from a lunch with their mother, they might turn the bitter relationship they have with her into a succession of humorous anecdotes involving the old lady and the waiter. But a tender lover schooled by therapy might add a small rejoinder: "It sounds like she still manages to hurt you every time you see her. It can't be easy." We would then, as the partner, perceive that we had landed on that most special of beings: someone—like the best sort of therapist and the most enticing of lovers—who knows us better than we know ourselves.

TOLERATING AMBIVALENCE

One of the ideas about which therapy remains most sanguine is that our feelings are seldom pure. There is rarely a love which is not, at some level, accompanied by a kind of hatred, just as there is rarely a disdain that doesn't have a strand of affection concealed somewhere within it.

Therapy knows that there are few loving mothers who do not, at points, wish their babies dead. And few respectful, affectionate children who do not fantasize that their parents might be annihilated, if only for a while. It knows, too, that it's wholly normal to love someone and fantasize about having sex with someone else; or to completely forget why we ever committed to a partner only to recover the thread of our story a few hours later. Therapy is unbothered by the strangeness of our disloyal and entangled feelings. It knows that we are all a good deal stranger than we're allowed to admit and it lets us be as unconventional as is helpful without judging or taking fright.

A lover schooled in therapy can adopt a similar sangfroid. Of course there will be moments of intense hatred and declarations of catastrophe and panic. But this is no reason to think a relationship is doomed—just as a two-year-old child who bites their mother in a fit of frustration in the kitchen is not to be understood as making any long-term statement about their feelings for her. With the example of therapy in mind, we'll be less upset by squalls, less frightened of viciousness, and better able to hear with wry patience that we are apparently a shit-faced bastard who ruined someone's life—only, ten minutes later, to hear an addendum that we are also someone our partner will love to eternity. Anger and irritation don't destroy love; they are inevitable parts of being genuinely close to and extremely dependent on another human being.

A therapeutic attitude taps into a proper recognition of the many contradictions of the mind. It prepares us for the fact that, if we are ever to make a good shared life together with someone, we'll have no option but to confront and accept—and in the end finally love—the infinitely strange and wondrous complexity of a fellow human.

3 Simpler Relationships

Many people, after they've been in a relationship for some time, will privately admit that they are in many ways frustrated and disappointed by the person they've chosen to share their lives with. If pressed for details, they will have no difficulty coming up with a list of complaints about their partner:

is too loyal to their irritating family

doesn't share their views on the layout of the living room

never wants to go camping

plays tennis every Wednesday evening, no matter what

doesn't like Moroccan food

doesn't share their enthusiasm for nineteenth-century Russian novels

has a friend who laughs for no apparent reason

likes doing jigsaws

drinks coffee from a big mug with "1984" inscribed on the side

has a habit of adding "actually" to every second sentence, when it's *actually* redundant . . .

As the list gets longer, they sigh. They still love their partner and long to be happy with them, it's just that it seems impossibly complicated to make this relationship work.

What's driving the frustration isn't that they've sadly fallen for an idiot as a mate; it's rather that we have all inherited needlessly complicated ideas of what a relationship is supposed to be for. We are told that love is meant to involve the almost total merger of two lives: We expect that a loving couple must live in the same house, eat the same meals together every night, share the same bed, go to sleep and get up at the same time, only ever have sex with, or even sexual thoughts about, each other, regularly see each other's families, have all their friends in common, and pretty much think the same thoughts on every topic at every moment.

It's a beautiful vision, but a hellish one too, for it places an impossibly punitive burden of expectation on another human. We feel our partner must be right for us in every way, and if they're not, then they have to be prodded and cajoled into reform.

But there's another perspective: relationships don't have to be so complicated and ambitious if we keep in view what in the end actually makes them fulfilling. If we boil matters down, there might really be—as we have seen—only five essential things we want from one another. The things we *have to* make an intelligent fuss about concern our core emotional requirements, which broadly give rise to our five fundamental demands. Our requests to our lovers might sound as follows:

- I need you to accept—often and readily—the possibility that you might be at fault, without this feeling to you like the end of the world. You have to allow that I can have a legitimate criticism and still love you. I need you to be undefensive.

- I need you to own up to what you are embarrassed or awkward about in yourself. I need you to know how to access the younger parts of you without terror. I need you to be able to be vulnerable around me.

- I need you to respond warmly, gently, and compassionately to the fragile parts of who I am; to listen to, and understand, my sorrows. We need a union of mutual tenderness.

- I need you to have a complex, nuanced picture of me and to understand the emotional burdens I'm carrying, even though I wish I weren't, from the past. You have to see me with something like the generosity associated with therapy.

■ I need you to regularly air your disappointments and irritations with me—and for me to do the same with you—so that the currents of affection between us can remain warm and our capacity for admiration intense.

If these five critical demands have been met, we will feel loved and essentially satisfied whatever differences then crop up in a hundred other areas. Perhaps our partner's friends or routines won't be a delight, but we will be content. Just as if we lack these emotional goods, and yet agree on every detail of European literature, interior design, and social existence, we are still likely to feel lonely and bereft.

By limiting what we expect a relationship to be about, we can overcome the tyranny and bad temper that bedevil so many lovers. A good, simpler—yet very fulfilling—relationship could end up in a minimal state. We might not socialize much together. We might hardly ever encounter each other's families. Our finances might overlap only at a few points. We could be living in different places and only meet up twice a week. Conceivably we might not even ask too many questions about each other's sex life. But when we do come together it would be profoundly gratifying, because we would be in the presence of someone who knew how to be kind, vulnerable, and understanding.

A bond between two people can be deep and important precisely because it is not played out across all practical details of existence. By simplifying and clarifying what a relationship is for, we release ourselves from overly complicated conflicts and can focus on making sure our urgent underlying needs are sympathized with, seen, and understood.

4 *Untragic Endings*

News of the end of a relationship tends to be greeted with deep solemnity in our societies. It is hard to think of a breakup except in terms of a minor tragedy. People will offer condolences as they might after a funeral.

This in turn reflects an underlying philosophy of love: we are taught that the natural and successful outcome of any love story is to remain with a person until their or our death. So, by implication, any breakup must be interpreted as a failure governed by overwhelming hostility on one or both sides.

But there's another scenario in which we understand that we are separating not because our relationship has gone badly but precisely because it has gone well. It is ending because it has succeeded. Rather than breaking up with feelings of hurt, bitterness, regret, and guilt, we're parting with a sense of mutual gratitude and joint accomplishment.

This counterintuitive but real possibility has an unexpected source. It comes from having kept a crucial question in mind throughout our time together: What is this relationship for? The enquiry may feel negative; we can imagine asking it in a deeply disillusioned tone of voice. But it can and should be asked positively and eagerly—with the aim of finding a good answer that goes to the heart of love.

Normally, we imagine love as a kind of ownership: full of admiration, two people agree to buy one another, as they might a static, beguiling object. But there is another, more dynamic and less hidebound way to interpret love: as a particular kind of education. In this view, a relationship essentially comprises a mutual attempt to learn from and teach something to another person. We are drawn to our partners because we want to be educated by them and vice versa. We love them because we see in them things that we long for that are missing in us; we aspire to grow under the tutelage of love.

For example, a partner might at the outset have been confident but gentle—a combination that, until we met them, seemed impossible. Or they knew how to laugh at themselves, while we were too withheld and solemn to do so. Or they had a practical competence that we found delightful and moving precisely because it was lacking in us. We could accurately say in such cases that the purpose of the relationship was to teach us confidence or gentleness, or how to laugh at our own idiocy or to become more dexterous—or a thousand other qualities depending on who we both are. The point is, there will be some specific and highly important things we need to do together that will define what the relationship is for.

By being with our partner, by intertwining our lives, by listening to them, even by being criticized or nagged by them, we will gradually be able to internalize what they have to teach us. But there may legitimately come a point where we have absorbed as much from them as we can. Thanks to our partner, we really are more mature beings than we were when we got together: we're more balanced and wiser; they've helped us to become a little more like the people we always wished to be.

Precisely because our relationship has had a great, intimate, loving purpose, it can get completed. It can be finished in the sense in which a novel can be finished—not because the writer has got sick of the trials of writing but because they have, through plenty of difficulties, brought the project to a good resolution. Or, more poignantly perhaps, a relationship can be finished in the way that childhood can be finished: a child—thanks to the immense devotion of their parents—reaches a point at which, in order to progress further, they need to leave home. They're not being kicked out in anger or running away in despair; they're leaving because the work of childhood has been done. This isn't a rejection of love; it is love's good consequence. Finishing isn't a sign of failure but of background success.

The difference in these cases is that we've clearly understood what all our efforts were for. There was a goal in mind: The writing shouldn't go on for ever, the child should leave home. But because, unfortunately, we have not asked what our relationship is for, we can't normally get to this sense of having reached a proper ending. Or else we are refusing to ask because the only motive for the relationship is to ensure that we are not alone—which is never, when we reflect on it, really a good enough reason to monopolize someone else's life.

In an ideal relationship, the sense of completion would be completely mutual. The painful reality, however, is that we may sometimes want to leave while our partner wants us to stay together. But the idea of love as education can still apply: Our unbearable conflicts mean that we've stopped being able to teach one another anything. We may know important qualities they should learn but we're not the right teacher: We currently lack the patience, the skill, the charm, or the self-confidence to transmit insights in a way that will work for them. We have done all we can. Our task is complete, not because our partner has nothing left to learn, but because we aren't the right person to guide them. We are entitled to leave without feeling we are abandoning anyone.

We can avoid feeling devastated by a breakup knowing that there are still so many other ways in which we need to develop. We may have learned so much but we're still far from complete. It's just that the lessons we now have to take on board are going to come from someone else—or from the always profoundly educative experience of being on our own for a while.

III : Art

Art can be a tool with which to combat some of our worst mental afflictions. When it shows us pretty and inspiring things and even—especially—when it shows us melancholy ones, it fortifies us against nihilism and hardness of heart.

We all benefit from having to hand a private gallery of images to shore us up. What follows is an example of such a museum of the mind. It has little to do with those grand national galleries of art sculpted from granite and marble where floors are dedicated to the important movements of art—and where, exhausted and overwhelmed, our thoughts wisely often soon turn to the cafeteria and—with luck—cake. This is a miniature gallery of images that we might look at in bed or in the bath to slow down and reverse a slide into self-hatred and terror. It wants us to hang on and wait for dawn.

Religions knew what art was for. It had nothing to do with remembering dates or understanding techniques. It was for crying with and imploring. It was for kneeling down in a solemn hall in front of, so that Vishnu or Guanyin, Mary or Nivaranaviskhambhin could hear what was tearing us apart: that there would be no more money at the end of the month, that our partner was cold-hearted, that we had seduced the wrong person, that our children had no love in them, that we felt like a failure, that we wanted to die.

We may no longer believe in gods very much, but this doesn't mean that art has abandoned its capacity to console and rescue us. Secular works of art—a careful painting of four daffodils in a jar in early April, a silvery photograph of the Sierra Nevada, an embroidered tapestry of a llama, an abstract canvas of dark blues and greens, a sketch of a sheep and its young, or a study of a river at dusk—retain the power to rescue our moods and rearrange our priorities.

In this small portable museum, we are invited to be as emotional as we might once have felt in a temple or a church. We can fall into solemn reflection, we can cry, we can feel sorry for ourselves, and we can vow to change our lives. The artists would have wanted us to do so very much.

It may be a time of distress right now; it might be night and we might be in a hotel, a clinic, or an unheated spare bedroom. It may feel as though we are entirely alone and that no one could possibly understand. They do.

As much as pills, therapy, walks, a thoughtful friend, baths, a lot of sleep, and perhaps the occasional fig, this gallery of images is a tool in the service of our frayed psyches. This is art against despair.

1 *Six Persimmons*

Everything has become abundant, everything is in reach. We can have produce from the four corners. Fruit is flown in from anywhere—even persimmons, which taste rich and honey-like when ripe, with the texture of an apricot and a skin like an apple's.

But the tragedy is also that we don't notice anything much of what we have. Buddhism takes aim at our haste and our neglect. In failing to appreciate the things before us, we become far more avaricious and dissatisfied than we need to be. We dream of fame and elevated status. We call our circumstances narrow and uninspiring, when in reality we have omitted to do them justice. We seek a better world without having taken stock of the one already to hand. If we were able to open our eyes, there would be so many universes for us to see right in front of us.

The Chinese Buddhist monk—no one is ever just an "artist" in Buddhism—Muqi Fachang completed his rendition of six persimmons in the middle of the thirteenth century, around the end of the Southern Song dynasty. Those with a sympathy for the lessons of his creed have been looking at them carefully ever since, especially after they reached Japan in 1606 and were given pride of place in a meditation hall in the Daitoku-ji temple in Kyoto.

There is ostensibly nothing very special about the persimmons—and that is precisely the point. Those who are in a hurry, those who are unable in the end to notice and draw value from anything, will rush past them as they will so much else. Muqi is trying to slow down our impatient gaze. He deliberately empties the visual field and sets these modest works of nature in front of us for reflective contemplation, daring us to ignore them while also beseeching us—with all the resources of his art—not to.

The painting's guardians in Kyoto traditionally asked that we pause

Muqi Fachang, *Six Persimmons*, 13th century.

to look at the work for at least three minutes, which can feel like an awfully long time. But when we accept the challenge, after around the first thirty seconds our breathing is likely to slow and we may start to see how much there is to appreciate. Each persimmon, though "the same" from a distance, emerges as distinct in size, shape, and color. What we might initially have thought of as identical declares itself as rife with difference. Each persimmon is, we can now see, as individual as a child is to its parent.

What Muqi asked us to do with pieces of fruit we might carry out with the world more broadly: We might take a second and third look at loaves of bread, clouds, paving stones, the books on our shelves, blades of grass and—most importantly—one another. Once we have learned to draw value from inexpensive things, we can never be poor, whatever our ostensible level of wealth, and we can never be bored, however quiet things might have become. The persimmons are with great humility doing momentous work for us: They are pointing us toward a path of liberation.

2 *Albrecht Dürer and His Pillows*

One of the most beautiful and unexpectedly moving sketches in the world was completed by the German artist Albrecht Dürer in 1493, when he was twenty-two years old and apprenticed in his native Nuremberg. It shows six pillows, probably his own, in a variety of shapes and positions.

On the other side of the paper, Dürer drew himself looking at us with penetration and inquisitiveness, alongside a version of his hand and, at the bottom, for good measure, another—seventh—pillow.

A pillow has no distinguished place in the order of the universe. We are unlikely ever to have paid much attention to this modest household object. We take its existence for granted, owe it no special gratitude and are unlikely ever to have been detained by its qualities. Like so much else that we are surrounded by, we see it without noticing it. It belongs to a vast category of things which we rely on without for an instant stopping to wonder at, or deriving any satisfaction from, them. We are—for the most part—wholly blind.

In the face of our customary inattention, it may help us greatly that, a long time ago, a genius arrested his gaze in order to tell us that, among the neglected detritus of a household, there might be something worth bothering with; that a pillow, properly considered, might be as interesting as a castle or as nuanced as a poem; and that we have all along been putting our heads down on a treasury.

It matters, too—though it shouldn't ideally—that Dürer's work is highly acclaimed; that the pillow image is stored in a special temperature-controlled room in New York's Metropolitan Museum of Art; that it has been the subject of extensive study by elaborately trained art historians; and that it has a higher value than a sports car. We are, by nature, immoderately snobbish creatures and appreciate principally

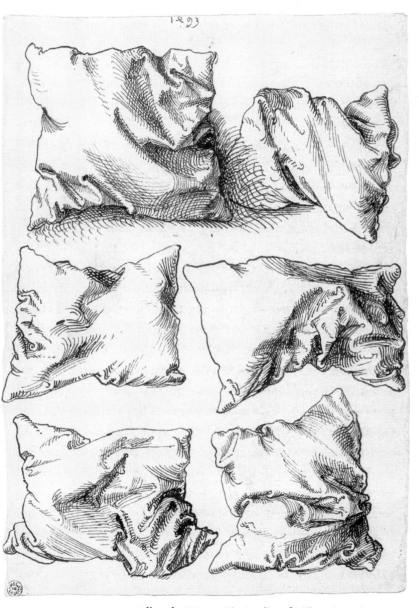

Albrecht Dürer, *Six Studies of Pillows* (verso), 1493.

what we have been encouraged to be curious about by the most prestigious voices in society. This means that we spend a lot of time thinking about fame and glory, and no time at all attending to most of what lies closest to us, which includes not just our pillows, but also the lemon on the sideboard, the light at dusk, an afternoon free of commitments, the flowers in the garden, the laughter of a child, the kindness of a friend, a history book on the shelf, and the many small moments of harmony and satisfaction that—despite our many difficulties—we have already witnessed.

One of the most acclaimed artists of the European Renaissance lends us his immense prestige in order that we might in turn learn to draw pleasure from thoroughly unprestigious things. We declare our lives to be worthless, we cast envious glances at the achievements of our rivals, but all along we trample on what keener, more alert eyes would know how to feast on.

Throughout his career, Dürer looked at ordinary life and saw it for the unlikely, ecstatic, jewel-filled pantheon it is. Some years after the pillows, he completed a study of a range of ordinary plants and grasses and wondered at the capacity of the smallest clod of earth to give life to so much beauty and interest.

Nothing could be further from the realm of worldly ambition than a few columbines. Such flowers grow freely in seemingly unpromising stony soil. There's no market for them; no one has ever boasted of owning what is more or less a weed. But for Dürer, such spectacles of nature were among the most serious sources of pleasure that exist, worth as much as any coat of arms and more likely to satisfy us than a love affair. He relished the delicacy of shoots. He admired the individuality of petals and the subdued yet subtle colors of new leaves. Fulfillment—which we are taught exists only in a good reputation, financial achievement, and costly decorative objects – may be already here, waiting for us in a crack in the sidewalk or in a window box.

We may not have Dürer's talent but we don't, in this instance, need it. We're not trying to become artists; we're trying to become people who have reasons to live. And in this regard, Dürer is generous. He is

Albrecht Dürer, *Self-Portrait, Study of a Hand and a Pillow* (recto), 1493.

Albrecht Dürer, *Columbine*, 1495–1500.

reminding us that there are reasons everywhere: in the way the light falls on a cup, in a few words with someone who still cares about us, in a banana cake we might make tomorrow. The lesson is not to focus on exactly the same things that Dürer studied—though we might do this too—it's to take his attitude of generosity, openness and modesty and apply it to our own circumstances. We might find our version of his satisfaction in a pattern of lichen on an old stone wall or in the refined elegance of a boiled egg.

So compelling was Dürer's skill as an artist that he came to the notice of the rich and powerful of his day, including—most consequentially—the Holy Roman Emperor Maximilian I. Maximilian loved horses, wars, armor, and pageantry. Most of all, he loved himself, for all the grand and important things he had done: expanding the Habsburg dynasty to Spain, recapturing Austria, checking the power of the French. He asked Dürer to make him a work of art that would fully celebrate his achievements, his character, and his place in history—and urged him to make it as big as possible. Money was no object. The result was one of the largest prints ever made, three meters high, laid out on thirty-six gigantic sheets of paper from 195 separate woodblocks. The central arch was called "Honour and Might," the right arch "Nobility" and the left arch—quite simply—"Praise." Each one was densely packed with illustrations highlighting Maximilian's wisdom, courage, strength, popularity, and good nature. In one area, there was a complicated family tree that traced his lineage back to Clovis I, the first king of the Franks, and in another, a table that equated his achievements with those of Julius Caesar and Alexander the Great.

Maximilian was delighted. He praised Dürer to all the aristocracy and had copies of the work delivered to every corner of his lands. But the artist was less content: He had done it for the money and his heart wasn't remotely into such bombast. Too much in his character went in other directions: toward the everyday, toward humility, and toward an awareness of how disaster might strike each one of us, even or especially the mighty ones, at any moment.

Dürer's mind was dominated by terrifying visions of what fate

Albrecht Dürer, *Triumphal Arch*, c. 1515.

Albrecht Dürer, *The Four Horsemen*, from "The Apocalypse," 1498.

Albrecht Dürer, *Portrait of the Artist with a Thistle Flower*, 1493.

might have in store: disease, famine, injustice, and war laying waste to our dreams and ambitions. In his self-portraits, he never disguised his anxiety. In a second early work, he showed himself holding in his right hand a shriveled thistle, a symbol of pain, decay, and defeat. His look of suspicion and wariness is directed not at us but at himself. He knew how quickly, and with how few wrong moves, we can all be undone.

Ruin or disgrace may well catch up with us. Things collapse, plans turn sour—shortly after the arch was done, for example, Maximilian fell into a depression and, inconsolable, insisted on sleeping in a coffin, which was carried around all day with him; he died a few years later. But we don't always need the very large elements of our lives to succeed in order for existence to be bearable. We can survive and in distinctive ways thrive through a disciplined focus on the smaller elements around us that lie more reliably within our command and that offer us pleasure without exacting envy or punishing effort. We can nourish ourselves on the sight of flowers, on the smell of freshly baked bread, on an evening writing our diary, or on a walk around the park. We can take pleasure in an apricot, in a hot bath, in some flowering weeds—and, not least, in our own set of pillows that have so often and so generously, in the wake of our disappointments, received our tears.

3 *Kersting and Lamplight*

We might be tempted to feel rather sorry for someone who confessed that their greatest pleasure in life was staying at home—or, yet worse, that their deepest satisfactions sprang from interior design. What would need to have gone wrong for someone to prefer their own bedroom or kitchen to the theaters and clubs, parties and conference venues of the world? How narrow would someone's horizons need to have grown for them to devote hours to choosing a flower-ringed vase for the sideboard or a brass lamp for the study? Our era has a hard time maintaining sympathy for domesticity. Reality lies outside our doors. There are really only two categories of people who can be forgiven for being heavily invested in staying at home: small children . . . and losers.

But after launching our ambitions on the high seas, after trying for a few decades to make a mark on our times, after exhausting ourselves sucking up to those in power and coping with gossip, slander, and scandal, we might start to think less harshly of those who prefer to remain within their own walls and think a lot—and with pride—about cushions and jugs, pencil pots and garlic crushers, laundry cupboards and cleaning products.

It might, of course, be preferable to manage to bend the world to our own will, to tidy up the minds of millions, or to fashion a business in our own image, but after a bit of time on the planet, some of us may be ready to look with new understanding and admiration at those who can draw satisfaction from making blackberry jam, planting beds of lavender, or waxing bedroom floors.

The painter Georg Friedrich Kersting was born in northern Germany in 1785 and as a young man wanted to become a great military general and perform heroic deeds in battle. He dreamed of helping to expel the French armies that, under Napoleon, occupied large areas of the German states. After briefly studying art in Copenhagen, Kersting joined the Lützow Free Corps, a Prussian volunteer force, and saw action at the Battle of the Göhrde, in which thousands lost their lives and after which he received the Iron Cross for bravery.

But after the defeat of Napoleon, during the political impasse that befell the German states, something changed in Kersting. He retired from the military, gave up on politics, moved to Dresden, got married, had some children—and became very interested in the idea of home.

He had had enough of the machinations of government and the schemes of generals, of German nationalism and wars of liberation. Such ventures and the ideals that supported them became bound up in his mind with hubris and overreach. He was haunted by the bloodletting that he had witnessed and the friends from the military he had lost. From now on, what would interest him was the challenge of leading a good enough ordinary life in domestic circumstances and of remaining sane and serene when there was so much that might unbalance and perturb him. He closed the door on the world and became a prophet of the consolations and beauty of home.

In 1817, Kersting completed one of the most quietly remarkable and beguiling of all paintings. *Embroiderer* shows a young woman in a dignified modest dress absorbed in her work at an open window. We cannot see her face but can imagine her lips pursed in concentration, the little finger on her right hand extended and taut as she struggles to thread her needle. The interior is peaceful and inviting, without being in any way showy or extravagant. Someone has thought hard about how the mauve couch will create an intriguing contrast with the green wallpaper, and the chunky wooden floorboards have been matched up with an especially graceful chair and table, suggesting a reconciliation between practicality and elegance.

A few years later, Kersting completed an equally iconic companion piece. This time it is night and a woman is again at work, doing some darning. A lamp has been swung into place and the room is bathed in a soft light—soon it will be time to make some camomile tea, kiss

Georg Friedrich Kersting, *Embroiderer*, 1817.

somebody on the forehead and rearrange their teddy and then, gradually, go to bed. The task isn't distinguished or obviously memorable, there will be no government medals or honors handed out as thanks for it, but, through Kersting's eyes, we're in no doubt that something very special is going on. The sitter has been cast as a secular saint of a new home-focused creed which rejects prevailing assumptions about where glory might lie and what must count as intelligent and purposeful. Perhaps those who focus on home will not gain distinction or renown, their graves will not commemorate any obviously glittering deed, but they will nevertheless have played a role in supporting civilization. It is to misunderstand where satisfaction lies to insist that fulfillment can exist only in cabinet rooms and boardrooms, stock markets and opera houses. The more imaginative will know the distinctive pleasures of preparing a family meal or painting a room, hanging a new picture or filling a vase with hyacinths and lilies of the valley.

We might once have wanted to tame and educate the entire world, to have millions of people agree with us and gain the adulation of strangers. But such plans are inherently unstable and open to being destroyed by envy and vanity. We should gain security from knowing how much a devotion to home can shore up our moods if our wider surroundings grow hostile. When we have become a laughing stock, when no one wants to know us any more, we can reactivate our dormant appreciation of our surroundings and find meaning in nothing greater or smaller than sewing on a few buttons in the late evening or choosing a new fabric for a chair. Kersting was not naive: he understood how war, politics, and business worked. But it was precisely because he did so that he was keen to throw his spotlight elsewhere. His art was—in the deep sense—political, in that it articulated a vision of how we should ideally live: It covertly criticized military generals and emperors, business leaders and actors. It told us that waving flags at rallies or sounding important at meetings was all well and good, but that the true battles were really elsewhere, in the trials of ordinary existence, and that what counted as a proper victory was an ability to remain calm in the face of provocation, not to despair, not to give way to bitterness, to

Georg Friedrich Kersting, *Young Woman Sewing by Lamplight*, 1823.

Georg Friedrich Kersting, *Man Reading by Lamplight*, 1814.

vanquish paranoia, to decode our own mind and to pay due attention to passing moments of grace.

Kersting spent much time in his own study, which he represented in a number of sketches and one especially famous painting. He must sometimes have regretted his old ambitions. It must have hurt that he never made a fortune and that he remained, in his lifetime, relatively undiscovered. There would have been days when he felt that he had made all the wrong choices. Nevertheless, his art continues to be a point of reference for those who have had enough of trying to bring order to the public square. It urges us to accept the consolation and peace available in ceasing to worry what others think and learning to limit our ambitions to the boundaries of our own dwellings and laundry cupboards.

Tonight, we might—once more—choose to stay in, do some reading, finish patching a hole in a cardigan, try a new place for the armchair, and be intensely grateful that we have overcome the wish to live too much in the minds of strangers.

4 *Hokusai and Melancholy*

There are two ways of looking at Mount Fuji. As a geological phenomenon, it is classified as an active basalt composite stratovolcano, 3,700 meters high and 10,000 years old in its most recent form, which last exploded in 1708. Located on the island of Honshu in central Japan, on the fault line where the Eurasian, Okhotsk, and Philippine plates meet, it has a mounting pressure inside its magma chamber of 1.6 megapascals and an average temperature at its summit of −5°C (25°F).

But Mount Fuji is simultaneously a psycho-spiritual phenomenon interpreted in both the Shinto and Zen Buddhist traditions as a conduit to, and guardian of, wisdom and enlightenment. There are temples and rituals in its honor. It is understood to have a meaning; it wants to tell us things. For Buddhism, humans are perpetually at risk of forgetting their true irrelevant position within the natural world. We overlook our powerlessness and unimportance in the universal order. This amnesia isn't a helpful illusion; it is responsible for much of our frustration, anger, and vain self-assertion. We rage at events because we cannot see the necessities we are up against. Buddhism regularly turns our attention to natural elements—rocks, rain showers, streams, giant cedar trees, the stars—because it sees in these ways we can gracefully come to terms with our denied subservience. We can be reminded that we have no alternative but to submit to nature's laws and that our freedom comes from adjusting our individual egos to what defies us. For Zen, Fuji is only the largest conveyor of a general truth, but it deserves special reverence because of the extraordinary elegance and primordial simplicity with which it delivers its message. Its beauty, visible on a clear day when its cone is newly sprinkled with snow, makes it a little easier to accept that we will die, that our plans will be ground to sand, that what we achieve will not matter and that we are as nothing next to the aeons of time to which the earth has been witness.

The printmaker and artist Katsushika Hokusai was in his seventies and already famous in Japan when he hit on the idea that would immortalize his name. The project was to capture Fuji obliquely, to make it feel almost by the by and yet also magnetically present in a series of "Thirty-six Views of Mount Fuji," published between 1830 and 1832. Hokusai never lets us forget the contrast between the eternal steadiness of Fuji, constantly resplendent and serene somewhere in the background, and the agitation, struggle, pain and overexcitement of human lives. We catch Fuji peeking out from behind a busy bridge over the Onagi river as it joins the Sumida; it's in the background as workers and travelers do business together in the Sundai district of Edo; it's there as a peasant leads a horse laden with saddlebags full of grass in Senju; it's watching as a half-naked craftsman makes a barrel in Owari province and as workers fix the roof of the Mitsui department store in Edo (a sign says: "Cash only"); it's discreetly in the frame as some clam fishermen fill their baskets in Noboto Bay and a group of pleasure seekers have refreshments at a *hanami* (cherry blossom viewing) on Goten-Yama Hill near Shinagawa.

In some of the prints, the contrast between the puny defenselessness of vainglorious humans and the indifference of mighty nature is at a pitch. We feel pity and melancholy for our pride and what we are up against. In the tenth view in the series, we see a group of travelers wending their way around rice paddies on the eastern sea route near Ejiri in Suruga province. It's fall and a gust of wind has just blown. That's all that may be needed to break our fragile hold on order. Hokusai's humans are at once thrown into chaos. They struggle to hold on to their hats, their possessions fly into the paddy fields, and most notably someone's papers—they might be anything from the manuscript of a novel to some tax returns, though what they really stand for is human logic and presumption—are being carried off into oblivion, to end up in an adjoining province or a nearby muddy ditch. This, Hokusai is telling us, is what man is: easily buffeted, one gust away from disaster,

Katsushika Hokusai, *Ejiri in Suruga Province* (*Sunshū Ejiri*),
from the series "Thirty-six Views of Mount Fuji
(Fugaku sanjūrokkei)," c. 1830–32.

defenseless before nature, trying to work out what it all means on bits of paper that are as evanescent as fireflies.

In the eighth view, the sun is setting over Fuji; it will be dark in half an hour. A couple of hikers are ascending the steep Inume Pass while, a long way behind them, two traders are following with heavily laden horses. We can tell this latter pair are in trouble. Those horses won't make it up the pass in the darkness; there's a strong risk someone will fall down a precipice. This may be the end of the road for the unfortunate traders. But the wider mood is not mournful or panicked. Fuji is serene, as it always is, even when in its shadow people are being buried or dying of cancer or imploring the heavens or regretting their lives. Nature doesn't care one bit about us—which is both the origin of our damnation and, when we have learned to identify with its motions, a source of redemption.

Then there is the most famous view of all, the first in the series. Three fishing boats are out at sea off the coast of Kanagawa. They are the fast *oshiokuri-bune* boats, each powered by eight muscular rowers, that would catch fresh fish—typically tuna, sea bass, or flounder—for the marketplaces and restaurants of Edo. But today nature has other plans. It doesn't care about this evening's *uramaki* or the lives of thirty little people with families and dependants and hopes of their own. It's decided to send a giant wave, twelve meters high, to toss things about and remind humanity of who is in charge. We shudder at the fate of the fishermen and the other passengers on board. This doesn't look like a picture of survival, more of a prelude to a wake. Fuji looks on impassively, appearing like a wave of its own, its tiny-seeming snow-capped peak impersonating the foaming sea closer by. We are pawns in the hands of forces that care nothing for us and will not mourn us a moment when we are gone.

Hokusai could have chosen to anchor his melancholy meditations on human powerlessness to any number of natural phenomena: "Thirty-six Views of the Moon," "Thirty-six Views of Drifting Clouds," "Thirty-six Views of the Constellation Cassiopeia"—a dim speck in the northern hemisphere 4,000 light years away. Against these, too, his

Katsushika Hokusai, *The Inume Pass in Kai Province* (*Kōshū Inume tōge*),
from the series "Thirty-six Views of Mount Fuji
(*Fugaku sanjūrokkei*)," c. 1830–32.

Katsushika Hokusai, *Under the Wave off Kanagawa*
(*Kanagawa oki nami ura*), also known as *The Great Wave*,
from the series "Thirty-six Views of Mount Fuji
(Fugaku sanjūrokkei)," c. 1830–32.

genius could have shown up our exploits in all their absurdity: a couple squabbling, a writer finishing a book, a person weeping at their medical diagnosis, a lover pining for companionship.

We are fated to have to take seriously ambitions and desires that make no sense in the wider scheme. We have to live knowing that most of what we do is in a cosmic sense ridiculous. Our lives are no more profound than those of an earthworm and almost as fragile. In so far as we can ever recover a little meaning, it is by ceasing to worry so much about ourselves and identifying instead with planetary reality—even to the point where we might contemplate our own mortality with a degree of resigned equanimity, fully and generously appreciating our absurdity—and using it as a springboard to kindness, art, and the right kind of sadness.

5 Mark Rothko and the Seagram Murals

The most unexpectedly uplifting and consoling artist of the twentieth century was the abstract painter Mark Rothko, the high priest of grief and loss, who spent the latter part of his career turning out a succession of sublime and somber canvases that spoke, as he put it, of the "tragedy of being human" and who in 1970, at the age of sixty-six, committed suicide in his studio in New York by overdosing on barbiturates and slitting an artery in his right arm.

Born in Dvinsk, Russia, Rothko emigrated to the United States at the age of ten and immediately grew to despise the aggressive good cheer and steely optimism of his adopted land. He was a latter-day Leopardi or Pascal adrift in Disney World. Appalled by the sentimentality around him, he learned to make art that was insular, unrelenting, and oriented toward pain. It was, one critic said, the visual equivalent of a condemned prisoner's last gasp. Rothko's favorite colors were a burnt burgundy, dark gray, pitch black, and blood red, occasionally alleviated by a sliver of yellow.

In 1958, Rothko was offered a large sum to paint some murals for a soon-to-be-opened opulent New York restaurant, the Four Seasons, in the Seagram Building on Park Avenue. It was, as he put it, "a place where the richest bastards of New York will come to feed and show off." His intentions for them soon became clear: 'I hope to ruin the appetite of every son of a bitch who ever eats in that room.' And to that end, he set to work on some large black and maroon color fields expressing a mood of terror and archaic anguish. It was an unlikely commission for Rothko to have accepted, but it became ever more so in his mind when, following a trip to Italy, where he had been much moved by Giotto's renditions of the crucifixion, in the fall of 1959 he took his wife, Mell, to the restaurant for lunch. His hatred became overwhelming. Believing it was "criminal to spend more than $5 on a meal," he couldn't get over the overpriced dishes, the fancy sauces and the ponderous waiting staff. "Anybody who will eat that kind of food for those kind of prices will never look at a painting of mine," he vowed. But he hated the clientele even more: suntanned, cheery rich people, out to celebrate and show themselves off, to cut deals and swap gossip, the apparent winners of life, the kind who invested in tennis lessons and whitened their teeth. His hatred of them had its roots in his sense that we only accede to our humanity when we face pain and commune around it with compassion and humility. Anything else is grandstanding and pride. He had remained Russian in his soul.

Following the lunch, Rothko called up his patrons, explained his feelings, and sent back the money. He then gave his paintings to London's Tate Gallery, where they were hung in a quiet, airy, contemplative, religious-seeming space that enclosed the viewer in an atmosphere of meditative mortification. The paintings remain ideal companions for visitors who drift into the gallery at their wits' end, who might be working through the loss of a partner or the ruin of their career and who need more than anything else to know that they are not alone. Rothko's art did not save his life but it will have prevented many others from taking theirs.

Rothko's canvases—though focused on the darkness—are never themselves depressing to look at because they lend our difficulties dignity and legitimacy. To bathe in their atmosphere is to gain a distinct sense of comfort, like lying in the arms of a tender person who says little other than a modest "I know" in response to our dejection and loss. With Rothko as our guide, it matters a little less that the world is mostly filled with noisy, brash, apparent winners, that no one much cares for us, that we have failed in numberless areas, that our name isn't in lights, that we have enemies, and that we are no longer young. We are offered a refuge from the boosterish voices of contemporary society and are able to locate in an external form works that echo our own confused and inchoate sorrows.

Mark Rothko, *Red on Maroon*, 1959.

A great part of our misery is caused by the cruel and erroneous assumption that life might fundamentally be a pleasant journey, capable of delivering satisfaction and delight to those who work hard and retain noble and purposeful hearts.

The truth could not be further from such a sentimental vision. Agony is baked into the human condition. We are suffering not by coincidence but by necessity. We may be focused on the particular errors and cruelties that have brought us to a low point, we may be narrowly concerned with what our enemies have done to us, how a few mistakes have cost us everything or how we have been abandoned by those who should have cared for us. But it isn't to minimize these problems to insist that they are merely local manifestations of more global and endemic troubles. They are in reality the specific mechanisms by which we have come to taste the sorrow that would—however fate had twisted our path—have been our lot and is the grisly birthright of every human. We must all ultimately drink the very same amount of poisoned liquid from the cup of sorrow, even if in different gulps and at different times. No one gets through unscathed.

Yet not only are we sad, we are isolated and lonely with our sadness, because the official narrative is remorselessly upbeat, insisting that we can find the right partner, that work can deliver satisfaction, that destinies are fair, and that there is no inherent reason for us to lament our state. However, we don't deserve—on top of everything else—to be forced to grin. We should be allowed to weep without being hectored into positivity. Our true overlooked right is not, after all, the right to happiness; it is the right to be miserable.

This may sound far from a reason to live, but the ability to look darkness in the face and accept its role in our affairs functions as its own very particular and intense reward. No longer must we be surprised by our suffering. No longer must we be taken unawares by misery. No longer do we have to feel that our reversals say something unique and shocking about us. We can start to rediscover a taste for life when we see that we're not alone in wanting to give up on it; that it is acceptable, even necessary, sometimes to hate the smiling "bastards" who so annoyed Rothko and anyone else with a heart. We can build friendships—imaginative, artistic, or real—around shared honesty about tragedy. We will have banked our first reason to live when we know that we aren't exceptionally stupid for finding matters very difficult. Unhappiness is just—as wise artists have always liked to remind us, and despite the suggestions of all the adverts, the brochures, and the confident-seeming people congratulating themselves in the world's fancy restaurants—very normal indeed.

6 Grief with Agnes Martin

If there were to be a patron artist of sadness, it might be the American abstract painter Agnes Martin. Over a long life (1912–2004), she produced hundreds of canvases, most of them 1.8 by 1.8 meters, showing not very much at all. From a distance, they can seem merely white or gray, though step nearer and you notice grid patterns hand-drawn in pencil, beneath which run horizontal bands of color, often a particular subtle shade of gray, green, blue, or pink. There is an invitation to slough off the normal superficiality of life and bathe in the void of emptiness. The effect is soothing and moving too. For reasons to be explored, we may want to start crying. The works can appear simple but their effects are anything but. "Simplicity is never simple," she explained, having studied Zen Buddhism for many years and learned that encounters with little can be frightening, because they remind us of our own ultimate nothingness, which we otherwise escape through noise and frantic and purposeless activity. "Simplicity is the hardest thing to achieve, from the standpoint of the East. I'm not sure the West even understands simplicity."

In the little town of Taos, in the north-central region of New Mexico, where Martin spent her last years, one can visit the Agnes Martin Gallery, an octagonal room empty except for seven of her paintings and four steel cubes by her friend and fellow minimalist artist Donald Judd. We know how far we generally drift from what is important, how often we lose ourselves in meaningless chatter or attempts to assert our interests. The paintings bid us throw aside our customary, relentless self-promotion. It is just us and the sound of our own heartbeat, the light coming in from an oculus above—across which a New Mexico cloud occasionally drifts—the patient work of thousands of hand-drawn grids repetitively punctuated by strips of the mildest hues of gray and

Agnes Martin Gallery at the Harwood Museum in Taos, New Mexico, on March 20, 2022.

pink, and the peace there would have been over the oceans when the Earth was first created. Martin once remarked that her work was fundamentally about love, not the noisy, exuberant, romantic kind, but the selfless, patient sort a parent might feel for their sleeping newborn or a gardener might experience in relation to their seedlings.

The German early twentieth-century art historian Wilhelm Worringer proposed that humanity had across history tended to make art of two kinds: abstract and realistic. On the one hand, there was an art of geometric non-concrete patterns—the abstraction one might see on a Navajo rug, a Persian mosque wall, or a Peruvian basket—and on the other, there was art made up of depictions of people, things and places—lions in prehistoric caves, mountain landscapes, battle scenes. Worringer made an additional suggestion. What determines the sort of art a society is drawn to at a given moment is often the degree of chaos, difficulty, and struggle to which that society is subject. The more cacophonous it is, the more it tends to be attracted to the serenity and peace implied by the sober repetition of geometric patterns, just as quieter eras may seek out new vigor in bold images of mounted generals or waterfalls. We attempt to correct via art imbalances in our own emotional economy.

By implication, we shouldn't suppose that Agnes Martin was herself anything like the peaceful canvases she turned out. When still a young woman, she was diagnosed as paranoid schizophrenic and suffered from repeated bouts of extreme depression. She would often hear voices in her head criticizing her and urging her to take her own life. It could be hell inside her mind. It is understandable that she might as an artist have felt compelled to produce some of the most serene works the world has ever known, that she gained boundless relief from spending hours—and overall decades—alone in a simple house on the edge of the New Mexico desert, listening to Bach and Beethoven, tracing grids on canvases and applying paint in colors that Zen Buddhism identifies with the renunciation of the ego and the alignment of the self with cosmic harmony.

If we are moved, if we are tempted to start crying, it's not because

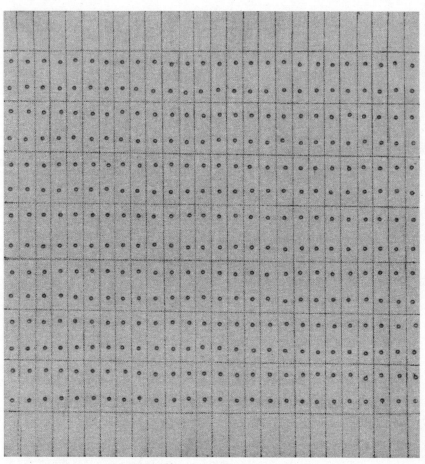

Agnes Martin, *Little Sister*, 1962.

Agnes Martin, *Untitled*, 1974.

our lives are themselves extremely serene. It's because—like the artist herself—we have for far too long been familiar with mental perturbation, because we know what it means to have inner voices insisting on our worthlessness and how right one might be to die. Martin matters because she gives dignity to a longing for something infinitely more harmonious and loving than the world can generally offer. The canvases are like a map to a destination we have lost sight of and can't get back to. They are our Ithaca. We might point to them and say that this is where we belong, this is the repository of everything we prize but have too fragile a hold on. The paintings lend us the courage to cut ourselves free from our unhealthy attachments, to say goodbye to concerns for status, to shun the pursuit of public esteem, to dismiss false friends who do us nothing but underhand harm, to accept the terror of disgrace, to reconcile ourselves to our own company, and to pursue connections with just a very few honest souls who have known struggles and been rendered kind by them. The paintings are what we could be if we sat with our own feelings and let their range course through us, if we gave up using our clever minds to ward off sadness and stopped trying to make sense of every experience, if we made our peace with mystery and the encroaching darkness that will soon subsume us.

Nowadays, by the typically perverse accidents of the art market, Agnes Martin's paintings cost as much as planes. They can only generally be seen in bustling public museums. In a better world, we'd all be able to own a few. As it is, we can at least spend time with them in high-quality online versions and printed reproductions. They are sad pictures, in the best of ways. They know of our troubles, they understand how much we long for tenderness yet how rough everything has been day to day, and they want us to have the simplicity of little children and the hearts of wise old people who have stopped protesting and started to welcome experience. The titles that Martin gave her paintings indicate some of what she was getting at: *Loving Love*, *Gratitude*, *Friendship*, and, best of all, *I Love the Whole World*, which implies the sort of love one experiences not when everything has been hunky-dory, but

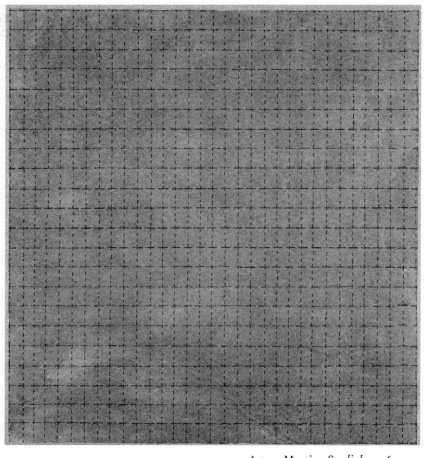

Agnes Martin, *Starlight*, 1963.

when one has after the longest time come through from the other side of agony.

We can follow the grids and be happy. There's one rectangle after another, one dot after another, nothing more troubling than lines of gray and white, no more surprises and departures, nothing unforeseen or cruel, only Martin's careful pencil, riding along the little bumps that tremble beneath unprimed canvas. It's as if she's guiding us step by step, as we might a small child or a very old person, from square to square, making the world more manageable again, reducing its strident, clattery riot to something we can ingest. She's cutting up the food of life for us into very neat and precise squares. She knows how unsteady we have felt. Occasionally, after a lot of grays, she goes for a pink, as if to hell with reserve, why not surrender to sweetness and take a risk with innocence? She's giving us a hug and inviting us to come to the window to watch a new day with her through her frame.

To those who don't see anything in her work, let's hope that life won't teach its lessons too painfully. To everyone else, her work will feel like a homecoming. We will know that someone else has understood, has been as ill and has been committed to hope, endurance, and kindness.

7 Cakes and Happiness

Wayne Thiebaud isn't being sarcastic or elaborately sly. This isn't a sophisticated mockery of ordinary appetites, or a nod to pop art—a movement he disliked. He just deeply adored confectionery. His mother had been a great baker and he was an excellent cook himself. When he went to Paris, his first destinations were not the Louvre or the Jeu de Paume, but Stohrer and Angelina's—and his favorite works were not Rembrandts and Van Goghs, but canelés and brioches, eclairs and roses des sables. Across a long career, he painted German chocolate cakes and king cakes, devil's food cake and baked Alaskas. He took us into the delights of buckeyes and Indiana sugar cream pies, banana puddings and snickerdoodles. In his 1963 *Cakes*, his precise, frank brushwork conjured up meringue and cream, icing sugar and melted chocolate.

When lying on our deathbeds, there will really be only two lovely things we will wish we had had more of. The other one is cakes. Our large and sophisticated brains do us a disservice when they lead us to forget how much the principal pleasures of life do not originate in their folds and downplay how much fun will ultimately need to come from elsewhere.

We are understandably wary of "escapism." We like our pleasures to be allied to grand, rationally founded, and enduring schemes: marriage and professional advancement, children and local politics. It appears demeaning to ask confectionery to provide us with one of the central constituents of the meaning of existence. But we should not fool ourselves. Most of what we scheme for in our clever minds will not come off; most of our sober larger hopes will not be realized. Friends will let us down, love will disappoint us, careers will go off at half-cock.

Thiebaud's art knows as much—and our stomachs concur. It is a

Wayne Thiebaud, *Cakes*, 1963.

superior form of intelligence to know the limits of intelligence; part of good thinking involves knowing when to stop thinking. To overlook the role of mille-feuilles and strawberry tartlets in underpinning contentment is a cold-hearted and senseless mistake. Great artists have always remembered to celebrate the real reasons to keep living.

8 *Seizing Melons*

Between 1973 and 1979, Stephen Shore made six trips across the United States, clocking up tens of thousands of miles along the way. What the photographer wanted to find and capture through his lens was nothing less than the idea of "America" in all its troubled glory, alienation, beauty, and horror. There were to be hundreds of pictures, many of them iconic and known even to those who have made no effort to know them.

But perhaps his most resonant image was taken by chance in the tiny town of Kanab in southern Utah in a diner—it still exists—early one summer morning in 1973. Sitting in the Trail's End Restaurant contemplating his just-arrived order of a plate of stacked pancakes lathered with foamy butter, a brim-full glass of cold milk, and half a shiny cantaloupe melon, Shore was struck by the sheer beauty and ecstasy of it all and, in a state of delight, with the manager's permission, stood up on a chair, pointed his 35mm Leica downward and captured an enduring testament to the sensory pleasures of life.

It doesn't feel coincidental that Shore was on a long journey and that he was in search of something large and intangible. In this respect, most of us are a version of him—though our destinations have names like "contentment" and "achievement." We dream of reaching a promised land where anxiety, restless questioning, and uncertainty will be at an end.

But we will, of course, never arrive. There is no true destination and there is definitely no end point. All there is is the journey—an idea which, though it has its tragic dimension, liberates us to make more of the true valuable increments of life: moments.

Without any promised land, there will be unexpected moments of

Stephen Shore, *Breakfast, Trail's End Restaurant, Kanab, Utah,
August 10, 1973*, 1973.

pure joy, instances of total, albeit fleeting, wonder. Our happiness must be counted in minutes, not years. But when those moments sneak up on us, we should be wise and old enough to embrace them as avidly as a child might, pushing back our chair, beholding them with awe and fixing them in our memory for ever.

9 *Wise Cows*

The mountains weren't made to deliver a message to us. No one created them to articulate a philosophy. But that doesn't mean that they aren't exceptionally well placed to do so—especially when framed through the talent of the Swiss artist Ferdinand Hodler, one of the greatest painters of any place and of any age.

We're looking up at the seven interconnected peaks of the Dents du Midi range, which rises in an almost sheer vertical up to 3,000 meters from the fertile valley floor of Switzerland's Valais region, creating an astonishing, impassable wall of granite capped for six months of the year with layers of ice and snow visited only by the occasional griffon vulture and marmot.

So much of our upset stems from being belittled by a world that refuses to accord us the respect and recognition we know should be our due. One way to appease our bruised sense of importance is to be made to feel small with definitive and magisterial force by something obviously mightier than any human. Our sense that we have been overlooked and treated badly by our fellow citizens can be subsumed by an impression of how petty and insignificant all our society's endeavors are next to the indomitable forces of nature, of which the peaks, created 60 million years ago by the titanic rippling of the Earth's crust in the continental collision, are an especially impressive symbol. It matters ever so slightly less, in the shadow of the peaks, that our projects were rejected and our reputation sullied, that we have recently rowed bitterly with our partner and been misunderstood by so-called friends.

The real stars of Hodler's painting—among his last; he died two years later—are not the mountains at all, but the three clever cows that he has carefully observed on the edge of a field. They care nothing for us and—with equal boldness—nothing for the spectacular scenery

Ferdinand Hodler, *The Dents du Midi from Champéry*, 1916.

either. They are exclusively focused on finding their next mouthful of grass and enjoying the warming rays of the August sun. The follies that agitate us have no analogies in their hearts. They are not scholars or monks but, through the good fortune of their biological makeup, have already reached the state of benign indifference and serene acceptance of fate that the wisest of humans struggle to attain after a lifetime of devoted effort.

10 *Healing Love*

There's some kind of story going on, a very lovely one, but we can't know the details for certain. We are, in this respect, standing outside a window ourselves—in the most agreeable of ways. What we can guess with some accuracy is that the relationship is an extremely kindly and tender one. This is Granny, Mommy, Nanny, or Auntie—and just beyond the window, through those thin, delicate panes of seventeenth-century Dutch glass, there is little Maries, Annelies, Sofie, or Wilma. Maybe it's a game: *I'll run outside and wave to you and your job is to wave back.* Or: *You cover your eyes, I'll duck beneath the window, give a little tap and then you have to rush to spot me before I drop down again.* Or, more simply: *When I have to go home after a day with you, I miss you so much and I like to say goodbye many times, four times in the room, twice from the hallway and then once again at the window.*

In other words, in some undefined way, this is a portrait of love. An adult, probably quite a serious one who has known many cares and has considerable responsibilities, is bending to the sweet and imaginative will of a small person, in whose reflection she sees a version of herself. Vrel hints that the window is a mirror: the old woman gazing at a version of her younger self. A grown-up who could so easily have humiliated the child—said she was busy or that it was all too silly—is joining in enthusiastically and giving the ritual or game her all, to the extent that she might even fall off her chair.

One of the unexpected origins of something as serious and consequential as adult mental health arguably begins right here. If we find ourselves as grown-ups feeling creative, knowing how to appreciate ourselves, understanding how to remain calm, and ready to give affection to others, it is almost certainly because at some point, a long way back, someone did for us what the woman in Vrel's painting is doing

Jacob Vrel, *Woman at a Window, Waving at a Girl*, c. 1650.

for the little girl: gave us attention, made us the focus of tenderness, appreciated us on our own modest but vital terms.

Children who end up sane have been spared the need to be very good or very reasonable too early. We can't know much about the economic status of Vrel's figures. What we do know is that such games and the love behind them belong to what it really means to have had that most invaluable of things: a privileged childhood.

11 *I'm Not Getting in the Car*

It was the summer of 1963 and Joel Meyerowitz was walking the streets of New York City with his M10 when, on the Upper East Side, somewhere around 76th and Madison, he came across a girl whose name we will never know having one of the worst mornings of her young life. The wails resounded all around the brownstones. No, she wasn't getting in. No, she didn't care about what the time was. No, she wasn't going to listen. No, no, no.

Part of what makes young children's lives so difficult is that they have extremely powerful antipathies, worries, loves, and dreads that make no immediate sense to grown-ups because children lack the language or wherewithal to be able to explain them with requisite adequacy. Their feelings are an outgrowth of the manic sensitivity, unconfined intelligence, and wild imagination of the infantile mind. Small people are, in the best and most inspiring of ways, slightly mad.

Let's imagine that perhaps the girl doesn't want to get inside because she really doesn't like the way the car looks. She hates the dark orange paintwork of its upper body; it reminds her of the color of a house she once had to go into where another girl said something extremely mean to her about her hair. Or maybe she doesn't want to get inside because the driver makes an odd noise when he swallows or because there's a strange smell in the toilets at school or because she's been forbidden from taking her soft rabbit with her and she doesn't want Floppy to spend all day alone with Maria in the apartment staring at the wall and getting bored. But because all this is so hard to explain, most children simply end up screaming, then being labeled "spoilt" or "difficult."

The child and the artist are in a sense in a very similar predicament: both are uncommonly sensitive, both notice and are marked by "small things" that it's easy to overlook or denigrate. Both might spend an age

Joel Meyerowitz, *New York City*, 1963.

looking at a sidewalk, a flower, or a conker. But artists are in a luckier position: They can bring to the sensitivities of a child the powers of communication of a robust and ingenious adult. They can turn their tears into pictures and essays.

With their examples in mind, we should strive not so much to become less sensitive as to grow better able to convey what we are sensitive about, so that we will have a slightly better chance of being understood even by people who are in a very great hurry to get us into the car.

12 *What Remains*

She should, it seems, have so little to be happy about. She's only got a few months left to live, she had to sell her bungalow after the diagnosis, both of her knees are giving her trouble, she can't hear anything in her left ear, she's seen too many of her close friends die. And yet, extraordinarily, she is smiling.

Furthermore, though it sounds strange, she's happier now than she was a while ago, when she ostensibly had so much more to feel happy about, when she could run and hear a pin drop. She's certainly happier than she was at twenty, when she was deciding between Vincent and Albert; or when she was forty, and the kids were teenagers; or after the marriage fell apart and she moved to a small place outside Lille on her own.

All the worries have faded into the background. She is living—as certain Eastern sages have always recommended—entirely in the present. She doesn't look much beyond tomorrow. She is surprised and amazed to have made it until the spring. She studies everything with patience and wonder. How extraordinary a rose is, she thinks, with the glee of a young child—one of the nurses brought it for her after her daughter mentioned the garden she had left behind. She had never been too interested in flowers until she was sixty. Then they started to matter a lot. By that time, all her larger aspirations had faded; she knew full well about the gap between her hopes and the available realities. So then flowers were no longer an insult to ambition, but a genuine pleasure amid a litany of troubles, a small resting place for hope in a turbulent sea of disappointment.

She doesn't care about the so-called big things any more. When the politicians argue on television, she looks away. She has seen so many babies turn into old men, and brilliant young things fade into nothing.

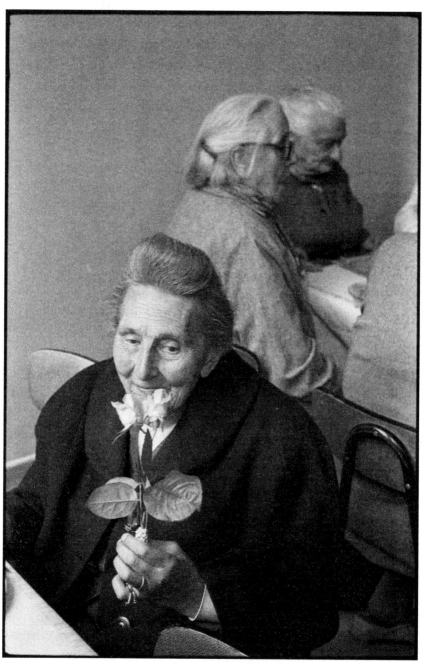

Martine Franck, *"Maison de Nanterre,"* Old People's Home,
Hauts de Seine, France, 1978.

She doesn't worry about what will happen to the planet or get excited about what the scientists might discover. If you visit her, she just wants to know how you are and whether you might be cold or after something to drink. She's happy that you exist and that she can put her hand on yours.

In the end, all we will care about will be kindness. We should—with the help of the right art—learn a little ahead of time.

13 *Hockney's First Day*

In 1963, the *Sunday Times* sent the already much celebrated 26-year-old artist David Hockney to Egypt on an assignment to record the great monuments of antiquity: the pyramids outside Cairo, the temples at Luxor and Karnak, and the tombs in the Valley of the Kings. Egypt astonished Hockney and induced in him a state of almost perpetual creativity where everything seemed to hold a secret, everything was worthy of investigation and reflection. He sketched on whatever was to hand: old envelopes, hotel room notepaper, and the inside covers of his books. However, what struck him most were not the obvious tourist destinations so much as the details of ordinary Egyptian life: the watch of the man at reception, the sandals of the newspaper seller, the signs for the dry cleaner, and the television repair shop.

On arrival in Alexandria, Hockney sat on the terrace of the Hotel Cecil and very carefully drew the label on a bottle of local mineral water from the El Natroon valley and a packet of cigarettes. In its delicacy and observational precision—Hockney knew no Arabic—this astonishing study of a bottle might be an emblem of what it means to be properly attuned to a place: to put aside our usual cares and surrender to the interest and beauty of the world, as a child might, as artists will—and as we almost never do.

Generally, we tend to notice nothing, but we may make an exception for one particular time and place: *the first day in a new destination*. There and then, for once, we too may be shaken from our customary lethargy. Everything leaps out at us: how peculiar the taxis are, the smells in the street, the sound of passers-by, the clothes of the old. Our eyes open properly, as they last did when we were two years old and it took us half an hour to get home from the park because there was so much for us to study on the way.

David Hockney, *Waiter, Alexandria*, 1963.

This state is unlikely to last long. After a few days, we usually go back to our habitual blindness. But even if we manage it for only a short while, the receptivity of that first day remains a possibility that we should strive to enact more regularly and generously, even in places closer to home. We shouldn't need another continent to start to appreciate the texture of existence. We knew how to do so as a small one and we might do so again. Artists are in this context only the emissaries of an appropriately appreciative relationship to the world of which we are all in theory capable.

Our travels have an overwhelming lesson to teach us: that we need whenever we can to try to look at our lives, with which it is so easy to get dispirited and about which it is so forgivable to despair, as though we were still in some ways on that hopeful, endlessly fascinating *first day* somewhere else, when even a label on a bottle of water has something important to whisper to us.

14 *The Greatest Artist*

This is a self-portrait by one of the greatest artists of the twenty-first century, a car-shaped contraption named Curiosity which has been moving around at a glacial pace – it would take an hour for it to complete a hundred-meter sprint—over the surface of Mars since its bumpy landing there in a cloud of dust on August 6, 2012, following a 560-million-kilometer journey from Earth.

Curiosity has ostensibly come to Mars in order to find out more about the planet's biological and geochemical properties. It's been trying to understand Mars's organic carbon compounds; it's been figuring out the relative proportions of sulfur, carbon, hydrogen, and phosphorus in the atmosphere. It's been mapping isotopic composition and measuring the spectrum of radiation, with a special interest in secondary neutrons and solar proton events.

But regardless of the stated purpose, what Curiosity has really been trying to do is to help our marriages, calm our anger with our colleagues, appease our disappointments, and bolster our capacities for calm and perspective. No one can look at any of the images it has sent back without a sense of awe that at once relativizes everything petty and regrettable that agitates and demeans us day to day. What can it possibly matter who said what to whom and in what tone of voice given that Curiosity has captured the sun going down at six in the evening below the rim of Gale Crater? Or that its mast camera has just sent thirty-two individual images that it has assembled into a panorama of a Martian outcrop nicknamed Mont Mercou?

The machine also reminds us of the beauty of our own planet. The bleakness of Mars emphasizes the lushness of our own world. Pictures

Curiosity self-portrait at "Glen Etive" site, 2019.

of this far-off place we will probably never go to ourselves can inspire wonder and gratitude for where we are already.

Like all great artists, and with comparable technical ingenuity, Curiosity has attempted to help us change our lives, away from superficiality and bitterness toward goodness, wisdom, and truth.

IV : Freedom

There are few more emotive or beguiling words than "freedom." Even without examining it very closely, and perhaps especially then, the term tends to evoke something especially honorable, enticing, and good, of which we would always want more and could never stand to be deprived.

In our societies, the word has been especially resonant at the collective level, so much so that when we nowadays think of freedom, it is first and foremost political freedom that we might have in mind. It's in the name of political freedom that millions have marched, chanted, and risked their lives in demonstrations and struggles over the centuries: in Paris in 1789 and Bucharest in 1877, in Lima's Plaza Mayor in 1885 and Leipzig's Karl-Marx-Platz in 1989.

The freedom that we can, in certain parts of the world, now take for granted—the right to own property, to express negative opinions about the government, and to live without fear of arbitrary arrest—is the result of five hundred years of fearless effort on the part of the defenders of liberty. It is because, in the cities of northern Italy and the Low Countries, medieval merchants rose up against their tyrannical feudal overlords, because seventeenth-century political theorists carefully took apart the claims of absolutist monarchies, and because groups of determined students in nineteenth- and twentieth-century Europe refused to kowtow to the rule of dictators that we can nowadays lob sarcastic remarks at our mediocre rulers and look at the security forces without fear.

But if politicians know that they can always be sure of drawing a powerful response from their audiences by brandishing the word "freedom"—and labeling their opponents as its enemies—it is in part on the basis of a subtle emotional sleight of hand. We are open to being mobilized by a promise of freedom in politics because it is a quality that, even if only in a semiconscious way, we long for in our personal and psychological lives.

Even when, at the level of the state, we have all the freedoms we need, we may lack freedom of the spirit. We might be free but not feel free. Without there being any formal chains around us, we may have an impression of being hemmed in or uncomfortably observed. We may be afraid of departing from convention and of doing things that our friends or people we went to school with wouldn't approve of. A sense of inward freedom turns out to be in its own way even more complicated than political freedom—and its enemies more subtle.

Were we to draw up a charter of what we can call psychological freedom, we might need to include some of the following constituents:

freedom from fear of judgment

freedom from the weight of public opinion

freedom from society's ideas of normality

freedom from society's definitions of a good relationship

freedom from standard beliefs about status

freedom from expected consumption patterns

freedom from fashionable opinions

freedom from the pressure to be normal, ambitious, or optimistic

All these will contribute, in their absence, to much more elusive forms of enmeshment than those we know in the political sphere. The prohibitions are much harder to track—and the forms of suffering they generate more insidious in their effects.

We lack the iron-clad reliable vocabulary open to those who seek to defend political freedoms. We know the importance of "freedom from arbitrary arrest"; we're still at the dawn of appreciating what it might mean to be free enough not to consult social media or to resist the pressure to parrot fashionable opinions—let alone take off for a hut in the woods, flout the latest shibboleth on relationships, or never go to another party again.

We are still feeling our way to an understanding of what a genuinely free life would be like: what we could refuse, who we could stop listening to, what we could dare to focus on if we were brave enough to take our own consciences *and sensations as our lodestars. We may remain, in our hearts, every bit as unfree as an unbeliever in a totalitarian religious regime or a dissident under observation of the state apparatus. We can be no less fearful, our choices just as constrained, our ability to roam as we would wish equally compromised.*

We have been fighting for liberty from state control for centuries. The quest now is to identify and then more robustly hold on to the key ingredients of psychological freedom. For this, we need humbly to accept how still relatively unfamiliar we might be with the idea of being free in and of ourselves. We should concede that shackles and obedience come to us far more readily than do indiscipline and the solitary path. Though we may flatter ourselves through identification with lone rebels and renegades, we are by nature docile, pliable, accommodating herd animals with a ready appetite to go meekly wherever our shepherds might dictate.

We need—though the phrase may sound peculiar—to learn to be free, to rid ourselves of the invisible hierarchies in our minds and the fears bequeathed to us by our histories. We need to lean on examples of once-timid people who grew into themselves, discern the bars of our cages, and properly identify who and what is wasting what remains of our years. We may have loved the idea of freedom for a long time already; now come the challenge and opportunity of leading a life that is truly our own.

1 *Sonnet 29 and Failure*

When, in disgrace with fortune and men's eyes,
I all alone beweep my outcast state,
And trouble deaf heaven with my bootless cries,
And look upon myself and curse my fate,
Wishing me like to one more rich in hope,
Featured like him, like him with friends possessed,
Desiring this man's art and that man's scope,
With what I most enjoy contented least;
Yet in these thoughts myself almost despising,
Haply I think on thee, and then my state,
(Like to the lark at break of day arising
From sullen earth) sings hymns at heaven's gate;
> For thy sweet love remembered such wealth brings
> That then I scorn to change my state with kings.

Sonnet 29, written around 1592, finds William Shakespeare, then in his late twenties, in a highly fragile state. He is worried about failure. He is contemplating a future in which he will be a social pariah, his mention enough to provoke revulsion. He will be in agony, pondering his stupidity and bad luck. He will lament that he can't practice the job he most enjoys—and he will look around and feel desperation and envy of all those who remain so much more successful than he is and who will still enjoy esteem and their good name.

It is, of course, a paradox that the most acclaimed writer in English literature should have worried so acutely about failure; that he should have been so like us in fearing that he would one day—through a mixture of his own idiocy and unfortunate outside events—be a disgraced nobody. Then again, "greatness" in literature doesn't come from living pompously among high-flown abstractions; great writers are ultimately simply those who know how to speak with special honesty about the panic and sadness of an ordinary life.

What had brought Shakespeare to this anxious, vigilant state? Why was he so afraid he was going to lose it all? Partly, it was because he was not yet very well established. He'd written only *Richard III* and the three parts of *Henry VI*. In the coming years, he would write—in quick succession—*A Midsummer Night's Dream*, *The Merchant of Venice*, *As You Like It*, and *Twelfth Night*. But as yet these would have been mere sketches in his mind. There was another problem. Shakespeare had a famous and very vicious enemy who was spreading rumors about him and seemed determined to bring him down. He was a fellow playwright called Robert Greene.

Greene loathed Shakespeare. He wrote an open letter warning that "There is an upstart Crow, beautified with our feathers, that with his Tygers heart wrapt in a Players hide, supposes he is as well able to bombast out a blanke verse as the best of you." He nicknamed him "Shakescene"—that is, a show-off and a popularizing fool—and, to further rub in how untalented he was, a jack of all trades or "Johannes Factotum." In different circumstances but with equal unfairness, we all have Robert Greenes around us. The world abounds in them and makes life a good deal more terrifying and nasty than it should be.

The London theater world was small, mean, and very gossipy. This kind of review from a respected playwright was intended to damage and it would have done huge harm. One can imagine Shakespeare, still young and finding his feet in the capital, panicking at how bad the sniping was getting, worrying that such insults would never stop, knowing how many people had had a mean laugh at his expense, fearful that his good intentions would never surface and that he would for ever be known as a cheap, unscrupulous idiot.

Furthermore, the bubonic plague had returned, as it did continually to England in the Elizabethan age. The year before Shakespeare's birth, an outbreak had killed 80,000 and now it was back. Between August 1592 and January 1593, 20,000 people died in the southeast of England,

15,000 of them in London. There was rioting in the streets and Queen Elizabeth moved out to Windsor Castle for her safety. The government shut down all pubs and theatres for six months. Every actor and playwright was out of work. Not only was his name being trashed, Shakespeare was facing financial ruin.

How to bear the terror of failure? With Shakespeare as our guide, though the impulse may be to turn away from fear, what can calm us down is to sit with what scares us most. We should dare to investigate the terrifying scenario so as to drain it of its strangeness and stop apprehending it only through the corners of our eyes in shame. Shakespeare openly meditates on what might happen: He pictures the worst that could unfold in order to see how it might be borne. He also renders himself cathartically vulnerable in the process; he makes no bones about his suffering to us in the future and, we can imagine, to the people more immediately around him. He is going to admit just how bad things are for him in order to break his isolation and sense of unacceptability. He will try to universalize what could otherwise feel like only a very personal and embarrassing affliction. He will dare to see if anyone else has ever suffered as he has—and hold out an imaginary hand of friendship to all his readers, as writers will.

But then comes the core of the consoling process. He recognizes implicitly that what is driving his wish to be successful is the desire to be respected and liked. It might be money and fame that he is drawn to, but beneath these there is another hunger: to be treated well and to avoid humiliation. There is a quest for love hiding within the drive to be somebody. Once that idea is established, a deeply redemptive maneuver comes into view. We don't actually ever need the whole of society to love us. We don't have to have everyone on our side. Let the Robert Greenes of this world—and their many successors in newspapers, living rooms, and social media down the ages—say their very worst and nastiest things and be done with them. All that we need is the love of a few friends or even just one special person and we can survive.

The love of a single sensitive and intelligent being can compensate us for the loss of love from the world and with such a gift we can, as

Shakespeare says, be in a better place than "kings." Popular success is an unreliable goal, at the mercy of fickle fortune. There are so many jealous people and we are prone to make mistakes that they can use to bring us down. What we must therefore try to do is cultivate—and look forward to leaning on—the affection and regard of sympathetic companions. Others may be scoffing, others may sneer every time our name comes up in conversation, but we will be secure. We will be somewhere far from the gossipy and plague-ridden city, living quietly with those who properly know us and for whom we won't need to do anything more to deserve a place in their hearts.

Shakespeare's Sonnet 29 has been prized for four centuries because it latches on with such sincerity to an anxiety that afflicts us all—and proposes a solution that we know must be correct. In the end, things may turn out all right: the plague may recede, business may pick up, the rumor mill may die down and leave us alone. But if none of this happens, if it does all go wrong and we become a definitive byword for awfulness, then in our moments of high anxiety, especially late at night, we should know the fallback: a few generous, sincere, emotionally mature souls who know about forgiveness and kindness, sympathy and charity, who won't reduce us to one horrid nickname, who will love us with the complex regard that a parent might bestow on a child or a god on its creations. Love will redeem us. We may well fail, but we don't need to fear it will be hell—and so we can afford to approach challenges with a little more freedom and light-heartedness. The cleverest and most humane writer who ever lived knew as much; in our panic we should trust him.

2 *How to Live in a Hut*

There's a dread that we normally keep at the far edges of our minds but that occasionally—particularly at three o'clock on a restless night—floods our thoughts: If we don't constantly strive to achieve, if we slip up, or if some new catastrophe strikes the economy, we'll lose pretty much everything and we'll end up having to live in a caravan, a tiny one-room apartment or—God forbid—a hut in the middle of nowhere.

The bleakness of this image spurs us to ever more frantic efforts. We'd settle for almost anything to avoid it: oppressively long working hours; a job that holds no interest; risky money-making schemes; a loveless marriage that keeps us in the family home; or, maybe, decades of suffering the whims of a grim relative for the prospect of an inheritance. The hut is a symbol of disaster and humiliation.

It's in this fear-laden context that we might consider the case of a man called Kamo no Chomei, who was born in Japan around 1155. His father was the well-to-do head of a prominent religious shrine near Kyoto, which was then the capital, and Chomei grew up in luxurious circumstances. He received a refined education and in the early part of his adult life had an elegant social circle. When he was still in his twenties, his grandmother left him a big house and his future looked bright. But then it all started to go wrong. He made enemies and was sidelined in his career; he got into financial difficulties and, by the time he was fifty, he had alienated his former friends, had practically no money left—and was going bald.

Chomei was forced to reform his existence and survive on the most slender material base. Far out in the country, where no one else wanted to live, he built himself a tiny hut—just ten feet by ten. It was, he reflected, one hundredth of the size of the mansion in which he'd

Kawai Shrine within the Shimogamo Shrine, Kyoto, Kyoto Prefecture, Kinki Region, Japan.

grown up. It wasn't even a permanent structure; his situation was so precarious he had to ensure that his home could be dismantled and carted away.

A modern reconstruction shows just how small and basic it was, but doesn't convey its isolated position in the hills at Toyama, which was considered the back of beyond. Rotting leaves collected on the roof, moss grew on the floor, and the water supply was just a rickety bamboo pipe leading from a nearby stream to a little pool by the door. Chomei cooked outside, though eventually he rigged up a small awning to keep the rain off in wet weather. He slept on a pile of bracken on the floor, he had no furniture, and he lived mainly on nuts, berries, and wild root vegetables which he foraged from the woods—and quite often he went hungry. The only people he saw were a family of peasants who lived at the foot of the hill whom his former grand friends would have dismissed as lowly rustics. He could afford only clothes made from the coarsest cloth and they soon became mere rags, leaving him indistinguishable from the beggars he used to see in the city. It was here, in this way, that Chomei lived for fifteen years, up to his death in his mid-sixties.

It was also here that he wrote a short book, *The Ten Square Foot Hut*, one of the great masterpieces of Japanese literature. It's not—as we might expect—a lament, poring over the misfortunes and betrayals that led him to this degraded condition. Instead it's full of good cheer, happiness, and pleasure. The most touching line in the whole of the essay is the simple affirmation: "I love my little hut, my simple dwelling."

What, we can ask, was it that enabled Chomei to find fulfillment in such an apparently unpromising place? It wasn't that he was naturally drawn to a minimal material life: No one who'd known him earlier, in his days of prosperity, would have imagined that he could thrive under such circumstances—least of all himself. He wasn't someone who for years had been hankering after the simple life. He moved to the hut in desperation and against his inclinations; it was only once he was there that he discovered that he liked it—that it was in fact his ideal home.

Chomei was guided by a distinctive philosophy. And this is a principle of hope, for we can't magically take on another individual's personality but we can understand, and perhaps come to share, their ideas. Temperament may be fixed but philosophy is transferable. From his book, we can identify four crucial ideas that together transformed what could have been a purely grim experience into one of deep and tranquil satisfaction.

BEAUTY IS VERY IMPORTANT

This might seem a strange place to start because normally beauty looks like the outcome of immense wealth: elegant possessions, a gracious home, and trips to Venice and St Petersburg. But these expensive things are just the most obvious instances of beauty. As our tastes become more sensitive and our imaginations more expansive, the link with money falls away—because a great many truly lovely sights are readily available almost everywhere to those who know how to look.

Around his modest home, Chomei—with a sensitive eye—discovered endless sources of beauty: fall leaves, fruit trees in blossom, melting snow, the sound of the wind rustling through the trees and the rain beating down on the roof. All were free. He was entranced by flowers: "In spring I gaze upon swathes of wisteria that hang shining in the west, like the purple clouds that bear the soul to heaven." He found a delightful spot on the hillside: "If the day is fine I look out over Mount Kohata, Fushimi Village, Toba and Hatsukashi" and "at night, the fireflies in the nearby grass blend their little lights with the fires the fishermen make at distant Makinoshima: no one owns a splendid view."

It's partly the idea of having to cope with constant ugliness that makes a lower-level economic life so frightening. Chomei's antidote is to stress the continuing opportunities for visual delight, even on the most minimal of incomes.

TIME IS MORE IMPORTANT THAN MONEY

Although we say that time is precious, our actions reveal our real priorities: We devote a huge portion of our conscious existence to making and trying to accumulate money. We tend to have a highly concrete and detailed sense of accounting around finances, while time invisibly slips away.

Chomei, on the contrary, had a keen sense of the value of his own time, without interruptions, impediments or duties: "I can choose to rest and laze as I wish, there is no one to stand in my way or to shame me for my idleness."

He had time to practice playing the lute, or *biwa*: "my skills are poor," he admitted – but then he had no audience, he wasn't trying to please or impress anyone. "I play music, I sing alone, simply for my own fulfillment."

He read and reread the same few favorite books, which he came to know almost by heart. He had time to reflect and to write. He meditated, took long walks, and spent a lot of time contemplating the moon.

His activities were self-directed: He did them simply because he found them enjoyable, not because anyone had asked him or because they were expected of a civilized individual. And he had this luxury only because he had disregarded the nexus of money and the pursuit of status which is so closely connected to it.

Theoretically Chomei could have found a job, however lowly. But he preferred to cut his expenses down to zero in the name of something truly valuable: his time.

EVERYTHING IS TRANSIENT

Chomei opens his book with a metaphor comparing human life to a river: "On flows the river ceaselessly, nor does the water ever stay the same. The bubbles that float upon its pools now disappear, now form anew, but never endure long. And so it is with people in this world, and with their dwellings." He's reminding himself—and us—of the half-terrifying, half-consoling fact that our existence and all our pleasures and troubles are fleeting.

Because our lives are so brief it is the quality of our experiences, rather than the extent of our possessions, that matters. The more things we own, the more we are exposed to random misfortune: A fashionable home will soon be dated; our prestige in the eyes of others will fluctuate for trivial reasons; we might build a palace and die before it is completed; and the monuments we hope will allow our names to last get misinterpreted or torn down. The simple hut makes an accommodation with impermanence: It might get blown down in a storm or washed away in a flood, officials might arrive at our door and tell us we have to leave, but our needs have been pared down so much that chance has less to work on.

"WORLDLY" PEOPLE ARE LESS HAPPY THAN THEY SEEM

A thought that erodes our willingness to live a simpler life—in a hut, if need be—is the haunting fear that other people are having a wonderful time. Perhaps we could manage to get by, but we'd always be conscious of how much we were missing out on.

Chomei continually reminded himself that a "worldly" life—which in his early and middle years he knew intimately—carries a heavy load of limitations, defects and sorrows. The life of the well-to-do is less enviable than it outwardly seems. The fashionable world is full of what he called "cringing": "You worry over your least action; you cannot be authentic in your grief or your joy." In high society, it is always paramount to consider how any opinion will be judged by the other members of the social beehive. Envy is widespread and there is perpetual anxiety around losing status—which takes the satisfaction out of prosperity: "without a peaceful mind, palaces and fine houses mean nothing."

Chomei's aim wasn't to disparage the rich. "I am simply comparing my past, worldly life with my present one," he wrote, and added that the balance of pleasures and contentment was distinctly in favor of the latter. What he had been denied wasn't, on examination, worth regretting.

Chomei is showing us that it's *possible* to live in materially minimal conditions while being good-humored, ambitious, and in search of true fulfillment. He is dismantling our fear that material modesty has to mean degradation and squalor. We can, if we embrace his ideas, live more simply anywhere, including a hut, should we have to. And in the meantime, as we now know, we do not need to be so afraid.

3 Become an Aristocrat

Aristocrats are, of course, a faintly ridiculous proposition: They wear tweedy clothes; they speak with improbable accents; they have odd-sounding, often very long names; they bury themselves in the depths of the country on estates that have been in their families for generations, devoting themselves to the slaughter of foxes and grouse; they are low on talent and ill-equipped for competition in a meritocratic society.

But they have one very enviable merit: They are utterly indifferent to popular opinion. It never occurs to them to worry whether what they care about will get a fair hearing in the media. They accept that they belong to a radical minority and it would be absurd to imagine that the average person would know about, let alone be sympathetic to, their world. This gives them the strength to approach the media with light-hearted indifference. They don't blame or even dislike the popular press for not understanding them—it's entirely inevitable. The vast majority of the population are, in their eyes, simply unfortunate people who at some level mean well but can't conceivably have opinions worth taking too seriously. Aristocrats are not politically anti-democratic but something quite different and more intriguing: They are psychologically above popular opinion.

We might rather wish we could share some of their unconcern, but how can we who lack castles and long lines of fancy ancestors possibly have access to this elevated and blithe state of mind?

The dilemma received one intriguing answer in France in the nineteenth century. Traditionally, aristocrats had been defined by their huge economic and political power. But in the Revolution of 1789, many of them lost their heads and even more lost their money, so a new definition started to be explored. A pivotal figure in this was the novelist and essayist Jules Barbey d'Aurevilly, who was born in 1808 into the Normandy gentry. His family had for generations been allied with the grand lords who ruled the nation. They had now lost their lands and their homes, but they still wished to signal that they were not like everyone else. Barbey d'Aurevilly tried to give form to a sense of superiority that did not depend on lineage or money: He might no longer have been at the top of society in sheer material terms but he possessed—so he thought—a different and more important title. He was one of the initiators of a new idea of aristocracy: an aristocracy of the spirit rather than the blood. To be an aristocrat in the modern world, he suggested, was a matter of possessing elegant taste, sensibility, lofty ideas, and refined emotions. This, rather than the possession of large tracts of land and a chateau or two, was what gave one the keys to the elite.

In his own life, Barbey d'Aurevilly expressed his attitude by adopting an extravagant mode of dress and self-presentation. He was very fond of lace cuffs and often wore an elaborate cravat; he grew a vast mustache, adopted a haughty posture, and perfected a way of lifting his chin, lowering his eyelids and gazing down his nose to convey a profound lack of concern for what people in general might think of him, or indeed of anything else. It wasn't his bloodline that he thought set him apart, it was his soul. He resolutely opposed the notion of popularity. The ideal, he said, was "to be a genius and to be obscure," although he was in fact rather widely read in his own time. Loftiness and intensity of mind did not need popular endorsement.

Barbey d'Aurevilly was putting a finger on a crucial possibility: that there might be a modern, workable version of a legitimate aristocratic disdain for public opinion. It could be reasonable to see oneself as being "above" the populist debate, without possessing an estate or an ancient name, just because one had a different sort of mind.

Sadly, Barbey d'Aurevilly was too emotionally attached to the vision of *looking* special to fully articulate the deeper implications of his thought. In reality, a pure aristocrat of the spirit could look entirely normal, live in a perfectly ordinary house and have a common enough

Émile Lévy, *Jules Barbey d'Aurevilly*, 1881.

job and never sport a cravat. None of the dandyish garb of nineteenth-century aristocrats of the spirit was really necessary. What should in essence set aristocrats of the spirit apart is a commitment to mental refinement.

Their disdain for popular opinion isn't the result of ill will or hostility. It arises from a sober and careful analysis of the human condition. Most people just aren't interested in understanding an opposed opinion; blind partisanship is simply far more tempting. It may be unfortunate that almost no one has a taste for unpicking the exact logic of an argument, but nothing in history should lead us to expect that they would. It's surely a pity that millions are more eager to denounce than to explain, but it's hardly surprising. A love of accurate explanation is almost as rare as the ownership of a castle.

The pure aristocrat of the spirit ignores public opinion not because they hate people but because they know them well and are sympathetic and compassionate toward the reasons why they won't be thinking straight. They feel an immense tenderness toward the ordinary preoccupations and struggles of daily life that make intricate argumentation, tenderness, open-mindedness, and the delicate weighing of possibilities unreachable luxuries for most. They are set apart not by haughty contempt but by a melancholic certainty that the disputes of the populace will be chaotic, brutal, partisan, deeply illogical, and unfair because this is the normal, unfortunate lot of the human animal. These aristocrats don't take any of it to heart. They never hoped to be widely understood or popularly appreciated.

Just as the aristocrat of the blood once did, the new aristocrat of the spirit takes pride in their genealogy. But they are no longer talking about DNA. They belong to the great dynastic family of everyone who has shared their sensitivity, their suffering, and their nobility of mind. They discover that Stendhal was an ancestor and Rembrandt was a member of their clan; Jane Austen perhaps was a relative and possibly Leo Tolstoy. They are, with great legitimacy, laying claim to a different but entirely real kind of nobility: one of ideas, responses, emotions, doubts, worries, pleasures, aspirations, and complications, the common heritage of a small, but very lovely lineage. And so they—we—can look on the disorders of democratic debate in the mass media without anxiety or distress. For we inhabit a very different kind of castle: one made of sensitivity rather than stone, just as enduring and open to all free-thinking newcomers, though invisible to the eyes of most.

4 *The Ecstatic Dance*

One of the strangest but also most intriguing and redemptive things that humans get up to, in almost any culture one cares to study, is occasionally to gather in large groups, bathe in the rhythmic sounds of drums and flutes, organs and guitars, chants and cries, and move their arms and legs about in complicated and frenzied ways, losing themselves in the bewilderment of a dance.

Dancing has a claim to be considered among the most essential and salutary activities we ever partake in. Not for nothing did Nietzsche, a painfully inhibited figure in day-to-day life, declare, "I would believe only in a God who could dance"—a comment that stands beside his equally apodictic pronouncement: "Without music, life would be a mistake."

But dancing is at the same time an activity that many of us, arguably those of us who might most need to do it, are powerfully inclined to resist and deep down to fear. We stand on the side of the dance floor appalled at the possibility of being called to join in, attempt to make our excuses the moment the music begins, and take pains that no one will ever, ever see our hips unite with a beat.

The point here is definitely not to learn to dance like an expert but to remember that dancing badly is something we might actually want to do and, equally importantly, something that we already know how to do—at least to the appalling level that is the only proficiency we need to derive key benefits.

In almost all cultures and at all points of history—except oddly enough perhaps our own—dancing has been widely and publicly understood as a form of bodily exercise with something very important to contribute to our mental state. Dancing has nothing to do with dancing well, being young, or revealing one's stylishness. Summed up sharply,

Shiva as the Lord of Dance, Tamil Nadu, India, c. 950–1000.

we might put it like this: Dancing has been valued for allowing us to transcend our individuality and for inducing us to merge into a larger, more welcoming, and more redemptive whole.

It should come as no surprise that one of the main gods of Hinduism was a dancing god and that Shiva's dance has a meaning with resonance far beyond a specific religion. By dancing, we may enter, as Shiva does, back into harmony with the cosmos. As limbs swing and bodies sway, the many details of our material and practical lives—our age, levels of prosperity, voting preferences, even our gender—drop away and we reunite with the totality.

A comparably rich vision of dancing developed in classical Greece. The Greeks were for the most part committed worshipers of the rational mind. One of their foremost gods, Apollo, was the embodiment of cool reason and disciplined wisdom. However, the Greeks understood—with prescience—that a life devoted only to the serenity of the mind could be at grave risk of desiccation and loneliness. And so they balanced their concern with Apollo with regular festivals in honor of a quite different god, Dionysus, a god that drank wine, stayed up late, loved music—and danced.

The Greeks knew that the more rational we usually are, the more important it is—at points—to fling ourselves around to the wild rhythms of pipes and drums. At the festivals of Dionysus, held in Athens in March every year, even the most venerable and dignified members of the community would join in with unrestrained dancing that, irrigated by generous amounts of red wine, lasted until dawn.

A word often used to describe such dancing is "ecstatic." It's a telling term. Ecstatic comes from two Latin words, *ex* (meaning apart) and *stasis* (meaning standing), indicating a state in which we are symbolically "standing apart" from ourselves, separated from the dense, detailed and self-centered layers of our identities which we normally focus on and obsess over and reconnected with something more primal and more necessary: our common human nature. We remember, through a period of ecstatic dancing, what it is like to belong, to be part

William Bouguereau, *La Jeunesse de Bacchus*, 1884.

of something larger than ourselves, to be indifferent to our own egos—to be reunited with humanity.

This aspiration hasn't entirely disappeared in modernity, but it's been assigned to very particular settings: the disco and the rave. These places often point us in unhelpful directions: toward being cool, a certain age and knowledgeable about very stylish kinds of clothes and sounds—criteria that leave many of us out. We need urgently to recover a sense of the universal benefit of dancing. The greatest enemy of this is fear, and in particular the fear—as we may put it—that we will look "like an idiot" in front of people whose opinion might matter. The way through this is not to be told that we will in fact be fine and, with a bit of effort, very far from idiotic. Quite the opposite: We should accept with good grace that the whole point of redemptive, consoling, cathartic communal dancing is a chance to look like total, thoroughgoing idiots, the bigger the better, in the company of hundreds of other equally and generously publicly idiotic fellow humans.

We spend a good deal of our time fearing, as if it were a momentous calamity that we did not even dare contemplate in daylight, that we might be idiots and holding back from a host of important aspirations and ambitions as a result. We should shake ourselves free from such inhibitions by loosening our hold on any remaining sense of dignity and by accepting frankly that we are by nature completely idiotic, great sacks of foolishness that cry in the night, bump into doors, fart in the bath, and kiss people's noses by mistake – but that far from being shameful and isolating, this idiocy is in fact a basic feature of our nature that unites us immediately with everyone else on the planet. We are idiots now, we were idiots then, and we will be idiots again in the future. There is no other option for a human.

Dancing provides us with a primordial occasion on which this basic idiocy can be publicly displayed and communally celebrated. On a dance floor filled with comparable idiots, we can at last delight in our joint foolishness. We can throw off our customary shyness and reserve and fully embrace our dazzling strangeness and derangement. An hour of frantic jigging should decisively shake us from any enduring belief in our normalcy or seriousness. We will no longer be able to bully others, persuade them of our superiority, humiliate them for their mistakes, or pontificate at length on weighty matters. We will no longer worry about how others see us or regret a few things we said to intimidating strangers. The gentle aches in our limbs and our memories of our moves will remind us of anchoring facts that will guarantee our ongoing sanity and kindness.

Whenever we have the chance to invite others around, especially very serious people by whom we're intimidated or whom we might be seeking to impress, we should remember the divine Dionysus and dare, with his wisdom in mind, to put on "Dancing Queen," "I'm So Excited" or "We are Family." Knowing that we have Nietzsche on our side, we should let rip with a playlist that includes "What a Feeling," "I Wanna Dance with Somebody" and "It's Raining Men." We should lose command of our normal rational pilot selves, abandon our arms to the harmonies, throw away our belief in a "right" way to dance or indeed to live, build the intensity of our movements to a frenzy, gyrate our heads to empty them of their absurd worries, forget our jobs, qualifications, status, achievements, plans, hopes, and fears—and merge with the universe or at least its more immediate representatives, our fellow new mad friends, before whom the disclosure of idiocy will be total.

Around us might be a formally shy accountant, an efficient dental nurse, or a white-haired school principal bending up and down and flinging their arms in the air, throwing their heads back, contorting their bodies. After a few songs, something astonishing will begin to happen: It won't matter any more that we said a slightly out of place thing in a meeting two weeks ago, that we haven't yet met the love of our life, or that we still don't understand very much at all. We will feel a part of something far more important than ourselves, a supportive community in which our individual errors and doubts will cease to weigh so heavily and punishingly upon us.

Through dance, we glimpse a huge project: how we might more regularly experience ourselves as vulnerable in front of other people in order to become better friends to ourselves and more generous and compassionate companions to others. The true potential of dancing has for too long been abandoned by thoughtful people to stylish elites who have forgotten the elemental seriousness of allowing themselves to be and look idiotic. We should reclaim the ecstatic dance and uninhibited boogie-woogie for their deepest universal purposes: to reconnect, reassure, and reunite us.

5 *Learning to be Angry*

There are many reasons to believe that one of the dominant problems in the world today is an excess of anger. We know all about the very shouty and their antics: their tantrums, their lack of reason, their unwillingness to compromise. Furthermore, it threatens to get a lot worse because we seem to be locked into a set of dynamics—political, technological, environmental—which promise an ever less patient, ever less serene, and ever less forgiving future.

But it may be rather more realistic, albeit odd-sounding, to insist on the very opposite: that whatever the impression generated by a publicly vocal angry cohort, the far more common yet, by nature, invisible problem is a contrary tendency: a widespread inability to get angry, a failure to know how rightly and effectively to mount a complaint, an inarticulate swallowing of frustration and the bitterness, the subterranean "acting out" and the low-level depression that follow from not allowing any of our rightful sorrows to find expression. For every person who shouts too loudly, there are at least twenty who have unfairly lost their voice.

We are not talking here of delirious rage, the sort that injures innocents and leads nowhere. The point isn't to rehabilitate barbarism but to make the case for a capacity to speak up, with dignity and poise, in order to correct a reasoned sense that something isn't right—and that those around us need to take our opposing perspective on board.

We are as a rule hopeless at being angry, from the very nicest of motives: in part, from a belief in the complexity of situations and the minds of other people, which undercuts enthusiasm for anything that smacks of self-righteousness or pride. We tell ourselves, in relationships or at work, that others must have good reasons for behaving as they do, that they must be essentially kind and good and that it would be an insult to their efforts to raise our hand about a problem that we surely don't even entirely understand.

We tend to import our modesty from childhood. It's a privilege to allow a child to manifest their frustration and not all parents are game. Some are very keen on having a "good baby." They let the infant know from the first that being "naughty" isn't funny and that this isn't a family where children are allowed to "run rings around" the adults. Difficult moods and tantrums, complaints and rages are not to be part of the story. This certainly ensures short-term compliance, but paradoxically, preternaturally good behavior is usually a precursor of bad feelings, and in extremes of mental unwellness, in adulthood. Feeling loved enough that one can flip off parental figures and occasionally fling something—soft—across the room belongs to health; truly mature parents have rules and allow their children sometimes to break them.

Otherwise, there is a species of inner deadness that comes from having had to be too good too soon and to resign one's point of view without a flicker of self-defense. In relationships, this might mean a tendency to get taken royally for a ride for many years, not in terms of outright abuse—though that too—but of the kind of low-level humiliation which seems the lot of people who can't make a fuss. At work, an unwavering concern for politeness, empathy, and gentleness may end up providing the perfect preconditions for being walked all over.

We need to relearn the neglected art of politely, on necessary occasions, being a pain. The danger of those who have never shouted is that they might, in compensation, end up screaming. That isn't the point either. The goal is a firm but self-possessed protest: *Excuse me, but you are ruining what's left of my life. I'm so sorry, but you are cauterizing my chances of happiness. I beg your pardon, but this is enough . . .*

We think a lot about going on vacation and trying new activities. There's plenty of enthusiasm for learning other languages and attempting foreign dishes. But true exoticism and adventure may lie closer to home: in the emotional sphere, and in the courage and originality required to give contained anger a go, perhaps tonight, after supper. We have the speeches written in our heads already. There is likely to be a spouse, a parent, a colleague, or a child who hasn't heard enough from us for far too long—and with whom it would be of incalculable benefit to our heart rate and our emotional and physical constitution to have a word. The timid always imagine that anger might destroy everything good. They overlook, because their childhoods encouraged them to, that anger can also be a fertilizer from which something a lot less bitter and a lot more alive can emerge.

6 *Hugo's Defiance*

There have been few writers as brave as Victor Hugo. Over a turbulent sixty-year career, he fought fiercely for what he believed in: republican government, medieval architecture, an end to capital punishment, school and prison reform, a United States of Europe, and the right to lead the kind of complicated private life that upsets prudes. We shouldn't allow his posthumous acclaim to disguise how much he was, in certain quarters, loathed in his lifetime.

And yet, as his portrait suggests, he knew full well how to face critics down. In 1845, Hugo's friend the academic and politician Abel François Villemain fell into despair because of rumors about his sexuality and attacks on his work by professional enemies. Only concern for his daughters prevented Villemain from killing himself. Fortunately, Hugo was both a good friend and a great consoler, and came over one evening to shake him from his sorrow:

You have enemies! Well who doesn't have them? Guizot has enemies, Thiers has enemies, Lamartine has enemies. Haven't I myself been fighting for twenty years? Haven't I spent twenty years being hated, sold down the river, betrayed, reviled, taunted and insulted? Have my books not been ridiculed and my actions travestied? I've had traps set for me; I've even fallen into a few . . . What do I care? I have contempt. It's one of the hardest but also most necessary things in life to learn to have contempt. Contempt protects and crushes. It's like a breast plate and an axe. Do you have enemies? That's simply the fate of anyone who has done anything worthwhile or launched any new idea. It's a necessary fog that clings to anything that shines. Fame must have enemies, as light must have gnats. Don't worry about it; just have contempt. Keep your spirit serene and your

Étienne Carjat, *Victor Hugo*, 1876.

life lucid. Never give your enemies the satisfaction of thinking that they've been able to cause you grief or pain. Stay happy, cheerful, contemptuous and firm.

People-pleasing carries grave risks, as Hugo knew only too well, and it's well-targeted contempt that can save our spirits.

7 Learning to Lay Down Boundaries

One of the reasons why our lives might be less sane than they should be is that we have missed out on an awkward-sounding but critical art whose absence we may until now never even have noticed: that of *laying down boundaries*.

Laying down a boundary involves informing those around us—colleagues, parents, children, lovers—of a given set of objectively reasonable things that we are going to require in order to feel respected and happy, while doing so in a way that conveys confidence, self-possession, warmth, and a mixture of kindness and strength.

Those who can successfully lay down boundaries will tell their small child that though they love them very much, once this game is over, Mommy or Daddy is not going to want to play another round and it will be time to go upstairs for hair-washing and there's simply no other way, darling chipmunk, however disappointing I know this will sound, and biting or kicking is not the answer, as we've discussed before. The good boundary-builder will wait until everyone is well rested to tell their partner that though they love them to take the initiative in a hundred areas, when it comes to their own family, they want to be left in charge—and therefore it wasn't right for the partner to call up their mother-in-law without warning in order to arrange the forthcoming holidays. And at work, the boundaried manager will tell their new hire that though they want to be supportive where possible, it simply isn't their role to complete schedules or manage budgets for others.

However, because most of us have not been educated in this byway of emotional maturity, the boundaries are either non-existent or else established in a random or destructive manner. As the technical language has it, we are either too compliant or too rigid. Mommy or Daddy might not, therefore, ever say they've had enough of the game and, even when wilting, play on late into the night, ensuring that chipmunk will be exhausted and cross the next day, as well as craving the security that comes from knowing that their grown-up is "grown up" enough to say no, even to what they ostensibly badly want—if there's one thing we crave more than that our wishes are granted, it's someone responsible enough to resist granting them all. In a relationship, we might never explain what we require in order to feel content and therefore either store up our resentments—and, usually, therefore grow unable to have sex—or else burst into unexplained rages that exhaust our partner's capacity for love. At work, meanwhile, we might develop a reputation as a friendly pushover or as an unreasonable tyrant whom it becomes a lot of fun to try to evade.

Those who can't lay down boundaries have invariably not, in their early lives, had their own boundaries respected. Someone didn't allow them to say when they were unhappy with a genuinely difficult situation; someone didn't give much of a damn about their hurt feelings or distinctive hopes; someone insinuated that being good meant falling in line, always, immediately. No one modeled the skill of winning, graceful objection. And so now, when the time comes to make a request of others, three powerful anxieties bedevil the boundary-less person:

if I speak up, they will hate me

if I speak up, I will become a target for retribution

if I speak up, I will feel like a horrible person

Though such fears manifest themselves as unquestionable certainties, they are amenable to gentle probing. People almost never hate those who make polite and reasonably framed demands; in fact, they tend to respect and like them a little more. They feel in the presence of a maturity and kindly authoritativeness that appear worthy of their time, as well as seeming rare and a bit thrilling. Frustrating someone's wishes doesn't have to be evidence of selfishness; it may signal a noble concern for another's long-term well-being and flourishing. We can adore someone, wish them the very best, have the kindest intentions toward them—and still, very diplomatically and yet very decisively, tell them no.

An alternative response to building boundaries is a habit of throwing up walls topped with razor wire ringed by machine-gun turrets, or, to put it more simply, a tendency to get swiftly and gratingly defensive. The manically defensive person is also laboring under a set of highly unfortunate misapprehensions:

that everyone is trying to hurt them badly

that no one will listen unless they hit back with immense force

that their needs cannot ever truly be met

Yet the alternative to lacking all boundaries is not violent defensiveness. We should not let boundary-building be undermined by its most zealous practitioners. There is always a means to make a sound case without reaching for a weapon.

It is notable that the problem of boundary-building is particularly acute not so much around strangers but in intimate life. We may well be able to fight our corner with people we care little about—the person at the car rental desk, the tax official; the problem comes when we are dealing with someone who loves us and whom we have allowed into our emotional inner sanctum. It is as if, in a deep part of our minds, we cannot reconcile the notion that someone might at once be genuinely caring *and* capable of betraying our best interests. We find it hard to be simultaneously intimate and always a touch vigilant. What should help us to absorb this eventuality is to remember that just as we can say no and still be kind, so another can have harmed us and yet remain, in their essence, *good*.

It takes a little self-confidence and courage to be able to notice just how bad we may be at the art of boundary-laying. We may have spent a large chunk of our lives already in an essentially passive relationship to everyday infringements by people close to us. But we aren't a piece of helpless flotsam on the river of others' wishes; we have agency, direction, and, as it were, a rudder. The price to pay for affection isn't compliance. We can gradually take on board a highly implausible-sounding but redemptive notion: that we can prove lovable and worthy of respect and at the same time, when the occasion demands it—as it probably will a few times every day—utter a warm-sounding but definitive "no."

8 *You Could Finally Leave School*

Technically, most of us leave school at eighteen—an event that tends to be vividly etched in the memory and surrounded by considerable ceremony and emotion. And yet rather oddly, despite appearances, many of us in fact don't manage to leave school at that point at all. In a deep part of our minds, we may still be there, well into adulthood, not sitting in a classroom precisely but, in terms of how our minds work, as much stuck within the confines of a school-based world-view as if we were showing up for assembly every day—generating immense and unnecessary degrees of unhappiness and compromise for ourselves in the process.

What beliefs might be some of the hallmarks of an enduring school-like way of thinking:

- First and foremost, those in authority know what they are doing and our task is to obey and jump through the hoops they set for us. We desire to please teachers and gain prizes, cups, and ribbons.

- There is an implicit curriculum out there—an externally mandated map of what we need to do to succeed—and a wise person must dutifully subscribe to its demands.

- Work should, when it's going well, feel substantially irksome, dull, and somewhat pointless. Schools teach us to forget, or ignore, the clues offered to us by our own boredom. They teach us dangerous degrees of patience, subtly training us in intellectual masochism.

- We're doing it for someone else—an audience: our teachers and our parents, and their substitutes in adult life. *Make us proud.*

You have to shine. We've given you so much. What matters is the performance, not any inner sense of satisfaction.

■ Authority figures are benign, wanting what is good for us and speaking on behalf of our long-term interests. *We'll look after you. If you follow our rules, you will thrive.* We don't think we could ever know better and we distrust our instincts.

■ Exams, and all their successors, are fundamentally accurate. Those who set them have worked out the ultimate test of our value and we are what we score.

■ Every school is, in addition, a miniature society, equipped with a strong sense of what values to revere and codes to follow. Bullies lurk, ready to mock and identify any departures from the norm. We can't escape them because they are next to us in class every day. They will spot and persecute the weirdos; they can ruin our lives. We learn to cower and adjust our attitudes. Following the herd is paramount.

None of these ways of thinking require us to be sitting in a geography class. We might be in an office selling garden furniture to the Belgian market and yet still think like this. We might have children of our own and yet inside still think that there are exams to pass and cups to be won. What would it mean to break the mold? What would it mean finally to leave school?

To know some of the following:

■ There is no one way, no guarantee of a set path to fulfillment, laid out by authority figures. They don't know because no one knows.

■ The safe path may be entirely dangerous to our flourishing.

■ Our boredom is a vital tool that tells us what is slowly killing us— and reminds us that time is monstrously short.

■ Authority is not by definition benign. The teachers and their substitutes have no real plan for us except in so far as it suits their own advancement. It might look as if they want our supreme good but in reality they want us to play their game for their own benefit. At the end, they have no proper prize to offer us.

- It doesn't matter what the bullies think. No one is normal. Dare to make enemies—indeed, we must do so as the price to pay for having developed a character and found something truly to believe in.

We shouldn't be tough on ourselves for lingering so long. School is an immensely impressive system. We start there when we are not much bigger than a chair. For more than a decade, it's all we know. It is the outside world and it is what those who love us most tell us we should respect. It speaks with great authority not just about itself, but about life in general. It is sold to us as a preparation for the whole of existence. But, of course, the main thing it does is to prepare us for yet more school. It is an education in how to thrive within its own profoundly peculiar rules, with only a tenuous connection to the world beyond.

Knowing all this, we might do a very strange-sounding thing. We might finally work up the courage to leave our inner school, be it at twenty-eight, thirty-five, or sixty-two, and enter the wider, boundless world we have been in flight from for too long.

9 *Grand Libraries*

The problem with libraries is that they can be so large, impressive, and filled with knowledge that they unwittingly embed in us an idea that everything worth registering, everything valuable and true, must lie "out there," must already have been classified on a shelf with an index number to await our discovery the moment we cease to be so preoccupied with ourselves.

But what this modest, respectful, and quietly self-hating conclusion disguises is that each one of us is an unparalleled and superlative center of knowledge in and of ourselves. Our minds have more ideas stored in them than are to be found in the collective catalogues of the Biblioteca Geral da Universidade de Coimbra, the Pierpont Morgan Library in New York, and the British Library in London. We have vaults filled with a greater number of moving and beautiful scenes than exist in all the world's greatest museums put together. We are just failing to wander the stacks and galleries as often as we should; we are failing to notice what we have seen. So convinced are we that insights of worth lie beyond us, we have omitted to consult the treasury of thoughts and visions generated every hour by our endlessly brilliant, fatefully unexplored minds.

The American essayist Ralph Waldo Emerson once remarked, "In every work of genius, we recognize our own rejected thoughts." In other words, geniuses don't have thoughts that are in the end so very different from our own; they have simply had the confidence to take them more seriously. Rather than imagining that their minds are only a pale shadow of the minds of infinitely greater thinkers who lived and died elsewhere long ago, they have been respectful enough of their existence to conceive that one or two properly valuable ideas might

Candida Höfer, *Biblioteca Geral da Universidade de Coimbra IV*, 2006.

plausibly choose to alight in the familiar aviary of their own intelligences. Thinking is—in a way we generally refuse to imagine—a truly democratic activity.

We all have very similar and very able minds. Where geniuses differ is in their more confident inclinations to study them properly.

10 *Learning to Listen to Your Boredom*

One of the most striking characteristics of small children is their militant aversion to boredom. With ruthless determination, they embark on one occupation after another, shifting their focus whenever an even marginally more attractive prospect comes into view. An average morning might involve taking out eight board games from the cupboard, then, just as it seemed it might be time for Snakes and Ladders, experimenting with turning the couch into a ski slope, then trying to pull toy rabbit's tail off, followed by exploring what happens to the chocolate chip cookies when you pound them with a hammer, before finally tipping up all the kitchen chairs and pretending they might be ships engaged in a sea battle.

What we call education is in large measure an attempt to bring order to this peripatetic chaos by teaching the child to ignore the welter of their own spontaneous enthusiasms and instead learn to sit with their boredom for a while in the name of getting something substantial done: listening to a lengthy speech about kindness by the head teacher without screaming, enduring a forty-five-minute maths lesson without getting up to dance, resisting the temptation to draw an imaginary world during an introductory French class. Becoming that most prized of things, a "good child," means mastering the art of suppressing our own boredom in the name of growing up.

The rationale for this pedagogical move is both solid and noble: there is clearly a great deal to be gained from not running away the moment a new fancy enters the mind. Yet the problem isn't that we're generally blind to this logic but that we're far too good at submitting to it. Most of us are fatefully too proficient at bearing our own boredom.

Along the way, we forget that boredom has many important things to teach us. It is, at its best, a confused, inarticulate but genuine signal from a deep part of our minds that something is very wrong. We may not quite know what, but the sensation of being bored frequently contains—especially for otherwise sensible adults—an apprehension of genuine danger. There are boring books that should in all fairness be tossed aside. There are boring people we should, in order not to wither inside, refuse to see. There are boring movies we should walk out of. And what should sharpen our courage to do so is an ongoing awareness that the fundamental currency of our lives is time, of which we are in desperately short supply, there being on average no more than 26,000 days or so in an entire existence on the planet.

Listening to our boredom will tug us back to our true concerns. We realize what our tastes in literature really are, what sort of entertainment we actually go in for, what properly enthuses us about other people. Boredom functions as the scalpel with which we can cut off all that is "dead" and extraneous about our lives. The courage to admit to our boredom allows us, gradually, to develop a personality. Boredom is the inarticulate voice of a fundamental idea: that something has been over-sold to us and needs to be discounted.

It is telling that, as they grow older, many artists instinctively get better at listening to their boredom and produce greatly superior work as a result—what critics commonly refer to as a "late style," marked by impatience, brevity, courage and intensity: one thinks of Bach's exceptional later choral works, the final short stories of Chekhov, or the sublime paper cut-outs of the dying Matisse. Poignantly, on a tour of a primary school an ageing Picasso once said, "At their age, I knew how to paint like Titian. It's taken me a lifetime to remember a greater achievement: how to paint like a child." What he meant was that it had taken him decades to shake off a compliant urge to paint "well" and "respectably" and to listen instead more closely to his own sense of fun—which is a serious business not to be confused with its lesser sibling, frivolity. Pushed by mortality into a new respect for his own centers of pleasure, Picasso had learned how to overcome every trace

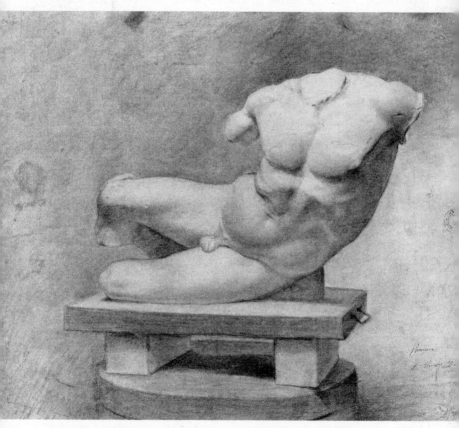

When he was fourteen: Pablo Picasso, *Academic Study*, 1895.

When he was seventy-six—and had finally remembered to listen to his boredom: Pablo Picasso, *The Pigeons*, 1957.

of the mannered approach of his youth in order to focus instead on the joy of decorating a canvas with the loose brushstrokes, exuberance, and bold colors well known to those natural artistic masters: five-year-old children.

We don't have to be a towering figure of twentieth-century art for the point to apply. All of us need to learn to develop a "late style," ideally as early on in our lives as possible: a way of being wherein we shake off the dead hand of habit and social fear and relearn to listen to what entertains us—and so can stand the best chance of properly pleasing others too. The results should apply not to works of art in a museum, but to aspects of our intimate lives: to the way we choose a career, host a dinner party, go on a vacation, have sex, tell an anecdote, or act around our friends. Here too lie multiple opportunities to cut to the chase, to say what really matters, and to express what we truly feel and want, while we yawn politely but defiantly at all that is slowly killing us.

11 *Gessner's Hedgehog*

Early in his career, the Swiss naturalist Conrad Gessner formulated an enviably ambitious plan: He would spend the rest of his life tracking down and describing every animal on the planet, from the armadillo to the green chameleon, the Egyptian mongoose to the rhinoceros. His labors resulted in one of the first and most beautiful works of zoology, *Historia animalium*, published in Zurich between 1551 and 1558.

Gessner got a lot of things wrong. He was muddled about names and numbers of legs. Many of his colors were off. He was confused about the numbers of stripes on the tiger and spots on the leopard. But it is Gessner's boldness that continues to impress. He didn't worry about the odd mistake, nor did he limit his aspirations for fear of treading on other experts' toes.

He did have one enormous advantage, however: he was early on in the game. He did not have to suffer from the dispiriting sense, which too often subsumes us today, that everything must surely already be known; that there is nothing at all we might think that hasn't already been better expressed somewhere else by someone else. The existence of so many books—130 million and rising—doesn't so much inspire as crush us: What more could we possibly add? What thought worth having could ever germinate in our naive minds? The virgin snow across which Gessner once drove his intellectual sledge is now criss-crossed with others' tracks. Increased knowledge has undermined our intellectual self-confidence.

But this cannot in truth be fair, for we still don't understand so much: how to have good marriages, run countries, educate children, create beautiful architecture, or overcome loneliness—just to start the list. We

Conrad Gessner, *Hedgehog*, from *Historia animalium*, 1551.

have mapped less than one billionth of the real map of knowledge. We are almost as much at the beginning as Gessner was. Nothing should legitimately stop us from imagining that we couldn't right now head out and, with a fair wind and a few years of toil, discover a menagerie of things at once unknown, colorful and essential.

12 *How to Lengthen Your Life*

The normal way we set about trying to extend our lives is by striving to add more years to them—usually by eating more couscous and broccoli, going to bed early, and running in the rain. But this approach may turn out to be quixotic, not only because Death can't reliably be warded off with kale, but at a deeper level because the best way to lengthen a life is not by attempting to stick more years on to its tail.

One of the most basic facts about time is that, even though we insist on measuring it as if it were an objective unit, it doesn't, in all conditions, seem to be moving at the same pace. Five minutes can feel like an hour; ten hours can feel like five minutes. A decade may pass like two years; two years may acquire the weight of half a century. And so on.

In other words, our subjective experience of time bears precious little relation to the way we like to measure it on a clock. Time moves more or less slowly according to the vagaries of the human mind: it may fly or it may drag; it may evaporate into airy nothing or achieve enduring density.

If the goal is to have a *longer* life, whatever the dieticians may urge, it would seem that the priority should be not to add raw increments of time but to ensure that whatever years remain *feel* appropriately substantial. The aim should be to densify time rather than to try to extract one or two more years from the grip of Death.

Why, then, does time have such different speeds, moving at certain points bewilderingly fast, at others with intricate moderation? The clue is to be found in childhood. The first ten years almost invariably feel longer than any other decade we have on earth. The teens are a little faster but still crawl. Yet by our forties, time will have started to trot; and by our sixties, it will be unfolding at a bewildering gallop.

The difference in pace is not mysterious but has to do with novelty.

The more our days are filled with new, unpredictable, and challenging experiences, the longer they will feel. And, conversely, the more one day is exactly like another, the faster it will pass by in a blur. Childhood ends up feeling so long because it is the cauldron of novelty; because its most ordinary days are packed with extraordinary discoveries and sensations. These can be as apparently minor yet as significant as the first time we explore the zip on a cardigan or hold our nose under water, the first time we look at the sun through the cotton of a beach towel or dig our fingers into the putty holding a window in its frame. Dense as it is with stimuli, the first decade can feel a thousand years long.

By middle age, things can be counted upon to have grown a lot more familiar. We may have flown around the world a few times. We no longer get excited by the idea of eating a pineapple, owning a car, or flicking a light switch. We know about relationships, earning money, and telling others what to do. And as a result, time runs away from us without mercy.

One solution often suggested at this point is that we should put all our efforts into discovering fresh sources of novelty. We need to become explorers and adventurers. We must go to Machu Picchu or Angkor Wat, Astana or Montevideo; we need to find a way to swim with dolphins or order a thirteen-course meal at a world-famous restaurant in downtown Lima. That will finally slow down the cruel gallop of time.

But this is to labor under an unfair, expensive, and ultimately impractical notion of novelty: that it must involve seeing new things, when in fact it should really involve seeing familiar things with new eyes. We may by middle age certainly have *seen* a great many things in our neighborhoods, but we are—fortunately for us—unlikely to have properly noticed most of them. We have probably taken a few cursory glances at the miracles of existence that lie to hand and assumed, quite unjustly, that we know all there is to know about them. We've imagined we understand the city we live in, the people we interact with, and, more or less, the point of it all.

But of course we have barely scratched the surface. We have grown bored of a world we haven't begun to study properly. And that, among other things, is why time is racing by.

Paul Cézanne, *Apples*, 1878–9.

The pioneers at making life feel longer in the way that counts are not dieticians but artists. At its best, art is a tool that reminds us of how little we have fathomed and noticed. It reintroduces us to ordinary things and reopens our eyes to a latent beauty and interest in precisely those areas we had ceased to bother with. It helps us to recover some of the manic sensitivity we had as newborns. Think of Cézanne looking closely at apples, as if he had never seen one before, and nudging us to do likewise.

We don't need to make art in order to learn the most valuable lesson of artists, which is about noticing properly, living with our eyes open and thereby, along the way, savoring time. Without any intention to create something that could be put in a gallery, we could—as part of a goal of living more deliberately – take a walk in an unfamiliar part of town, ask an old friend about a side of their life we'd never dared probe, lie on our back in the garden and look up at the stars or hold our partner in a way we never tried before. It takes a rabid lack of imagination to think we have to go to Machu Picchu to find something new to perceive.

In Fyodor Dostoevsky's novel *The Idiot*, a prisoner has suddenly been condemned to death and been told he has only a few minutes left to live. "What if I were not to die!" he exclaims. "What if life were given back to me – what infinity! . . . I'd turn each minute into a whole age . . ." Faced with losing his life, the poor wretch recognizes that every minute could be turned into aeons of time, with sufficient imagination and appreciation.

It is sensible enough to try to live *longer* lives. But we are working with a false notion of what long really means. We might live to be a thousand years old and still complain that it had all rushed by too fast. We should be aiming to lead lives that feel long because we manage to imbue them with the right sort of open-hearted appreciation and unsnobbish receptivity, the kind that five-year-olds know naturally how to bring to bear. We need to pause and look at one another's faces, study the sky, wonder at the eddies and colors of the river, and dare to ask the kinds of questions that open others' souls. We don't need to add years; we need to densify the time we have left by ensuring that every day is lived consciously—and we can do this via a maneuver as simple as it is momentous: by starting to *notice* all that we have as yet only *seen*.

V : Hope

For most of our lives, the majority of us don't require anything as specific and formal-sounding as "reasons" to keep living. We take hope for granted, rising out of bed with purpose and direction; we may be preoccupied by this or that challenge, but the business of existence as a whole is never in question.

Then there are other moods, more somber and confused in nature, in which what we are doing on the earth comes to seem like a far more doubtful and painful matter. An accumulation of reversals—some perhaps minor, others more severe—undermines our will to endure much longer; the automatic reflex of living escapes us. There seems no point in getting up, we have no will to eat, we fall into a reverie halfway through pouring a glass of water, there is nowhere we can think of traveling, there is no one we want to talk to. We are going through the motions, but our spirit is elsewhere.

In our sad state, we can't any longer say why we should take the trouble to get dressed or shower, why we should go to work or utter a word—or in fact take another breath. None of it seems obvious in the slightest. We might look around us in the park—at parents with children, pensioners with their dogs, or planes crossing the skies—and wonder by what peculiar, deluded and mysterious forces the whole vainglorious show is kept in motion.

It isn't as if, when we are feeling purposeful and optimistic, we necessarily have a conscious grasp of the reasons why we have a taste for life. We have our reasons but we don't have any need to identify them. They are so much in our command and are so many in number, we don't single them out. We think it's life itself we love, so don't pay homage to any singular set of ingredients: for example, our health or our friends, our good name or our prospects of promotion. But when despair strikes, we can't any longer be so casual about what might have the capacity to buoy us up.

We must learn to think through in rigorous ways what we had been accustomed to locate by reflex. We have to go in careful search of reasons why we should be. We have to ask ourselves, in a way the blessed never have to, how we are going to get through the coming years—or why we should bother, given the pain involved.

What follows is a set of small essays to assist us in our search for hope. They seek to lay before us some representative reasons why, despite everything, we might continue with tomorrow. Some are deliberately dark: It isn't always optimism that best cheers. Our spirits can be sunk by a punishing impression that everyone else is content and that we are alone in our misery—and accordingly, there can be relief in learning that sadness is in fact very widespread and that there are solid grounds for why life is often hellish.

But we also need thoughts that can restore perspective and situate our woes in a larger context of time and space. Finally, we can shift to some positive pleasures that, like the caress of morning light on the blind in the convalescent's room, await the recovering soul.

If we are to make a sustained recovery, we need to work our way toward our own well-defined list of arguments for pushing back against the forces of depression. The making of a list of hopeful things begins here.

1 *The End of the* Macrauchenia

Given the scale of the perils that face humanity, it is hardly surprising if serenity and peace of mind are hard to come by. Reasons to panic are daily brought before our eyes by the ever-inquisitive and always alarming modern media: There are wildfires raging across South America and Australia, currency manipulation is rife, people smugglers are working with impunity in Eastern Europe, bureaucracy is stifling innovation across the prosperous world, the air in large cities is more polluted than ever, soon there will be no more snow leopards, orangutans, or leatherback sea turtles, and there's a gigantic new kind of pink seaweed threatening the health of the southern oceans. It's a wonder we ever sleep.

At moments of particular alarm, we might turn our thoughts to the *Macrauchenia*. For millions of years, these delightful camel-sized animals flourished across what we now call South America, being found in their largest numbers in the north of Argentina. They were placid herbivores, with an endearingly droopy nose, a soft fleecy coat, and warm, contemplative eyes. They lived in small family groups, browsing inoffensively on the leaves of the jacaranda tree and in the evening trooping down to the many shallow lakes of the region to bathe.

Though the *Macrauchenia* had a very good run, they sadly didn't make it in the end. They flourished from the Late Miocene period, about 7 million years ago, but then their fortunes ran out. The species was decimated by newer, aggressive creatures that came down from North America during the Great American Interchange, after the establishment of the Central American land bridge. The last *Macrauchenia* are estimated to have died—probably in the jaws of some kind of prairie dog—about 10,000 years before the arrival of stooped early humans at the end of the Pleistocene period. It was Charles Darwin who, on a

Macrauchenia. This extinct prehistoric mammal lived
7 million to 20,000 years ago (the Late Miocene to
the Late Pleistocene).

short stopover in Puerto San Julián in Patagonia in 1834, uncovered the first *Macrauchenia* skeleton and it was given this name by Richard Owen in 1838.

The *Macrauchenia* would have been charming to get to know and deeply helpful to the farmers of South America—as well as its tourist industry. But their loss was not unusual. Some 99.9 percent of all organisms that have ever existed have been wiped out across the five mass extinctions of history. Five times over the last 500 million years life has more or less had to begin again from scratch. It is hugely unlikely that any of the species we are currently so attached to, and worried about—the Bornean elephant, the Ganges dolphin—will make it in the long term.

Our own fate necessarily hangs in the balance as well. It would take a resolute optimist to venture that we will not in time follow the example of most of our forebears, including the narrow-nosed rhinoceros, the flat-headed peccary, and the dwarf hippo. This might seem like an entirely tragic thought, but it has its relieving aspect as well. We are commonly overburdened by a momentous sense of responsibility for what is to come. We worry about peace conferences, the path of gas pipelines, the vagaries of unemployment insurance, and the levels of nitrogen in the soil. These are fine ways to mop up anxiety but, in the grander scheme, we might as well be weeping over the long-distant demise of a friendly South American odd-toed ungulate.

The news constantly provides us with a ringside seat at the most compelling and horrendous issues of our times, which feed both our outrage and our sense that there must be something we can do to try to prevent disaster. But in the process, we forget the radical limits on our powers to intervene effectively in pretty much any of the dilemmas that bedevil our species. It is our particular historical fate to know more than we have ever done about the troubles of our fellow humans and yet to remain almost wholly ineffective at finding solutions, not because we are uncreative or lethargic but because we have been granted, at best, a teaspoon with which to drain an ocean. Our planet is shaped by gigantic forces—financial, political, biological, extraterrestrial—against which our individual wills are doomed to be substantially powerless. We have about as much chance of altering the dynamics behind our catastrophes as we have of shifting the orbital patterns of the moons of Jupiter.

There may be a few steps we can take to dampen our crises, but they will tend to be close to home and to concern the welfare of only a handful of people. We should not be harsh or unjust toward ourselves. We didn't personally make the world and we aren't individually responsible for its fate.

As we contemplate the extinct *Macrauchenia*, we are seeing an image of our own small innocence and admitting a liberating truth: A great many things, fortunately, are not really for us to try to control or feel in charge of. A few of the more nervous, fretful *Macrauchenia* might once have worried about the survival of their race as evening fell and giant anteaters rustled in the bushes, but the truly wise and contented ones would have loved their families, planned the evening meal for the little ones, and refrained from fretting too much about what was to come over the next million years.

2 *After the Catastrophe*

It's been a lovely day with Grandfather. Aunts Tricia and Julie came by with their children, Christopher and Jennie.

It's all pleasantly normal and average, except that the grandfather is Richard Nixon and he used to have the nuclear codes in his office and he engineered the end of the Vietnam War—and in 1974 he would have been put on trial for obstruction of justice and abuse of power and sent to prison, if he hadn't received a pardon from his successor as president of the United States, Gerald Ford.

We'll never face the level of condemnation that he did; no disgrace of ours can ever match his. And yet, after years of soul searching—and with the sheer passage of time—Richard Nixon was able to pull together a worthwhile existence. It was eventually possible to take pleasure in digging the garden, in spending the afternoon with the family, and in catching up with old acquaintances.

For many people, of course, Nixon was simply an appalling man utterly undeserving of sympathy. But we might be tempted to think of him in a different light when we—in our own way—have badly messed up and earned the contempt of others. Nixon is then, for us, not just a famously bad person but a version of our own flawed selves. Nixon's failings were played out on the largest scale; our own disasters are more modest and local, but we too have—very often—been the shamefully guilty party.

What Nixon is sending us, via an ordinary family snap, is a message about the possibilities of recovery. He wasn't an adept apologist, he didn't make a grand return, he never shook off the widespread conviction that he was a devious character. But he was able to adjust and still find genuine sources of goodness and contentment in existence. What makes his example all the more touching is that he did this without being

President Nixon and his daughters, Tricia and Julie, with their children
Christopher Nixon Cox and Jennie Eisenhower, 1979.

in any way specially skilled at redemption. He was still a flawed, awkward man. He wasn't coming to the task of recovery with better chances than we have. At a dark moment, the image is speaking to us of our own future: modest, ordinary, but genuinely OK—which at troubled times seems almost more than we can dare to hope for.

3 *The Bones of the Chief*

In life, he was a great chieftain. After the withdrawal of the Roman army from Britain, he and his clan carved out a kingdom for themselves in the area that today lies just west of London. He led his people on daring raids on villages across the river. They sang his praises as they caroused around the campfire at night. He was a tall man for the time, evidently a ferocious fighter. He was famous and feared in the surrounding lands.

When he died, they buried him with all possible honor on a small hill overlooking a bend in the River Thames: the strategic center of their territory. Even in death, he would be the one to guide and protect them. They laid him out in his grave with his great sword and his treasured glass beaker—a prestigious rarity—beside him. The women wailed for days; the men lit funeral bonfires.

And then time passed. His kingdom was conquered and his Anglo-Saxon people became serfs to the new invading masters, the Normans. Quiet tenant farmers grazed their sheep on the lands he had won in battle. A railway line was constructed nearby, suburban villas sprang up, and, on tranquil evenings, retired solicitors and affable bank clerks and their wives would walk their dogs on the springy turf above his grave. The Winter Hill golf club laid out its fairways and sand bunkers where he had once mustered his loyal troops. A branch of a major supermarket chain opened within sight of his resting place and, on windy days, families would come over to fly kites, not realizing that they were standing just a few feet above the fragments of his skull.

All carried on as normal until, in 2018, a couple of local amateur archaeologists, armed with a metal detector, decided to explore the field. Alerted by the beeping of their machine, they began to very carefully remove the topsoil. His fine sword was half eaten away by rust and its

Archaeologists excavating at the site of the
"Marlow Warlord," Berkshire.

Anglo Saxon Military Chief.   Trumpeter and Warr[...]

"Anglo-Saxon military chief, trumpeter and warriors, Anno 975," from Sir
Samuel Rush Meyrick and Charles Hamilton Smith, *The Costume of the
Original Inhabitants of the British Islands . . .*, 1815.

beautiful leather scabbard had all but disintegrated; worms and beetles had consumed his flesh. Most of his bones had disintegrated and the roots of a gorse bush had grown through his ribcage.

There's a shocking, poignant contrast between what he once was and what became of him. His status, his possessions, and his strength were entirely forgotten. The pagan gods he worshiped were replaced first by Christianity and then by an indifferent atheism. But, of course, this is not a fate peculiar to him. With time it will happen to every one of us. All the great people of today will eventually be forgotten. Their graves will be lost, the entire culture which gave them their prominence and rich rewards will disappear, and archaeologists will one day strive to decipher the identities of people we now find it unimaginable not to know.

It's an oddly comforting thought. The distinctions and achievements which seem to matter so much in life will eventually lose their meaning and an ultimate equality of neglect will unite everyone. It won't matter who was the chief and who the pauper. Even better, we don't have to wait centuries for this sense of equality to take hold: We can summon the inevitable future into our imaginations right now. The youthful billionaire, the celebrity athlete, the handsome entrepreneur, the glamorous socialite—all will be returned to unity with us. As we look at their faces in a magazine or watch them on our screens, it is as if we can already see the future in which they will, like us, be crumpled anonymous bones in a forgotten patch of our gloriously indifferent earth.

4 *Mick Jagger and the Jesuit Priest*

One of the great moments of television history occurred in July 1967. Mick Jagger—then at the height of his fame and cultural influence—was helicoptered into the gardens of a large country house in the southeast of England to discuss his views on modern life with a group of distinguished establishment figures. The producers had picked these for one provocative reason above any others: they knew nothing about Jagger or his music.

One of the desperately out-of-touch interlocutors was a Jesuit priest and former master of an Oxford College, Fr Thomas Corbishley, S J—seen in the center of the picture in his round clerical collar. He immediately admitted that not only did he know nothing about the Rolling Stones, he'd never heard a single song by any modern band. But he was extremely interested in Mick Jagger nevertheless and, in a patient and kindly way, probed the star to reveal more about his positive beliefs rather than saying what he was against.

To the many millions of people who watched the show, Corbishley must have seemed comically out of touch, a ridiculous antiquarian relic cut off from the atmosphere of freedom, authenticity, and liberation of modernity. But in his own way, the priest was the truly heroic and independent figure with much to teach his own times and our own. He had opted—against massive societal pressure—not to follow the herd and to pursue issues that were dear to him instead. Whatever the widespread enthusiasm for "Sympathy for the Devil" and "Honky Tonk Women," Corbishley's interests lay elsewhere: he had translated the *Spiritual Exercises* of Ignatius Loyola, written commentaries on St Augustine, published a biography of the Jesuit priest Pierre Teilhard de Chardin, and, in a number of books, explored what it meant to be a Catholic in the wake of the Second Vatican Council.

Mick Jagger, during the filming of *World in Action*, July 31, 1967.

The priest was pursuing what one might term a strategy of voluntary exile from the current preoccupations of his society. He didn't feel any need to keep up with the flotsam and jetsam of contemporary culture. He felt closer to what was happening in Paris in 1254, when Thomas Aquinas wrote *De Ente et Essentia* (*On Being and Essence*) in defense of the Dominican community, than what was unfolding in Mary Quant's store on the King's Road in London in October 1965, where the first batch of miniskirts had just been launched. Corbishley was content to be thought ridiculous because he had his own well-defined concept of seriousness to hand.

We may not quite realize the extent to which we have mortgaged our inner lives to received ideas that are grievously alien to our true selves. We start to be free when we can dare to become—in selected areas—wilfully ignorant, when we no longer have to know the names of certain musicians that everyone esteems, when we don't feel compelled to read particular books that have won prizes, when we are left cold by vacation destinations, clothes, foods, exercise regimes, political scandals, and ideas that are dominant, when we can stay home rather than attend parties with people we dislike—and when we can hear of a celebrity and genuinely wonder who they might be. It is hard enough to have to exist in any given era; we don't in addition have to mold our souls in its image.

5 *The Aztecs and Tezcatlipoca*

At the height of the Aztec Empire in the late 1400s, a major, daily preoccupation for a great many people involved worshiping and placating the god Tezcatlipoca. He was a one-legged divinity of smoke, darkness, hurricanes, and destruction—and a great many darkly beautiful representations of his head were made by affixing precious stones to the skulls of people who had been sacrificed in his honor.

It was believed that when an earlier version of human society had failed to worship him appropriately, the god had flown into a rage and unleashed a titanic storm that had annihilated everyone on earth. To avoid such a catastrophe ever recurring, every year a young man—selected for his supposed likeness to Tezcatlipoca—would be sacrificed to the god and his remains eaten by priests and royalty. The testy deity would then be induced to send benign rains to end the dry season and implored to resist his more apocalyptic instincts.

These were deeply and sincerely held beliefs, propounded by the most learned people of the day. To doubt or disregard them would have been reckless. Of course, dangerous questions must, in secret, sometimes have crossed people's minds: *How do we know Tezcatlipoca really exists? How do we know that he wants us to do these things?* But to utter such heresies aloud would have been to invite imprisonment and death.

Today Tezcatlipoca has no power to frighten anyone: he's a carefully labeled exhibit in a museum and a point of reference in obscure academic treatises on the history of weather deities. Our own attempts to predict rainfall involve sober investigations of surface ocean temperatures and the intensity of the currents of El Niño.

The beliefs about Tezcatlipoca have no possible basis in reality, but the Aztecs were not unusually credulous in holding them. On the contrary they were, measured against the broad span of history, entirely

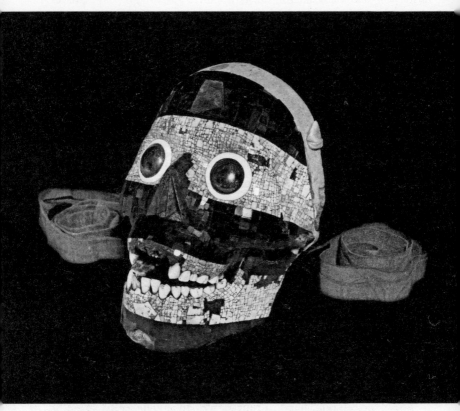

Turquoise mosaic skull representing the god Tezcatlipoca,
c. 1400–1521.

normal for doing so. All societies have collectively clung to highly peculiar ideas that in time have been revealed to be deeply mistaken and—often—close to insane. It would be impossible if the same were not true of our own times. The focus of mass delusion may change, but the phenomenon of delusion never abates. Central elements in what is now popularly taken to be the truth are almost certain to be mistaken—because crowds, almost by definition, are not out to discover the actual dimensions of reality. They don't get agitated by subtle lapses in reasoning; they don't urgently demand higher standards of evidence; they don't march through the streets insisting on more thorough research. They merely want to find a sense of reassuring togetherness while demonizing and shaming those who disagree with them.

Far from clearing the air, modern democracy plays straight into this tendency in our nature, equating the majority view with justice and righteousness. Markets, too, emphasize the primacy of popular senti- ment by rewarding companies that have no inclination to disabuse their customers of their errors of taste. It's our strange fate to be born into an age of crowds in which the best, most precise thoughts are unlikely ever to meet with popular recognition.

Such an aristocratic attitude can sound absurdly outdated, but it offers us something that remains vital—and has nothing to do with genealogy or connections to the landed gentry. It's the idea of being convinced from the outset that a popular outlook will frequently be riddled with errors and at odds with the beliefs of a thoughtful few, and that sanity must involve a willingness not to be ashamed, embarrassed, or even much saddened at being repeatedly out of sync with the dominant culture.

By understanding, without rancor, why most people subscribe to the myths of any age, we are released from waging a hopeless and dis- piriting struggle against public opinion. We don't expect our reasoned mentality to spread or to be easily absorbed. We know that most people will—as a matter of course—worship whatever version of Tezcatlipoca happens to be in vogue. We don't have to blame them; we can just— quietly—keep to ourselves and hope never to end up on the wrong side of a sacrificial frenzy.

6 I Will Survive

In October 1978, one of the greatest pop songs of the twentieth century was heard for the first time: Gloria Gaynor's eternal assertion of defiance: "I Will Survive." It was initially released as a B-side but it quickly became one of the bestselling singles of all time thanks to its power to touch something universal in the human soul.

Gloria Gaynor hadn't written the song herself. The words had in fact been penned by Dino Fekaris, a rather successful but temporarily disgruntled professional songwriter who'd just been sacked by Motown Records.

The song is in part a recollection of being trampled upon, of being taken for granted, but it's not really about the wrong others have done to us; it's an honest appraisal of the way we have let them do these things to us, because we have been insufficiently on our own side.

The other has undoubtedly harmed us, but the deeper problem is that we have not known how to esteem ourselves highly enough to stop them doing so. If they thought that we would crumble and lie down and die they did so for a good reason: because that is what we did so many times before. The beauty of the song is that it doesn't deny that we have been accomplices to the bad treatment that we have traditionally been accorded. We identify with its heroine because she is frank enough to admit that she has been the architect of her own humiliation.

Gloria identifies with the overcompliant, fearful part of ourselves. But it's because she understands our submissive tendencies so well that her deep encouragement to say a resolute "fuck off" to the world is so rousing. This is not the voice of someone who has never been put upon, it is that of a weak and timid being who is no longer going to let her fears rule her life.

Gloria Gaynor, 1979.

Defiance doesn't mean asserting that I *know* I will survive. At the moment when we belt out the song on the dance floor or—more likely—in the kitchen, we don't really know what will happen to us: our fears are still raw. We may have been bullied throughout our childhood or our relationships, we may only recently have instructed a lawyer to initiate divorce proceedings or written an email to a colleague. When we join in joyfully with the chorus, we're making a great and precious leap of faith. We're finally insisting that our ability to cope is greater than our past has traditionally led us to imagine.

Gloria is backing us up to attain what we might term emotional escape velocity. She's instilling—with the encouragement of deceptively simple yet mesmerizing chords—the state of mind in which we can bear to take on those who have injured us.

An attitude of defiance is never the whole of what we need. For things to go well, we also have to call on reserves of conciliation, compromise, acceptance, and tolerance—the mature virtues by which genuinely good things are kept afloat in an imperfect world. But that's not where we are right now. At this point, we still need to gird ourselves for a fight. And this is when the voice of Gloria Gaynor is not just a magnificent instance in the grand history of pop but for us—in a way that might feel embarrassing to admit to anyone else—what our soul needs to hear to save us from the weak but agonizingly familiar side of our nature that has so often given up so soon, too soon, on our hopes of freedom.

7 Budai

Buddhism gives every sign of being an unremittingly pessimistic philosophy: It loses few opportunities to remind us that life is suffering, that disappointment is the rule, and that we are fated to witness all our hopes and aspirations destroyed with time.

It can therefore feel a little paradoxical to come across the cult of Budai, a Chinese monk who became a saintly figure within Buddhism in the tenth century and is frequently represented in statues and on wall hangings, celebrated for his laughter, quick wit, and large belly, which he loved to rub while throwing back his head and chuckling warmly. What is a portly comedian doing in this religion of lamentation and sorrow? Why should we want to laugh, given what Buddhism has to tell us about our earthly prospects?

The paradox is only superficial. In essence, Buddhism wants to shake us from our pretensions, our complacency, and our misplaced perfectionism—and if these are its goals, then it sees no logical reason why they might not be accomplished as much via a set of witticisms as via a funereal lament.

Buddhism cannily understood that most humor arises from the omnipresent gap between our hopes and the available reality. We laugh not because things are happy but precisely because we have been helped to recognize that they are so damnably and incorrigibly sad. Our laughter represents a release of tension at the awfulness of everything.

We might laugh darkly at a joke that tells us that going on vacation will offer us a chance to be unhappy somewhere else with better weather. Or that celebrates marriage as an institution that generously offers us one very specific person to blame for all of our hitherto free-floating misery. Or that describes adolescence as a phase kindly designed by nature to ensure that we won't end up overly sad that our children are

Liu Zhen, stoneware figure of Budai Hesheng, 1486.

soon going to be leaving home. Laughter is an involuntary spasm provoked by a pithy and skilful assessment of the fundamental misery of existence.

Importantly, we tend to laugh in company. Humor is a social activity. Dark truths that we had contemplated alone, with embarrassment and a sense of having been persecuted by fate, are given a chance to be shared among friends. That we are all laughing together is proof that we are not—whatever our suspicions—actually alone. We are fellow suffering humans facing up to similar sources of frustration and grief. We have not been accorded an especially unpleasant destiny. It turns out that everyone is crying—and therefore laughing—about careers, marriages, ageing, money, and children.

The secular West has traditionally relegated comedy to the realm of "entertainment"; it is "just" for laughs. Buddhism has been more ambitious. It understood that trying to elicit laughter can be the most effective means of prompting people to confront their pain and isolation. It isn't a diversion from so-called serious things but rather the most graceful and kindly way of helping us to acknowledge and make our peace with them.

8 *Cultivate Your Own Garden*

It is crucial to note the subtitle of *Candide*, eighteenth-century Europe's most famous novel, which was written in three inspired days in 1759: *or Optimism*. If there was one central target that its author wanted satirically to destroy, it was the hope of his age, a hope that focused on science, love, technical progress, and reason. Voltaire was enraged. Of course science wasn't going to improve the world; it would merely give new power to tyrants. Of course philosophy would not be able to explain away the problem of evil; it would only show up our vanity. Of course love was an illusion, power a chimera, humans irredeemably wicked, and the future absurd. Of all this his readers were to be left in no doubt. Hope was a disease and it was Voltaire's generous goal to try to cure us of it.

Nevertheless, his novel is not simply a tragic tale; nor is his own philosophy mordantly nihilistic. The book ends on a memorably tender and stoic note. The tone is elegiac and we encounter one of the finest expressions of the melancholic viewpoint ever written. Candide and his companions have traveled the world and suffered immensely: they have known persecution, shipwrecks, rapes, earthquakes, smallpox, starvation, and torture. But they have, more or less, survived and, in the final pages, find themselves in Turkey—a country Voltaire especially admired—living on a small farm in a suburb of Istanbul. One day they learn of trouble at the Ottoman court: Two viziers and the mufti have been strangled and several of their associates impaled. The news causes upset and fear in many. But near their farm, Candide, together with his friends Martin and Pangloss, pass an old man who is peacefully and indifferently sitting under an orange bower next to his house:

Pangloss, who was as inquisitive as he was argumentative, asked the old man what the name of the strangled Mufti was. 'I don't know,' answered the worthy man, 'and I have never known the name of any Mufti, nor of any Vizier. I have no idea what you're talking about; my general view is that people who meddle with politics usually meet a miserable end, and indeed they deserve to. I never bother with what is going on in Constantinople; I only worry about sending the fruits of the garden which I cultivate off to be sold there.' Having said these words, he invited the strangers into his house; his two sons and two daughters presented them with several sorts of sherbet, which they had made themselves, with kaimak enriched with the candied-peel of citrons, with oranges, lemons, pine-apples, pistachio-nuts, and Mocha coffee . . . – after which the two daughters of the honest Muslim perfumed the strangers' beards. 'You must have a vast and magnificent estate,' said Candide to the Turk. 'I have only twenty acres,' replied the old man; 'I and my children cultivate them; and our labour preserves us from three great evils: weariness, vice, and want.' Candide, on his way home, reflected deeply on what the old man had said. 'This honest Turk,' he said to Pangloss and Martin, 'seems to be in a far better place than kings . . . I also know,' said Candide, 'that we must cultivate our garden.'

Voltaire, who liked to stir the prejudices of his largely Christian readers, especially enjoyed giving the idea for the most important line in his book—and arguably the most important adage in modern thought—to a Muslim, the true philosopher of the book known only as "the Turk": "*Il faut cultiver notre jardin*" ("We must cultivate our garden") or, as it has variously been translated, "We must grow our vegetables", "We must tend to our lands" or "We need to work our fields."

What did Voltaire mean with his gardening advice? That we must keep a good distance between ourselves and the world, because taking too close an interest in politics or public opinion is a fast route to aggravation and danger. We should know well enough at this point that humans are troublesome and will never achieve—at a state level—anything like the degree of logic and goodness we would wish for. We should never tie our personal moods to the condition of a whole nation or people in general, or we would have to weep continuously. We need to live in our own small plots, not the heads of strangers. At the same time, because our minds are prey to anxiety and despair, we need to keep ourselves busy. We need a project. It shouldn't be too large or dependent on many. The project should send us to sleep every night weary but satisfied. It could be bringing up a child, writing a book, looking after a house, running a small shop, or managing a little business. Or, of course, tending to a few acres. Note Voltaire's geographical modesty. We should give up on trying to cultivate the whole of humanity; we should ignore things at a national or international scale. Take just a few acres and make those your focus. Establish a small orchard and grow lemons and apricots. Dig some beds and grow asparagus and carrots. Stop worrying yourself with humanity if you ever want peace of mind again. Who cares what's happening in Constantinople or what's up with the grand mufti? Live quietly like the old Turk, enjoying the sunshine in the orange bower next to your house. This is Voltaire's stirring, ever-relevant form of horticultural quietism. We have been warned—and guided.

It was no coincidence that Voltaire put his lines about the cultivation of the garden into the mouth of a Muslim. He had done a lot of reading about Islam for his *Essay on Universal History*, published three years before, and properly understood the role of gardens in its theology. For Muslims, because the world at large can never be rendered perfect, it is the task of the pious to try to give a foretaste of what is to come in the afterlife, which can be seen as a well-tended garden—and where that is not possible, in the depiction of a garden in a rug. There should be four canals that allude to the four rivers of paradise, in which were said to flow water, milk, wine, and honey, and where they intersect represents the *umbilicus mundi*, the navel of the world, where the gift of life emerged. Gardening is no trivial pastime. It's a central way of shielding ourselves from the influence of the chaotic, dangerous world beyond while focusing our energies on something that can reflect the goodness and grace we long for.

We melancholics know that humans—ourselves foremost among

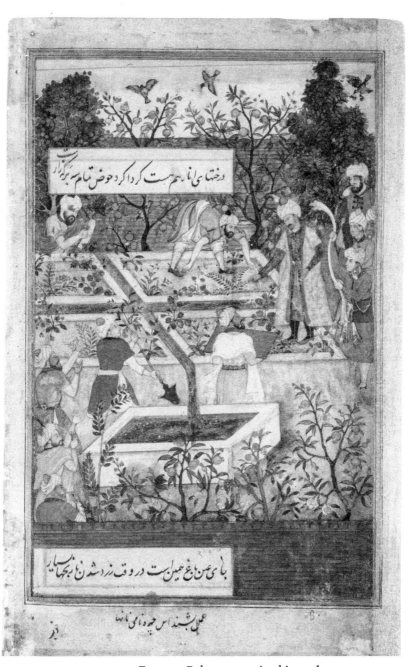

Emperor Babur overseeing his gardeners, c. 1590.

The "Wagner" Garden Carpet, early 17th century.

them – are beyond redemption. We melancholics have given up on dreams of complete purity and unblemished happiness. We know that this world is, for the most part, hellish and heartbreakingly vicious. We know that our minds are full of demons that will not leave us alone for long. Nevertheless, we are committed to not slipping into despondency. We remain deeply interested in kindness, in friendship, in art, in family life—and in spending some very quiet local afternoons gardening.

The melancholic position is ultimately the only sensible one for a broken human. It's where we get to, after we have been hopeful, after we have tried love, after we have been tempted by fame, after we have despaired, after we have gone mad, after we have considered ending it—and after we have decided conclusively to keep going. It captures the best possible attitude to pain and the wisest orientation of a weary mind toward what remains hopeful and good.

9 *The* Hotaru

One of nature's odder creatures is the firefly, a soft-bodied beetle that emits a warm yellow glow from its lower abdomen, typically at twilight, in order to attract mates or prey. Though relatively rare in Europe and North America, the firefly is a common sight in Japan, where it is known as the *hotaru*. *Hotaru* are at their most plentiful in June and July and can be seen buzzing in large groups around rivers and lakes. The glittering light is so enchanting, the Japanese have traditionally held firefly festivals—or *hotaru matsuri*—in order to watch these creatures caper and to recite poetry in their honor.

Something more magical has happened to the firefly in Japanese culture: it has become philosophical. Zen Buddhist poets and philosophers—the two terms are largely interchangeable—have urged us to look at fireflies as sources of a distinctive wisdom and serenity. What we are truly being invited to see in the firefly is not an insect but a version of ourselves. We too are tiny against the darkness, we too have no option but to put on a desperate light show in the hope of enticing possible partners, and we too won't last very long: Fireflies all die within three weeks.

Importantly, the metaphor is a generous one. We aren't being likened to rats or flies, with whom we have a few less flattering similarities as well. Fireflies are graceful and mesmerizing. They appear bold and touching, protesting bravely against the blackness in the limited hours afforded to them.

Many of our mental troubles spring from an overambitious sense of who we are. We ascribe to ourselves an importance that the natural world and our fellow humans turn out not to recognize. We protest in a bad temper at our puniness and lack of agency.

The metaphor of the firefly bids us to loosen our hold on arrogance

Kobayashi Kiyochika, *Fireflies at Ochanomizu*, c. 1880.

and irritation. We should not complain at our slightness but submit to it with wonder and poise. It isn't a personal curse that we aren't going to live very long and that our actions are but a short merry dance. We should know and accept our nature: A firefly does not mistake itself for a lion or a tortoise. We can imagine our cities from outer space looking much like the frantic swirls of fireflies across a lake: touching, absurd, beautiful, and minuscule within the order of the cosmos.

The art of locating important philosophical themes in the natural world is one that Zen makes repeatedly: for example, in relation to bamboo, which is evocative of resilience; water, which is a symbol of patient strength, capable of wearing down stone; and cherry blossom, which is an emblem of the brevity of happiness. Zen seeks to hang its ideology on to everyday things because it wants to make use of what is most ordinarily in our sight to keep us tethered to nourishing truths.

It also imbues its lessons with poetry. In a legendary haiku, the great seventeenth-century poet Matsuo Bashō attempts to quieten our egoistic ambition by focusing on a firefly, through which we may grow more attentive to our own finitude:

Falling from
A blade of grass, to fly off —
A firefly.

On its slender wings, the firefly is an ideal carrier of Zen reminders of the need for dignified resignation in the face of the mightiness and destructiveness of the natural order. Kobayashi Issa, an eighteenth-century Buddhist priest as well as a haiku master, wrote 230 poems on fireflies. In one of the most celebrated, he captures a moment in high summer when time is momentarily stilled as the insects put on their show:

The fireflies are sparkling
And even the mouth of a frog
Hangs wide open

It is a tiny moment of *satori* or enlightenment. The frog is as wonderstruck as the poet at the movements of the brave, doomed fireflies—much as we should fairly be amazed, grateful, and ultimately joyous to have been allocated a few brief moments in which to dance and give off a burst of light against the darkness of an always largely impenetrable universe that is already 13.8 billion years old.

10 *The Emperor's Giraffe*

We may be sad because we think we know it all, because everything has grown stale and familiar—because we have, for very understandable reasons, lost the ability to wonder.

Yet the world is always stranger and more unexpected than we can bring ourselves to believe in our depressed moods. Zhu Di, the Yongle Emperor, the third emperor of the Ming dynasty (r. 1402–24), had by middle age grown tired of his role as royal intermediary between heaven and earth. He had a thousand mistresses, he'd conquered Vietnam and tamed the Mongols, and he'd commissioned the largest book ever written, the *Yongle Encyclopedia*, which explained every element in the history of Chinese civilization. But, weary in his soul, the Emperor made a move that none of his predecessors had ever attempted. He sent some ships to explore the wider world. Chinese rulers knew their country to be the most interesting and blessed on the planet and therefore generally felt no need to go elsewhere—beyond at most subduing a near neighbor. Yet Zhu Di asked his explorer and mariner, the eunuch Admiral Zheng He, to venture out and make a thorough survey of all the barbarian lands he could find. With a more or less unlimited budget, Zheng He had a vast fleet built in the Longjiang shipyard near Nanjing and, after a banquet presided over by the Emperor at which sacrifices were made to Tianfei, the patron goddess of sailors, China's largest-ever expeditionary force set off. It dropped in on Brunei, Java, Thailand, Sri Lanka, and India before crossing to Arabia and Africa, stopping at Hormuz, Lasa, Aden, Mogadishu, Brava, Zhubu, and Malindi.

Along the way, the admiral picked up a panoply of gifts and treasures that he hoped would amuse and delight the Emperor: manuscripts, sculptures, clothes, gold, palm and date trees, figs, all manner of spices, a few slaves, and many new concubines. But what Zhu Di really loved

Unknown artist (formerly attributed to Shen Du),
Tribute Giraffe with Attendant, 16th century.

was animals and the admiral picked up a veritable zoo-full that had never been seen before in China: lions, leopards, dromedary camels, ostriches, zebras, a rhino, and antelopes.

One animal in particular took the Emperor's fancy: a giraffe that his admiral had bought from a couple of intrepid Kenyan traders in eastern India. Laying eyes on it for the first time, he stroked the animal's hide, marveled at its long neck and graceful but slightly awkward way of walking—and gave it his blessing. His spirits having lifted, Zhu Di invited the entire court to take a look. He had an enclosure especially built for the giraffe in his palace and often took walks with it around the grounds. Unsurprisingly, he asked his favorite artist to capture his new friend, an honor he did not bestow on any other foreign animal.

We probably all had some of Emperor Zhu Di's excitement when we first laid eyes on a giraffe, at the age of three. We too would have marveled at that long neck and admired the bright patterning and strange gait. But somewhere along the line, we stopped wondering—about giraffes and pretty much everything else as well. The world became familiar and then stale.

We should not, perhaps, have given up so easily. Giraffes remain hugely odd and importantly wonderful. We do not live on a dull planet, but we have allowed our sorrows to drain our capacity for joy. We should, when depression weighs us down, strive to remind ourselves that the world remains full of giraffes and what they symbolize: renewed charm and creativity, new opportunities for interest, and fresh reasons to keep going.

11 *An End to Suffering*

Hinduism is both salutary and original in proposing that there is nothing especially noble or interesting about being alive. Once we look at matters dispassionately, a lot of what we have to go through is misery and suffering: we need—with great effort—to grow up, to assume responsibilities, to master a profession, to have a family, to take our place in societies full of backbiting and hypocrisy, to watch those we love get ill, and eventually to succumb to old age ourselves. To think highly of life is, through a Hindu lens, a fundamental intellectual error.

As Hinduism sees it, our real purpose is to be done with life for ever. That is the true summit of existence. Hinduism reverses the Western equation: The sinful and blinkered are forced to live for ever, while the righteous and awakened are privileged enough to be able to die. If we are not careful, if we do not show sufficient mercy and imagination toward others, we may well—Hinduism suggests—be subjected to the ultimate punishment: We will have to carry on into eternity.

The symbol of this ghastly ongoingness is the eight-spoked wheel of *samsara*, the most commonly depicted element in the religion, which evokes the pitiless and unceasing nature of life—to which we are committed unless we take a disciplined series of averting actions that together comprise the central components of Hindu ethics.

Hinduism does not suggest that we will carry on for ever in our own bodies. According to the process of *samsara*, we are reborn into a succession of different outward envelopes, each of which is eroded away and disintegrated by time. Because *samsara* is at work across the whole animal kingdom, we might find that our enduring *atman* or soul transmigrates at our death into the body of a woodlouse, a pelican, or a house spider, though we might also be reborn as a paediatric nurse or a president. What determines the quality of the migration is the degree of

An eight-spoked wheel decorating the Hindu Konark Sun
Temple in India, 13th century.

karma or virtue that we have accrued in our lives. Among the many reasons we might have to be kind to others is an awareness that unkindness might leave us having to suffer a cycle or two of life as a cockroach or a naked mole rat.

Along the way, Hinduism generates an uncommon degree of respect and tenderness for all living things. When we look at a wasp or a crab, we aren't contemplating creatures fundamentally different from ourselves; a few turns of the wheel of life ago their *atman* might have been located in a High Court judge or a dental hygienist. We might as a result—as most Hindus do—feel it appropriate to stick to a vegetarian diet, lest we unwittingly eat our old uncle or geography teacher.

The suspicion that life is constantly painful and anxious is one that we largely have to bear in a very lonely way in the philosophies of the West. In those of the East, however, pessimism is ennobled and takes center stage. We are permitted to feel weary and amply dissatisfied. We have, without quite knowing it, been alive since the start of creation, and it is untenably exhausting and frustrating. The trick, and the true prize, will be to be good and wise enough to learn to die once and for all.

For Hindus, the way to step off the treadmill of eternal existence relies, first and foremost, on a piece of intellectual insight. We cease to be subject to *samsara* and are delivered into the comforting repose of nothingness known as *brahman* once we realize that, despite many appearances to the contrary, however paradoxical or absurd the idea might sound, we and the universe are in truth one.

From the earliest age, we tend to assume the very opposite. It seems self-evident that we are one kind of thing and the tree over there, the relative over here, the clouds in the sky, the monkey on the parapet, and the river wending its way to the sea belong to quite different categories. Yet Hinduism insists that our belief in difference belongs ultimately to a realm of *maya* or illusion. If we look more deeply into the nature of things, through the help of teaching and spiritual exercises, we stand to discover the remarkable unity of all elements. Contrary to appearances, everything we see and experience around us belongs to the same life force: the leaves unfurling on the tree, the child learning to read, the earthworm digging its tunnels, the lava bubbling from the earth – all belong to a single unitary power which only egoistic prejudice has hitherto prevented us from acknowledging as one.

Most of our pain, Hinduism argues, arises from an overeager attachment to the differences between ourselves and the rest of the world. We pay inordinate attention to who has slightly more money or respect than we do. We are constantly humiliated by people and events that don't seem to honor our sense of uniqueness.

But through a process known as *moksha* or liberation, we can throw off the veil of illusion that works to separate us from the universe and start to identify with cosmic totality. It no longer matters exactly where we end and others begin; everything belongs to the same whole that we have mistakenly and unnecessarily carved up into parts. There is a little less reason to grasp, to be puffed up, to be proud, or to become embittered. We can survey the course of our lives and of our societies with calm indifference. We can cease to identify happiness with the working out of our will upon the world and instead take in with compassion and serenity whatever destiny throws our way. We will then enjoy *paripurna-brahmanubhava*, the experience of oneness with *brahman*, the principle of all things.

Once we have let go of our ego like this, we may have a few more years left to live, but we can be sure that—eventually—we will not need to keep returning. Constant rebirth is the fate of those who cleave too tightly to their own selves. By contrast, those who have learned to surrender can at their demise merge with the universe and will never need to suffer the indignities of individual life again.

12 *The Deckchairs of the Titanic*

There remain few expressions better able to capture the futility of a task than one which compares our efforts to "rearranging the deckchairs on the Titanic." The hull has been breached and the ship is sinking, so to concern ourselves with the position of the loungers would be the ultimate folly, the deepest possible failure to recognize the true hopelessness of the situation.

The point seems grimly apt because we are, many of us, a little like the passengers on a stricken liner. Our larger hopes in life have been fatally holed: We see now that our careers won't ever particularly flourish; our relationships will always be compromised; we've passed our peak in terms of looks; our bodies are going to fall prey to ever more humiliating illnesses; society isn't going to cure itself; significant political progress looks deeply improbable. Our ship is going down. It can feel as if trying to improve our condition, let alone find pleasure and distraction, would be an insult to the facts. Our instinct is to be as funereal and gloomy as our ultimate end.

But there's one crucial element that distinguishes our predicament from that of the passengers who lost their lives on the RMS *Titanic* in the early hours of April 15, 1912: time. They had little more than two hours between feeling the ominous shudder of the impact and the moment when the once-majestic vessel broke apart and sank into the North Atlantic. We're going down too, but far, far more slowly. It's as if the captain had let it be known that the hull had been breached, there were not enough lifeboats, and there was zero chance of ever reaching port, but then added that it would probably be many decades before we finally slipped beneath the waves.

So though we can't be saved, though the end will be grim, we still have options as to how to use our remaining time. We are involved in

Francis Browne, *Titanic*'s port side A-Deck promenade, April 11, 1912.

a catastrophe, but there are better and worse ways of filling the days. In those circumstances, expending thought and effort on "rearranging the deckchairs" is no longer ridiculous at all; it's an eminently logical step. There could be no higher calling.

When our large hopes for ourselves become unattainable, we have to become inventive around lesser, but still real, options for the time that remains. Keeping cheerful and engaged in spite of everything becomes a major task. If we were on a very gradually sinking luxury liner in the early twentieth century, we might every evening strive to put on a dinner jacket and go to dance the foxtrot to the music of the string quintet, sing a cheerful song, or settle into the second-class library on C Deck as, all the while, bits of seaweed and debris lapped at our ankles. Or we might look out for the best spot for our collapsible recliner so that we could watch the seabirds wheeling in the sky or seek some privacy for a long, soul-exploring conversation with a new friend to the sound of crockery smashing somewhere in a galley down below. We might try our first game of quoits on the slightly tilting deck or drop in—contrary to our habits up to this time—on a wild party in steerage. Of course, from a wider perspective our lives would remain a thorough disaster, but we might find we were starting to enjoy ourselves.

Such inventiveness is precisely what we need to learn how to develop in order to cope with our doomed state. How can we invest the coming period with meaning even though everything is, overall, entirely dark? It's a question our culture hasn't prepared us for. We've been taught to focus on our big hopes, on how we can aim for everything going right. We crave a loving marriage, deeply satisfying and richly rewarding work, a stellar reputation, an ideally fit body, and positive social change. We've not been prepared—as yet—to ask ourselves what remains when many of these are no longer options: when love will always be tricky, politics compromised, or the crowd hostile. What are the viable ways of seeking the best spot for a deckchair on a listing liner?

If marriage is far less blissful than we'd imagined, perhaps we can turn to friendship. If society won't accord us the dignity we deserve, perhaps we can find a group of fellow outcasts. If our careers have irretrievably faltered, perhaps we can turn to new interests. If political progress turns out to be perennially blocked and the news is always sour, we might absorb ourselves in nature.

We are turning to what our society might dismiss as Plan Bs: what people do when they can't do the things they really want to do. But there's a surprising catch—or, really, the opposite of a catch. It may turn out that the secondary, lesser, lighter reasons for living are in fact more substantial than we'd imagined. And once we get to know them, we might come to think that they are what we should have been focusing on all along. It has taken a seeming disaster to get us to realize how central they should always have been.

13 *Calvary Cemetery*

In the city behind the cemetery are some of the most driven, clever, productive, ruthless, and cynical people ever to have been gathered into a single space in the history of humankind. On the island of Manhattan, we don't exist aside from the money and fame we accrue. There is no friendship or pity. Everyone is longing to see everyone else disgraced. People are proud of their cynicism. We need to triumph rapidly—or leave town.

It's to defend ourselves against the fear and panic induced by this terrifying piece of real estate that we should take a subway out to Calvary Cemetery in Queens: 365 acres tightly packed with the bodies of military heroes, Wall Street Titans, Fifth Avenue princesses and the ordinary heart attack and cancer victims of the northeastern United States. It might sound sad to spend a few hours communing with the dead in this way but it may, in these parts, be a great deal more reviving than attempting to connect with the living. Amid the graves, there is at least room for sympathy; there is space for thoughtfulness and tenderness. No one mentions an IPO.

Whatever their wealth, everyone slips into a similar-sized coffin. The most famous and awe-inspiring are reliably forgotten within two generations and each corpse—however large its last tax return—is quickly gnawed at by similar armies of undiscriminating worms. Death is beautifully democratic: To microbial life, the Upper East Side tastes much the same as the Bronx. The former leave exclusive penthouses on Park Avenue feet first in the morning and by evening are interred for eternity in a plot no larger than one of their former bathtubs. Everyone is silent, there is no more gossip, the journalists have gone, and the invitations dried up.

The largest cities of modernity excel in their powers to shatter our

Paige Lipsky, *Calvary Cemetery, Queens, with Manhattan Skyline*, 2017.

sincerity and peace of mind. It becomes impossible not to worry that we have been excluded and not to have nightmares about our downfall. We know that we should leave time for introspection, creativity, and vulnerable conversation, but we are too scared to remember how to begin. We forget all that is gentle and touching and that we understood so well when we were five. We cannot turn away from a mass media which appals us with news of never-ending threats to our reputations and livelihoods or those of others. We fear we can never be loved outside of what we can boast about at dinner.

The cemetery cares nothing for all of this. It bids us to sit on a bench and commune for a while with its stable and heartfelt verities. It asks us to live in such a way that we do not dishonor ourselves from the perspective of death. We should worry only about those things that still seem serious when contemplated from the far side of the grave. We should measure our thoughts against the implied verdicts of a skeleton.

We can be grateful to the dead of Queens for trying to save us from the living of Manhattan.

14 *Meteor Crater*

Day to day, the evidence for the idea is so slight, and the entire concept so peculiar and contrary to our sense of things, it's no wonder that we push it to the back of our minds and have resisted giving it its due place in public consciousness. And yet the evidence is incontrovertible: Much of who we are and of how life on the planet has taken hold is to be explained by the arrival of asteroids and comets.

In the Earth's early days 4.5 billion years ago, things were entirely dry, lifeless, and inert until, around 3.8 billion years ago, the planet underwent what is known as the Late Heavy Bombardment, a period of up to 200 million years in which giant planets were knocked off their normal circuits and objects scattered into the path of the terrestrial planets. Some 100,000 asteroids and comets of all different sizes smashed into the atmosphere-less Earth and on board these extraterrestrial objects came the central ingredients for life: the water in the oceans, the calcium in our teeth, the potassium in our brains, the carbon in our hair, the glycine in our cells, and the ribose in our DNA.

The evidence has since then been well concealed. We can see the pockmarked surface of the moon or Mars well enough through our telescopes, but here on Earth the mantle of life has cleverly disguised the story of its origins. Most of the craters have been filled in by vegetation, water, or erosion. There remain only a hundred or so pristine impact sites to be seen anywhere on the planet.

For a long time, the locals in Winslow, Arizona, refused to accept that this is what the place could be. They took it to be a volcano; many just called it a mountain. But one local meteoriticist, Harvey Nininger, insisted on the extraterrestrial theory, toured the area picking up small fragments of the alleged meteorite, wrote a book called *A Comet Strikes the Earth*, and set up the American Meteorite Museum a few miles from

Aerial view of Meteor (Barringer) Crater, Arizona.

the crater's rim. Settled scientific opinion now agrees: The big hole in the ground exists because 50,000 years ago during the Pleistocene epoch, a nickel-iron meteorite fifty meters wide slammed into Arizona at 12.8 kilometers a second and released energy equivalent to 10 megatons of TNT.

Fortunately, it's one of the most photogenic of all craters and so we might choose to pin it to the refridgerator door and turn to it whenever we feel any temptation toward self-righteousness or grandiosity. If one was founding a new religion dedicated to wisdom and maturity, Winslow might have a good claim to be considered the new Jerusalem.

15 *San Juan River*

One of our greatest difficulties—it gives us problems in so many areas—is that we can't understand time. However often the facts are explained to us, they keep slipping from our minds. Our myopia is partly rooted in our lifespan: The eighty or so years we have on the planet tend to power a steadfast background sense of what a "long time" might mean. Our brains dwell predominantly on the here and now, for there seems no efficiency or reward in having too many thoughts about what used to be or what is to come. Three months from now already feels very remote; a decade before our birth has a primeval sheen to it; five years away is unimaginable.

These biases are understandable but they make things far harder than they need to be. We continually exaggerate both the importance of setbacks in our individual lives and, more broadly, the significance of these lives within the greater span of planetary existence. And as a result we panic far more than we should and we laugh far less than we might. Anyone who thinks of a five-hour journey as "long" or a three-minute download time as "slow" is going to have problems finding perspective around a great many travails.

The sharp bends in the San Juan river in southeastern Utah appear to know our problem well enough and offer us a powerful solution to it. We cannot spend more than a moment in their company without sensing that we are being told something very powerful about time and, more specifically, how much of it there has been—and how little of that has been about us, or government ministers, or shocking headlines, or mesmerizing scandals. The San Juan river has very slowly cut a winding 300-meter-deep canyon through 300 million years of time. The rocks at the bottom date back to the Palaeozoic period, some 60 million years *before* the dinosaurs. The Earth's continents were at that point fused

San Juan river, Utah, 2010.

together into the giant landmass of Pangea, the apex predator was the Dimetrodon, the land was populated by synapsids and diapsids, and the seas were filled with mollusks, echinoderms, brachiopods, and ammonoids. The air buzzed with dragonflies the size of eagles.

We forget most of what we've ever been taught about time, but it pays to keep a few basic facts in mind:

the Earth was formed 4.543 billion years ago

life on Earth started 3.77 billion years ago

the first land animal dates back 428 million years

the first dinosaurs date back 243 million years

the first *Homo sapiens* date back 200,000 years

agriculture started 10,000 years ago

the early dynastic period in Egypt began 3,000 years ago

the Roman Empire was at its height 1,920 years ago

the first photograph was taken 196 years ago

the first powered flight took place 120 years ago

my last moment of despair was 5 days ago

Even as we scan the list, our attention may blur: a few million here or there is a hard concept to fix in the mind. The San Juan river appreciates the difficulty and won't set us any tests. It is content—through its majestic beauty—to make an overall point that should reach us through our senses as much as it does through our understanding. It really only wants to say one very simple thing to us non-experts in its ancient gravelly voice: that it is very, very old and that we are very, very short-lived. And on that basis alone, we should probably surrender our absurd and painful sense of the seriousness and importance of all that we are and do.

16 *Arco di Riccardo*

The Roman gateway now known as the Arco di Riccardo—the Riccardo in question may or may not be Richard the Lionheart—was erected in the city of Tergeste (modern Trieste) at some point during the first century AD.

It formed part of an extensive program of works for the city which included new walls, baths, and a library. The architect would have been well known and newcomers would have been awed. But as the centuries passed the Romans lost their empire. The statues that had once adorned the area were vandalized. The city was annexed by one warlord after another. The surroundings decayed and anyone who could do moved away. People chiseled out lumps of stone from the arch to repair their own homes. In winter ice expanded in the cracks, gradually weakening the entire fabric.

A tenement building was erected beside the arch, casually making use of one of its piers as part of the side wall and destroying its once-noble symmetry. Today, the arch juts straight out of a restaurant famed locally for its orecchiette with fresh tuna and its swordfish with aubergine purée.

For those who knew the arch when it was built, it might be confounding to see it battered, mutilated, and half buried. But we can take pride in its survival as well. The past may be substantially submerged but bits of it live on; things don't disappear entirely. We can make our peace with what remains, integrating its irregular masonry into our present. We can live promiscuously among the debris of different ages. An old gateway might magnanimously offer to hold up a beam of a family restaurant where, after much thought, we may order the maccheroncini with red shrimp.

Surprising us in the middle of a street with its ancientness, the arch

Arco di Riccardo, Trieste, Italy, 2017.

offers to release us from the intimidating aspects of our own times. Everything that seems impressive or important today will gradually lose its prestige. Our urgent debates will be known only to a few scholars who will struggle to find an audience. Our current celebrities will seem like the most old-fashioned people in the world and then will be forgotten entirely. Our most radical ideas will sound incomprehensible and everything that motivates or disturbs us will be forgotten. Our personal errors will count for nothing in the sweep of history. No one will remember or care about our failings. The things that loom so large and are so painful and agitating in our own picture of our lives will leave almost no trace.

To the Romans who built the arch, it would have seemed that the fall of their world was the fall of the entire world. They could not begin to imagine that the planet would ultimately survive well enough without them and that new and, in significant ways, much better forms of society would eventually emerge.

At some point in the future, someone will look on a decayed fragment of New York, Tokyo, or London and wonder for a moment about what we who lived then were like—and all their ideas will be wrong and we will be free.

17 *The Fennec Fox*

It's hard to think of an animal better adapted to the strange and difficult place it has to live than the fennec fox. In its native Saharan and Sinai deserts, the fennec has to cope with daytime temperatures of 40°C (104°F), a near-complete lack of water, boiling sand, sparse food supplies, and predatory vultures and jackals. Yet for each of its many challenges, it has arrived at an ingenious solution: its vast ears, up to fifteen centimeters long, help dissipate heat and detect the slightest movement of lizards and geckos; it can allow its body temperature to rise to 40.9°C (105.6°F) before it begins to sweat; it pants at a record-breaking 690 breaths a minute; it has specially adapted kidneys that produce hyperosmotic urine; and its fur covers its feet to give them traction and stop them burning as it runs across the hot sand.

To look at a fennec is to see evidence of 8 million years of evolution in relation to the rigors of one very specific habitat. We humans don't need to be jealous. We too were entirely well adapted to our original habitats: We acquired intensely fearful reactions that would alert us to predators, lusts that would help us find fertile mates, appetites for sugar that would help us maintain body weight, and minds favoring snap judgments to evade snakes and sabretooth tigers. We also had perfect spines for being on our feet all day.

But there is a major difference between us and the fennec. We no longer live in the environments to which we were originally adapted. Backs evolved to walk for kilometers in the savannah now slouch on office chairs; eyes honed to detect wild berries now focus in on another slice of polenta cake.

There have, it is true, been a few changes in our DNA over the last 60,000 years. Humans living in the Arctic have evolved to carry thicker layers of fat on their faces to reduce the risk of frostbite. Rice- and

Fennec fox (*Vulpes zerda*).

wheat-cultivating populations have gained an ability to better digest starch thanks to the salivary enzyme amylase. Around 6,000 years ago, a mutation in the OCA2 gene tweaked levels of melanin in northern populations and gave some of them blue eyes.

But no animal on earth whose original habitat has altered as radically as ours has survived while evolving as little as we have. We are doing well enough, but we should be forgiving when aspects of our historically evolved constitutions interact awkwardly with distinctive features of modernity. We are, at points, like a fennec forced to live in Hampshire, an African elephant trying to make its way in Baden-Württemberg, or a tropical rock lobster making a go of it in the waters off Antarctica.

Genetic evolution moves a lot less quickly than human history, making relics of much about our minds and bodies. It should be no wonder that we often eat too much, watch porn all day, develop backache, tremble at the thought of sharks, and get statistics entirely wrong. Narrowly speaking, it isn't our fault. It's just that a lot of who we are and what we want made a lot more sense in a world that no longer exists.

18 *The Happy Few*

One of the leading ambitions of modern society has been to make as many of life's pleasures and opportunities open to as many people as possible. "Accessible" has become one of our greatest terms of praise, democracy is our highest political ideal, and inclusivity can feel like our most urgent social aspiration. We retain, by contrast, nothing but contempt and anger for concepts like exclusive, aristocratic, and elite.

But because there is always value in studying what is outlying and contrary, we can in the modern context usefully turn to the example of the French novelist, diarist, and travel writer Marie-Henri Beyle (1783–1842), more commonly known by his pen name Stendhal, author of two of the greatest novels of French literature, *Le Rouge et le Noir* and *La Chartreuse de Parme*. Born into a prosperous middle-class family in Grenoble, as a young man Stendhal worked for the Napoleonic regime in a number of minor diplomatic and military roles. But after Bonaparte's exile, he grew disenchanted with his native country, which he came to associate with illiberalism, prudishness, anger, and cynicism. He knew plenty of people but had few real friends. In company, he had difficulty articulating his thoughtful, sweet, impish nature—the waspish critic Lytton Strachey once described him as someone who combined the penetrating intelligence of a High Court judge with the soft heart and weepy nature of an eleven-year-old girl.

Stendhal was no political reactionary. He wanted the vote to be open to all and for the talented to progress whatever their backgrounds. Nevertheless he became increasingly drawn to the idea of an "aristocracy"—that is, the existence of a distinguished elite who could be favored above others. This had nothing whatsoever to do with an aristocracy of the blood. What Stendhal cared about was an aristocracy of the heart: an elite who knew how to feel, think, long for, connect,

The Baptistery, Florence, Italy, c. 1890–1900.

and be quiet and sad in ways that few seemed to favor. He came to the view that though modern democratic society proclaimed the equality of all peoples and stridently sought to place everyone on the same footing, the sad reality was that only a narrow group would ever really understand matters in the profound, generous, witty, and kind way that he did.

Stendhal left France for Italy. He moved from Florence to Naples to Rome, eventually serving as the French consul in Trieste and Civitavecchia. It was in Italy that he began to use a phrase with which we still associate him. He remarked, in letters and in books, that he was going to dedicate his work and his life not to the masses, not to society in general, but to "the happy few." The phrase comes from Shakespeare—a line in *Henry V*: "we few, we happy few, we band of brothers"—but Stendhal gave it his own meaning. He understood by it a minority of people, all of them his imaginary friends, who had the kind of sensibility he revered though it was very much out of step with modern times: people who were hugely emotionally sensitive, thoughtful, loved to be on their own a lot, adored art and culture, hated political hysteria and vindictiveness, were sexually generous and open, and loved the sort of peaceful, unambitious, aesthetically sensitive life that he had discovered in Italy. People would know they had stumbled upon one of "the happy few" when they saw someone who had often known unrequited love, was full of regrets about their career but couldn't abide the fierce tactics needed to succeed at it, was moved by Mozart and Correggio, liked to laugh warmly at the tragedies of existence—and might swoon and well up with tears at a building like the Baptistery of St John in the center of Florence, the beauty of which contrasts so sharply with the chaos and ugliness of the world at large, and which had especially touched Stendhal by its graceful symmetry.

We often feel wretched for thinking, in our hearts, that we don't like many people, that most of those we meet are disappointing, and that we don't hold out much hope for the future of our species. It isn't fun to be misanthropic in a modern, upbeat, excited democracy. But we can in dejected moods turn to Stendhal as our own imaginary friend who will never punish us for our reservations. We may not even be misanthropes at all; we may just secretly, without having known it ourselves, have all along belonged to that narrow aristocracy of the heart: the happy few. Cynics are only idealists with awkwardly high standards. No wonder we have been so lonely—and how hopeful to think that we might no longer always have to be so.

19 *Astronomy and Melancholy*

It is a mark of the melancholy mind to be unable to side neatly with dominant ideas of what is supposed to count. We know well enough what we're meant to care about: our careers, the gossip around us, the opinions of the community, the latest stories in the news, our identities in the eyes of others, where the human race is headed in the next decade. We know the purported significance, but we may also, in a private part of our mind, feel at odds with our collective struggles and excitements, peering at them as though through dense glass, distanced from the passions held so dear by those around us. Without anything urgent or despairing being meant by this, we may not feel immensely bothered whether we live or die.

In such moods, we may be advised to shake ourselves from our torpor and rejoin the clamor, the ecstasy, and the panic. But another move might be to try to honor, and then deepen, the origins of our intuitions. We're not merely cold or unfeeling. It's just that we have ended up prone to seeing our species and our planet from a less human-centric perspective. Our eyes naturally settle not on what is directly in front of us but on how we might appear from 6 billion kilometers away. We're thinking not of what tomorrow will bring but of how the present moment might seem in relation to the age of the Earth.

The natural place to take such feelings of disengagement is not – as society sometimes tells us—a psychotherapist's chair, but rather our planetariums and our departments of astronomy, our charts of the lunar surface and our galleries of images from the Voyager space probes. We may redeem our disconsolate intuitions with the help of the swirls of the Canis Major Dwarf Galaxy, 236,000,000,000,000,000 kilometers from the sun, or photographs of late afternoon on the Aeolis Palus plain of Mars. Astronomy is the true friend of the melancholy mind, NASA and ESA its presiding deities.

Through our immersion in space, our alienated perspectives can be confirmed and returned to us with dignity. We are allowed to anchor our disengagement with the human drama to the sides of passing meteorites or the moons of Jupiter. Our loneliness can find a true home on the vast, silent dune fields of Sputnik Planitia in the southern hemisphere of Pluto. Some of our sense of loss can be absorbed by the asteroid-pockmarked surface of the moon. Our insignificance can be framed within the context of the 1,000,000,000,000,000,000,000,000 stars in the observable universe.

It can seem that planetariums are trying to show us the stars in order to equip us with the knowledge required one day to become astronauts or physicists. But in truth they offer us a means with which to diminish ourselves in our own eyes. They are a tool with which to take the sting out of our nagging sense of unimportance, our frustration at our modest achievements and our feelings of isolation.

There can be good reasons for us to strive to live in the here and now. But there may be yet more powerful reasons to dwell at least part of the day in the Proterozoic period, 2.5 billion years ago, when single-celled eukaryotes developed deep in the silence of giant undisturbed oceans. We don't need to blame ourselves unduly if we feel at odds with our nagging fellow humans when we can establish imaginary companionship with some of the many wondrous forms in which life has manifested itself across planetary history, such as the beguiling *Psittacosaurus* parrot lizard, which lived over 100 million years ago, or its near contemporary, the dog-sized, tuft-tailed, two-legged *Chaoyangsaurus*.

The best consolation for our sadness at how little ever works out is to cheer ourselves with the thought that the average stable lifespan of a star is only 8 billion years and that our sun has already burned for just under half of that. Soon enough, this middle-aged star's increased brightness will cause our oceans to evaporate. It will then run out of hydrogen and become a giant red star, expanding as far as Mars and

NASA's *New Horizons* spacecraft captured this image of Pluto
on July 14, 2015.

absorbing the whole of our planet, including the atoms of everyone and everything that is annoying us so much today.

We should drown our tears in the ocean of suffering to which every living thing is subject. We should align our feelings of purposelessness with detailed news of the five mass extinctions to have already befallen the planet. To every reversal, we should simply answer that there are 40 billion planetary systems at large in our galaxy. Before every anxiety-inducing date or speech, we should mutter to ourselves, like a talismanic prayer, that the Milky Way is 100,000 light years across and that the most distant known galaxy is GN-z11, 32 billion light years from the restaurant or conference center.

The melancholy mind often suspects that everything may be a bit meaningless. Through astronomy, we can discover, in the most engaging and inadvertently life-affirming way possible, why and how it truly is exactly that.

20 *Winter*

Every year, nature quietly takes us through a moral lesson that has much to teach us about how we might relate to certain of the more dispiriting and despair-inducing moments in our own development. Beginning in mid-October in the northern hemisphere, the temperature drops, the nights draw in, the earth turns cold and hard, fog lies low over the land, and rain drives hard across the austere, comatose gray-brown landscape. There is nothing immediate we can hope for. We now have nothing to do but wait, with resigned patience, until something better shows up.

Far more than we generally accept, our minds too have cycles. We cannot be permanently fruitful or creative, excited or open. There are necessary times of retrenchment when, whatever we might desire, there seems no alternative but to stop. We can no longer be productive. We lose direction and inspiration. We are immovably numb and sterile.

It can be easy to panic. Why should such a paralyzed and detached mood have descended on our formerly lively minds? Where have all our ideas and hopes gone? What has happened to our previous animation and gladness?

We should at such times take reassurance from the late November landscape. Certainly things are lifeless, cold, and in suspension. But this is not the end of the story. Earth is like this not as a destination but as a phase. The deadness is a prelude to new life; the fallow period is a guarantor of fecund days to come. All living organisms need to recharge themselves: old leaves have to give way, tired limbs must rest. The dance and ferment could not go on. It may look as if nothing at all is happening, as though this is a trance without purpose. Yet, deep underground, at this very moment, nutrients are being gathered, the

Alfred Sisley, *Winter Landscape, Moret*, c. 1888.

groundwork for future ebullience and dynamism is being laid down, another summer is very slowly collecting its strength.

As nature seeks to tell us, we cannot permanently be in flower. We need moments of repose and confusion. There is nothing to fear. Things will re-emerge. We should make our peace with our own midwinters and lean on nature's wise accommodation to strengthen us in our pursuit of serenity and patience.

21 *Not the End*

When Spain's greatest painter completed this drawing he was about eighty and had only two years left to live. He was almost totally deaf, his eyesight was failing, and he couldn't walk unaided. But he had not given up. He was still making great art, traveling, being read to, deepening his friendships, and, most of all, looking. Despite everything, as he wrote with heartbreaking defiance at the top of the page: *Aun aprendo*—I'm still learning.

What was he still learning? Not so much about art; he knew most of what there was to know in that field. He was learning the large, central, ostensibly simple but always elusive lessons that life insists on: about forgiveness, the importance of courage, the need to appreciate the beauty of the world, saying yes again and again to the universe despite the horrors, making time for small children, the beauty of lemons and olives, and the tenderness of dusk.

Such lessons are never complicated in themselves once we mention them. It's the remembering and the feeling that are hard. Great art strives to convince us in our bones of things that are, intellectually, very basic: love today, don't lose yourself to grudges, don't feel singled out by sadness, let joy overwhelm you, don't be afraid, resist bitterness, care less about what other people think.

The aged, hobbit-like Goya advancing toward us on his sticks has a twinkle in his eye. He is indomitable. He has come out of bed, even though cautious voices told him not to, because he wants another look at the world. There's a park he wants to visit, a bookstore he's heard about, a friend he wants to see. Death may be calling but he won't listen. He is ancient, he can't walk straight, he winces in pain but he retains the curiosity and energy of his very young self.

We have wasted a lot of time. We have refused to learn so much and

Francisco de Goya, *Aun aprendo (I'm Still Learning)*, c. 1826.

on so many occasions. We have been flighty, stubborn, blinkered, dull, and hard-hearted. But our spirit isn't vanquished—which is why we're here. There are so many pictures left to see and ideas to recall and rehearse.

It wasn't too late for him—and it isn't too late for us.

Conclusion

We would, of course, like any encounter with mental unwellness to be as brief as possible and, most importantly, to be isolated and singular. But the reality is that for many of us the illness will threaten to return for visits throughout our lives; it is a condition to which we will be permanently susceptible. So the challenge isn't to learn to survive only a one-off crisis but to set in place a framework that can help us manage our fragility over the long term. Some of the following moves, practical and psychological, suggest themselves.

ACKNOWLEDGMENT

Being ready for a return of the illness will help us calibrate our expectations and render us appropriately patient and unfrightened in the face of relapses. We should be aware of the special price we have to pay when we allow ourselves to declare the battle over, when we announce to ourselves and to friends that we are well again—and then recognize that we have actually been hasty and naive and need to return to the front once more. It can feel especially bitter to have to crouch low again when we felt we now had the right to stand tall. But it's better to adopt a stance of ongoing, permanent readiness than submit to cycles of hope followed by panic. We fell ill over many years—our whole childhood might have been the incubating laboratory—and it should not surprise us if we are never totally impervious again.

VIGILANCE

We'll need to monitor ourselves with special care, vigilant for signs of deterioration and vortices of despair. Our minds are prone to amnesia: We forget what we have learned about ourselves and what has kept us steady. We may have worked out the basic structure of our illness in therapy. We may know that we are prone to self-sabotage, that we carry a trauma with us from the past, that we are inclined to destroy everything that is good about our lives and alienate those who want to care for us. But such knowledge will always be vulnerable to destructive impulses that can sweep away our patient intellectual labor and catapult us back into a state of helpless and frightened infancy. We should be ready to be submerged by negativity and not experience our retreat as a humiliation, confident that ebbs and flows are normal and that we will be able to hold on to at least some of our gains.

REPETITION

Our minds don't just need good lessons, they need to learn good habits: that is, they need to fashion routines in which helpful rituals, activities, and ideas are repeated until they become second nature. Like someone learning a new language, we need to go over certain points again and again, rehearsing notions of self-love, self-forgiveness, kindness, and self-acceptance on a daily basis. Things are so slow because we aren't just trying to acquire intellectual concepts—something that might need only a minute—we're trying to alter our personalities. It will be a life's work.

MENTAL MANAGEMENT

We need to be rigorous with our patterns of thinking. We cannot afford to let our thoughts wander into any old section of the mind. There are thoughts that we need to nurture: about our worth, about our right to be, about the importance of keeping going, about self-forgiveness. And there are thoughts we should be ruthless in chasing out: about how some people are doing so much better than us, about how inadequate and pitiful we are, about what a disappointment we have turned out to be. The latter aren't even "thoughts," they have no content to speak of, they cannot teach us anything new. They are really just instruments of torture and symptoms of a difficult past.

A SUPPORT NETWORK

A decent social life isn't, for the mentally fragile, a luxury or a form of entertainment. It is a resource to help us to stay alive. We need people to balance our minds when we are slipping. We need friends who will soothe our fears and not accuse us of self-indulgence or self-pity for the amount of time our illness has sequestered. It will help immensely if they have struggles of their own and if we can therefore meet as equal fellow ailing humans, as opposed to hierarchically separated doctors and patients. We'll need ruthlessness in expunging certain other people from our diaries: people who harbor secret resentments against us, who are latently hostile to self-examination, who are scared of their own minds and project their fears on to us. A few hours with such types can throw a shadow over a whole day, as their unsympathetic voices become lodged in our minds and feed our own ample stores of self-doubt. We shouldn't hesitate to socially edit our lives in order to endure.

VULNERABILITY

The impulse, when things are darkening, is to hide away and reduce communication. We are too ashamed to do anything else. We should fight the tendency and, precisely when we cannot bear to admit what we are going through, we should dare to take someone into our confidence. Silence is the primordial enemy. We have to fight a permanent feeling that we are too despicable to be looked after. We have to take a gamble on an always implausible idea: that we deserve kindness.

LOVE

Love is ultimately what will get us through—not romantic love but sympathy, tolerance, and patience. We'll need to watch our tendencies to turn down love from an innate sense of unworthiness. We wouldn't have become ill if it were entirely easy for us to accept the positive attention of others. We'll have to thank those who are offering it, make them feel appreciated in return and, most of all, accept that from the outset our illness was rooted in a deficit of love and therefore that every encounter with love will strengthen our recovery and help keep the darkness at bay.

PILLS

Ideally, we would of course prefer not to keep adding foreign chemicals to our minds. There are side effects and the eerie sense of not knowing exactly where our thoughts end and alien neurochemistry begins. But the medicines set up guardrails around the worst of our mental whirlpools. We may have to be protected on an ongoing basis from forces inside us that would prefer we didn't exist.

A QUIET LIFE

We may, in our stronger moments, want to take on the world again and revive our largest ambitions. We should be careful of our motives. We don't need to be extraordinary to deserve to be. We should see the glory and the grandeur that are present in an apparently modest destiny. We are good enough as we are. We don't need huge sums of money or to be spoken of well by strangers. We need time to process our feelings and—lying in bed, say, or in the bath—soothe our frightened minds. We should take pride in our early nights and undramatic routines. These aren't signs of passivity or tedium. What looks like a normal life on the outside is a singular achievement given what we are wrestling with inside.

HUMOR

There is no need for gravity. We can face down the illness by laughing heartily at its evils. We are "mad" and "cracked" and can say so honestly—but luckily so are many others with whom we can wryly mock the absurdities of mental life. We shouldn't, on top of everything else, accord our illness too much portentous respect.

SMALL AND BIG WINS

Many of the steps we take toward recovery could appear relatively small: a week in which we have not denigrated ourselves, a relationship in which we are allowing ourselves to enjoy kindness, a sequence of peaceful evenings . . . The temptation might be to brush off these achievements a bit too lightly for our own good. Given what we may have gone through, these are milestones that deserve celebration and commemoration, so that we can notice how far we have come and gain strength from a glance back at the peaks and troughs of our mental lives.

We can think in this context of the work of the English walking artist Hamish Fulton. Fulton has spent his long career turning out large black-and-white photographs of places in the world where he has gone walking. Some of these walks have been epic in scale—whole weeks spent trekking across the Himalayas and the Andes; others have been

Hamish Fulton, *Walking to Benicadell, Spain,* 2016.

Hamish Fulton, *A Five Day Circular Clockwise
Walk Round London*, 2011.

more domestic—a few hours in the Welsh mountains. But Fulton always accompanies his images with solemn text, a written record of where he has been, how many miles he went, and how long it took him. He arrests a moment that might ordinarily be lost and lends it weight and dignity. Through immaculate lettering and sober photography, he is signaling to us how much a walk may—when fairly be viewed—be life-changing and as worthy of commemoration as a battle or a premiership.

We could imagine performing a similar exercise of commemoration on the business of recovering from mental illness. Here, too, there are plenty of moments that are quietly extremely arduous and important—and that would warrant being frozen and highlighted. We could picture a vast photograph of an ordinary bathtub to which a caption might say: "May 12, evening, two hours of soaking, rethinking my relationship to what other people think." Or a picture of an armchair by a window: "September 3, an hour reflecting on my right to be free and content." A shot of an unmade bed at night might say: "An evening of self-forgiveness."

We should be proud of ourselves for making it this far. It might at times have looked as if we would never make it. There might have been nights when we sincerely thought of taking our own lives. Somehow we held on. We reached out for help, we dared to tell someone else of our problems, we engaged our minds, we tried to piece together our histories and to plot a more endurable future—and we started reading about what might be up with our minds. We are still here, mentally ill at times, no doubt, but more than ever committed to recovery, appreciative of the light, grateful for love, hungry for insight, and keen to help anyone else whose plight we can recognize. We are not fully well, but we are on the mend and that, for now, is very much good enough.

Without all those awful things that happened, all those fears, all those people who didn't understand, what would we have learned? What would we have ever understood? The journey was almost worth it. What looked like a pure waste of time was in fact our own personal education.

Permissions

Vincent Van Gogh, *The Garden of the Asylum at Saint-Rémy, May 1889*, 1889. Oil on canvas, 91.5 x 72 cm. Rijksmuseum Kröller-Müller, Otterlo. Photo akg-images.

Henri Cartier-Bresson, *A Café, 2nd Avenue, Brooklyn, NYC, USA*, 1947. © Henri Cartier-Bresson © Fondation Henri Cartier-Bresson/Magnum Photos.

Leonardo da Vinci, *Studies of the Foetus in the Womb*, c. 1510–13. Red chalk and traces of black chalk, pen and ink, wash, 30.4 x 22 cm. Royal Collection Trust/© His Majesty King Charles III, 2023/Bridgeman Images.

Francisco Goya, *The Sleep of Reason Produces Monsters*, plate 43 from "Los Caprichos," 1799. Etching with aquatint, 18.8 x 14.9 cm. The Metropolitan Museum of Art, New York, Gift of M. Knoedler & Co., 1918, Acc. 18.64(43).

A group of devotees and Buddhist monks pray inside Wat Lang Ka pagoda during Pchum Ben festival, September 23, 2014, Phnom Penh, Cambodia. Photo © Omar Havana/Getty Images.

Ferdinand Hodler, *The Disappointed Souls*, 1892. Oil on canvas, 120 x 299 cm. Kunstmuseum, Bern. Photo André Held/akg-images.

Chino Otsuka, *1982 and 2005, Paris, France*, from the series "Imagine Finding Me," 2005. Chromogenic print, 30.5 x 40.6 cm. © Chino Otsuka.

Chino Otsuka, *1976 and 2005, Kamakura, Japan*, from the series "Imagine Finding Me," 2005. Chromogenic print, 30.5 x 40.6 cm. © Chino Otsuka.

Chino Otsuka, *1980 and 2009, Nagayama, Japan*, from the series "Imagine Finding Me," 2009. Chromogenic print, 30.5 x 40.6 cm. © Chino Otsuka.

Gustave Caillebotte, *Yerres, Effect of Rain*, 1875. Oil on canvas, 80.3 x 59.1 cm. Sidney and Lois Eskenazi Museum of Art, Indiana University; Gift of Mrs Nicholas H. Noyes, Eskenazi Museum of Art, Indiana University, Acc. No. 71.40.2.

The Yongzheng Emperor Admiring Flowers, c. 1725. Palace Museum, Beijing, China.

J. M. W. Turner, *Valley of Aosta: Snowstorm, Avalanche, and Thunderstorm*, 1836–7. Oil on canvas, 92.2 × 123 cm. Art Institute of Chicago; Frederick T. Haskell Collection, 1947.513.

Vilhelm Hammershøi, *Interior in Strandgade, Sunlight on the Floor*, 1901. Oil on canvas, 46.5 x 52 cm. Statens Museum for Kunst (SMK), Copenhagen.

Muqi Fachang, *Six Persimmons*, Southern Song dynasty, China, 13th century. Makota Sakurai/Alamy Stock Photo.

Albrecht Dürer, *Six Studies of Pillows* (verso), 1493. Pen and brown ink, 27.8 x 20.2 cm. Metropolitan Museum of Art, New York, Robert Lehman Collection, 1975, Acc. 1975.1.862.

Albrecht Dürer, *Self-Portrait, Study of a Hand and a Pillow* (recto), 1493. Pen and brown ink, 27.8 x 20.2 cm. Metropolitan Museum of Art, New York, Robert Lehman Collection, 1975, Acc. 1975.1.862.

Albrecht Dürer, *Columbine*, 1495–1500. Watercolor and opaque paint on parchment, 35.5 x 28.7 cm. The Albertina Museum, Vienna.

Albrecht Dürer, *Triumphal Arch*, c. 1515. Woodcut, 45.7 x 62.2 cm. Metropolitan Museum of Art, New York, Harris Brisbane Dick Fund, 1928, Acc. 28.82.7–.42.

Albrecht Dürer, *The Four Horsemen*, from "The Apocalypse," 1498. Woodcut, 38.7 x 27.9 cm. Metropolitan Museum of Art, New York, Gift of Junius Spencer Morgan, 1919, 19.73.209.

Albrecht Dürer, *Portrait of the Artist with a Thistle Flower*, 1493. Oil on vellum, transferred to canvas, 56 x 44 cm. Louvre, Paris. Photo Tony Querrec. Photo © 2022 RMN-Grand Palais/Dist. Photo SCALA, Florence.

Georg Friedrich Kersting, *Embroiderer*, 1817. Oil on board, 47.1 x 36.8 cm. National Museum, Warsaw.

Georg Friedrich Kersting, *Young Woman Sewing by Lamplight*, 1823. Oil on canvas, 40.3 x 34.2 cm. Neue Pinakothek München—Bayerische Staatsgemäldesammlungen. Photo © 2022 Scala, Florence/bpk, Bildagentur für Kunst, Kultur und Geschichte, Berlin.

Georg Friedrich Kersting, *Man Reading by Lamplight*, 1814. Oil on canvas, 47.5 x 37 cm. Kunst Museum Winterthur, Stiftung Oskar Reinhart. Photo © SIK-ISEA, Zürich (Philipp Hitz).

Katsushika Hokusai, *Ejiri in Suruga Province* (*Sunshū Ejiri*), from the series "Thirty-six Views of Mount Fuji (Fugaku sanjūrokkei)," c. 1830–32. Woodblock print; ink and colour on paper, 25.1 x 37.5 cm. Metropolitan Museum of Art, New York, Henry L. Phillips Collection, Bequest of Henry L. Phillips, 1939, Acc. JP2953.

Katsushika Hokusai, *The Inume Pass in Kai Province* (*Kōshū Inume tōge*), from the series "Thirty-six Views of Mount Fuji (Fugaku sanjūrokkei)," c. 1830–32. Woodblock print; ink and color on paper, 25.1 x 37.8 cm. Metropolitan Museum of Art, New York, Henry L. Phillips Collection, Bequest of Henry L. Phillips, 1939, Acc. JP2968.

Katsushika Hokusai, *Under the Wave off Kanagawa* (*Kanagawa oki nami ura*), also known as *The Great Wave*, from the series "Thirty-six Views of Mount Fuji (Fugaku sanjūrokkei)," c. 1830–32. Woodblock print; ink and color on paper, 25.7 x 37.9 cm. Metropolitan Museum of Art, New York, H. O. Havemeyer Collection, Bequest of Mrs H. O. Havemeyer, 1929, Acc. JP1847.

Mark Rothko, *Red on Maroon*, 1959. Oil paint, acrylic paint, and glue tempera on canvas, 266.7 x 238.8 x 3.5 cm. Tate, London. © 1998 Kate Rothko Prizel & Christopher Rothko ARS, NY and DACS, London.

Agnes Martin Gallery at the Harwood Museum in Taos, New Mexico, on March 20, 2022. Photo Joshua Ware. Agnes Martin: © Agnes Martin Foundation, New York/DACS 2023; Donald Judd: © Judd Foundation/ARS, NY and DACS, London 2023.

Agnes Martin, *Little Sister*, 1962. Oil, ink, and brass nails on canvas over wood, 25.1 x 24.6 cm. Solomon R. Guggenheim Museum, New York, Gift, Andrew Powie Fuller and Geraldine Spreckels Fuller Collection, 1999. Photo The Solomon R. Guggenheim Foundation/Art Resource, NY/Scala, Florence. © Agnes Martin Foundation, New York/ DACS, 2023.

Agnes Martin, *Untitled*, 1974. Acrylic, pencil, and Shiva gesso on canvas, 182.9 x 182.9 cm. Collection Cranbrook Art Museum, Bloomfield Hills, Michigan. Gift of Rose M. Shuey, from the Collection of Dr John and Rose M. Shuey (CAM 2002.22). Photograph by R. H. Hensleigh. © Agnes Martin Foundation, New York/DACS 2023.

Agnes Martin, *Starlight*, 1963. Watercolor and ink on paper, 29.8 x 26.7 cm. Private Collection. Photo © Christie's Images/Bridgeman Images. © Agnes Martin Foundation, New York/DACS, 2023.

Wayne Thiebaud, *Cakes*, 1963. Oil on canvas, 152.4 x 182.9 cm. National Gallery of Art, Washington, DC, Gift in Honor of the 50th Anniversary of the National Gallery of Art from the Collectors Committee, the 50th Anniversary Gift Committee, and The Circle, with Additional Support from the Abrams Family in Memory of Harry N. Abrams/National Gallery of Art, Washington, 1991.1.1. © Wayne Thiebaud/VAGA at ARS, NY and DACS, London 2023.

Stephen Shore, *Breakfast, Trail's End Restaurant, Kanab, Utah, August 10, 1973*, 1973. Chromogenic color print, 22.9 x 28.3 cm. © Stephen Shore. Courtesy 303 Gallery, New York.

Ferdinand Hodler, *The Dents du Midi from Champéry*, 1916. Private Collection. Photo Heritage Images/Fine Art Images/akg-images.

Jacob Vrel, *Woman at a Window, Waving at a Girl*, c. 1650. Oil on panel, 45.7 x 39.2 cm. Fondation Custodia, Collection Frits Lugt, Paris.

Joel Meyerowitz, *New York City*, 1963. © Joel Meyerowitz. Courtesy Howard Greenberg Gallery.

Martine Franck, *"Maison de Nanterre," Old People's Home, Hauts de Seine, France*, 1978. © Martine Franck/Magnum Photos.

David Hockney, *Waiter, Alexandria*, 1963. Pencil and colored pencil on paper, 30.5 x 24.5 cm. © David Hockney.

Curiosity self-portrait at "Glen Etive" site, 2019. Photo NASA/JPL-Caltech/MSSS.

Kawai Shrine within the Shimogamo Shrine, Kyoto, Kyoto Prefecture, Kinki Region, Japan. Photo Zairon/Wikipedia (Creative Commons Attribution-ShareAlike 4.0 International (CC BY-SA 4.0)).

Émile Lévy, *Jules Barbey d'Aurevilly*, 1881. Oil on canvas, 114 x 86 cm. Châteaux de Versailles et de Trianon, Versailles. Photo RMN-Grand Palais/Dist. Photo SCALA, Florence.

Shiva as the Lord of Dance, Tamil Nadu, India, c. 950–1000. Copper alloy, 76.20 x 57.15 x 17.78 cm. LACMA (Los Angeles County Museum of Art), Anonymous gift (M.75.1).

William Bouguereau, *La Jeunesse de Bacchus*, 1884. Oil on canvas, 331 x 610 cm. Photograph courtesy of Sotheby's, Inc. © 2019.

Étienne Carjat, *Victor Hugo*, published in *Galerie contemporaine, littéraire, artistique* (Goupil & Cie, Paris, 1876). Universitätsbibliothek Heidelberg.

Candida Höfer, *Biblioteca Geral da Universidade de Coimbra IV*, 2006. Chromogenic print, 204.5 x 247.3 cm. Private Collection. Photo © Christie's Images/Bridgeman Images. © Candida Höfer/VG Bild-Kunst, Bonn/DACS, London 2023.

Pablo Picasso, *Academic Study*, Barcelona, 1895. Charcoal and black pencil strokes on laid paper, 47 x 61 cm. Museu Picasso Barcelona. Gift of Pablo Picasso, 1970, MPB 110886. Museu Picasso, Barcelona., Photo Fotogasull. © Succession Picasso/DACS, London 2023.

Pablo Picasso, *The Pigeons*, Cannes, September 7, 1957. Oil on canvas, 81 cm x 99.5 cm. Museu Picasso, Barcelona, Gift of Pablo Picasso, 1968, MPB 70.454. Museu Picasso, Barcelona, Photo Fotogasull. © Succession Picasso/DACS, London 2023.

Conrad Gessner, *Hedgehog*, hand-colored woodcut, from Gessner's *Historia animalium*, 1551. Courtesy of Linda Hall Library of Science, Engineering & Technology, Kansas City, Missouri.

Paul Cézanne, *Apples*, 1878–9. Oil on canvas, 22.9 x 33 cm. Metropolitan Museum of Art, New York, The Mr and Mrs Henry Ittleson Jr Purchase Fund, 1961, Acc. 61.103.

Macrauchenia. Illustration by Michael Long/Science Photo Library.

President Nixon and his daughters, Tricia and Julie, with their children Christopher Nixon Cox and Jennie Eisenhower, 1979. Courtesy of the Richard Nixon Foundation.

Archaeologists excavating at the site of the "Marlow Warlord," Berkshire. Reproduced with permission of Dr Gabor Thomas, University of Reading, England.

"Anglo-Saxon military chief, trumpeter and warriors, Anno 975". Aquatint from Sir Samuel Rush Meyrick and Charles Hamilton Smith, *The Costume of the Original Inhabitants of the British Islands* . . . (R. Havell: London, 1815). British Library, London. Photo © British Library Board. All Rights Reserved/Bridgeman Images.

Mick Jagger, during the filming of *World in Action*, July 31, 1967. Photo ITV/Shutterstock.

Turquoise mosaic skull representing the god Tezcatlipoca, c. 1400–1521. Turquoise and lignite mosaic on a human skull, 19 x 12.2 x 13.9 cm. British Museum, London . Photo © The Trustees of the British Museum, London.

Gloria Gaynor, 1979. Photo Richard E. Aaron/Redferns/Getty Images.

Figure of Budai Hesheng decorated in polychrome enamels and with biscuit-fired areas, by Liu Zhen (according to inscription), China, Ming dynasty, 1486. Stoneware, 119.2 x 65 x 41 cm. British Museum, London, UK. Photo © The Trustees of the British Museum.

The Emperor Babur (1483–1530) overseeing his gardeners, by Bishndas and Nanha. Tempera and gouache on paper. India, Mughal period, c. 1590. Victoria and Albert Museum, London. Photo © Victoria and Albert Museum, London.

The "Wagner" Garden Carpet, early 17th century, Safavid period, Kirman, Iran. Cotton warp; wool, cotton, and silk weft; wool pile; overall 530.9 x 431.8 cm. Burrell Collection, Glasgow. Photo © CSG CIC Glasgow Museums Collection/Bridgeman Images.

Kobayashi Kiyochika, *Fireflies at Ochanomizu*, c. 1880. Color woodblock print, 21.27 x 23.18 cm. LACMA (Los Angeles County Museum of Art), Gift of Carl Holmes (M.71.100.82).

Unknown artist (formerly attributed to Shen Du), *Tribute Giraffe with Attendant*, 16th century. Ink and color on silk; mounted as a hanging scroll, 80 x 40.6 cm. Philadelphia Museum of Art, Gift of John T. Dorrance, 1977-42-1.

An eight-spoked wheel decorating the Hindu Konark Sun Temple in India, 13th century. Photo bajjibala/123RF.com.

Titanic's port side A-Deck promenade. Photo taken by Francis Browne, SJ, April 11, 1912. © Fr Browne SJ Collection.

Paige Lipsky, *Calvary Cemetery, Queens, with Manhattan Skyline*, 2017. © Paige Lipsky.

Aerial view of Meteor (Barringer) Crater, Arizona. Photo © Chon Kit Leong/123RF.com.

San Juan river, Utah. Photo Finetooth, 2010. Wikimedia Commons.

Arco di Riccardo, Trieste, Italy, 1st century AD. Photo bozac/Alamy Stock Photo, 2017.

Fennec fox (*Vulpes zerda*). Photo © Wrangel/Dreamstime.com.

The Baptistery, Florence, Italy. Photo taken c. 1890–1900. Library of Congress Prints and Photographs Division, Washington, DC (LC-DIG-ppmsc-06457).

NASA's *New Horizons* spacecraft captured this image of Pluto on July 14, 2015. Photo NASA/JHUAPL/SWRI.

Alfred Sisley, *Winter Landscape, Moret*, c. 1888. Pastel on paper, 38 x 55.4 cm. Von der Heydt-Museum, Wuppertal, Inv. No. G 0994. Photo Medienzentrum Wuppertal.

Francisco de Goya, *Aun aprendo* (*I'm Still Learning*), Album G. 54, c. 1826. Black pencil on laid paper, 19.2 x 14.5 cm. Prado, Madrid. Image Copyright Museo Nacional del Prado © Photo MNP/Scala, Florence.

Hamish Fulton, *Walking to Benicadell, Spain 2016*, 2016. Image courtesy of Hamish Fulton.

Hamish Fulton, *A Five Day Circular Clockwise Walk Round London*, 2011. Image courtesy of Hamish Fulton.

Index

Page references in *italics* indicate images.

Also available from The School of Life:

The School of Life: An Emotional Education

How to live wisely and well in the twenty-first century-an introduction to the modern art of emotional intelligence.

Emotional intelligence affects every aspect of the way we live, from romantic to professional relationships, from our inner resilience to our social success. It is arguably the single most important skill for surviving the twenty-first century. But what does it really mean?

One decade ago, Alain de Botton founded The School of Life, an institute dedicated to understanding and improving our emotional intelligence. Now he presents the gathered wisdom of those ten years in a wide-ranging and innovative compendium of emotional intelligence that forms an introduction to The School of Life. Using his trademark mixture of analysis and anecdote, philosophical insight and practical wisdom, he considers how we interact with each other and with ourselves, and how we can do so better. From the beloved expert of popular philosophy, *The School of Life: An Emotional Education* is an essential look at the skill set that defines our modern lives.

ISBN: 978-1-912891-45-0

THE SCHOOL OF LIFE

RELATIONSHIPS

Learning to love

The School of Life: Relationships

Learning to love

A book to inspire closeness and connection, helping people not only to find love but to make it last.

Few things promise us greater happiness than our relationships – yet few things more reliably deliver misery and frustration.

Our error is to suppose that we are born knowing how to love and that managing a relationship might therefore be intuitive and easy. This book starts from a different premise: that love is a skill to be learnt, rather than just an emotion to be felt.

It calmly and charmingly takes us around the key issues of relationships, from arguments to sex, forgiveness to communication, making sure that success in love need never again be just a matter of luck.

ISBN: 978-1-915087-13-3

THE SCHOOL OF LIFE

CALM

The harmony and serenity we crave

The School of Life: Calm

The harmony and serenity we crave

A guide to developing the art of finding serenity by understanding the sources of our anxiety and frustrations.

Nowadays almost all of us wish we could be calmer; it is one of the distinctive longings of the modern age. Across history people have sought adventure and excitement, however a new priority for many of us is a desire to be more tranquil. This is a book designed to support us in our endeavours to remain calm against all the adversities life throws at us.

A calm state of mind is not a divine gift, we can alter our responses to everyday things and educate ourselves in the art of remaining calm, not through slow breathing or special teas, but through thinking.

This is a book that explores the causes of our greatest stresses and anxieties and gives us a succession of highly persuasive, beautiful and sometimes dryly comic arguments with which to defend ourselves against panic and confusion.

ISBN: 978-1-915087-14-0

The School of Life: Small Pleasures

What makes life truly valuable

**Explores and appreciates the small pleasures
found in everyday life.**

So often we exhaust ourselves and the planet in a search for very large pleasures, while all around us lies a wealth of small pleasures, which if only we paid more attention could bring us solace and joy at little cost and effort.

This is a book to guide us to the best of life's small pleasures: the distinctive delight of holding a child's hand, having a warm bath or the joy of the evening sky. It is an intriguing, evocative mix of small pleasures to heighten the senses and return us to the world with new-found excitement and enthusiasm.

Small pleasures are points of access to the great themes of our lives. Every chapter puts one such moment of enjoyment under a magnifying glass to find out what's really going on and why it touches, moves and makes us smile.

ISBN: 978-1-915087-16-4

The School of Life: On Being Nice

A guide to friendship and connection

A guide to rediscovering niceness as one of the highest of all human achievements.

Many books seek to make us richer or thinner. This book wants to help us to be nicer: less irritable, more patient, readier to listen, warmer and less prickly. Niceness may not have the immediate allure of money or fame, but it is a hugely important quality nevertheless, and one that we neglect at our peril.

On Being Nice gently leads us around the key themes of the often-forgotten quality of being nice. It discusses how to be charitable, how to forgive, how to be natural and how to reassure, as well as the importance of navigating interpersonal relationships with compassion and kindness. Ultimately, the book encourages us to understand that niceness is compatible with strength and is not an indicator of naivety.

ISBN: 978-1-915087-15-7

The School of Life: A Job to Love

How to find a fulfilling career

A practical guide to finding fulfilling work
by understanding yourself.

Along with a satisfying relationship, a career we love is one of the most important requirements for a fulfilled life. But it can be difficult to know where we should direct our energies.

For anyone at the crossroads of their next big career move, this is a fresh take that will help you succeed in identifying a satisfying occupation. *A Job to Love* is a guide to how you can better understand yourself and locate a career that is right for you. With compassion and a deeply practical spirit, the book guides us to discover our true talents and to make sense of our confused desires and aspirations before it is too late.

ISBN: 978-1-915087-31-7

To join The School of Life community and find out more,
scan below:

The School of Life publishes a range of books on essential topics
in psychological and emotional life, including relationships,
parenting, friendship, careers and fulfilment. The aim is always to
help us to understand ourselves better and thereby to grow calmer,
less confused and more purposeful. Discover our full range of
titles, including books for children, here:

www.theschooloflife.com/books

The School of Life also offers a comprehensive therapy service,
which complements, and draws upon, our published works:

www.theschooloflife.com/therapy